What people are

A New Dictionary of Faries

I cannot recommend this book highly enough. Indeed, I would call it a worthy successor to the work of the late, great Katherine Briggs, the most highly regarded expert on fairies in the last half of the 20th century.
Segomaros Widugeni, author of *Ancient Fire: An Introduction to Gaulish Polytheism*

This is a truly impressive work – Daimler moves seamlessly between Celtic and Germanic experiences of Fairy, and provides the reader with a well-sourced guide for anyone curious about all the different aspects of Fairylore. From the earliest Irish texts to modern encounters, Daimler takes in the full scope of the subject, and presents the reader with one of the best-researched volumes on the subject. Everyone curious about the Other Crowd needs this on their shelf.
Mary Jones of the Celtic Literature Collective

A comprehensive and delightful guide of essential information for those interested in fairy lore. Daimler has created a long-needed resource for those interested in fairy lore. She's compiled a comprehensive list of subjects related to fairies, from alien abductions to Shakespeare, from Goethe to Dungeons and Dragons. She touches upon origin stories, Icelandic and Anglo-Saxon correlations, and the Seelie and Unseelie Courts. Her writing style is accessible and her scholarship impeccable. As an author who delves into the worlds Daimler recounts, I find it incredibly useful in my own research. I highly recommend this essential guide for those who wish to delve more deeply into the

lore, the background, and the various traditions surrounding the Gentry.
Christy Nicholas, author of the *Druid's Brooch* series

The New Dictionary of Fairies by Morgan Daimler is a treasure trove of rare information: brimming with scholarship and exquisite detail. It quickly dispels all childish and romantic notions about Fairies. It is time that we educate ourselves about Fairies if we are to be in right relationship with our world and other worlds. Daimler now provides us with the user manual and sage advice.

This is a book to read and re-read. I will put it on the reading list for my students!
Imelda Almqvist, international teacher of Sacred Art and Northern Tradition Shamanism, author of *Natural Born Shamans: A Spiritual Toolkit for Life*

A New Dictionary of Fairies is comprehensive and firmly rooted in scholarship with a genuine understanding of the Good People and their lore. With entries concerning Celtic and Western European fairies it is an essential reference book and establishes Daimler as the modern successor to the folklorist Katherine Briggs.
Jane Brideson, artist & blogger at The Ever-Living Ones

Morgan Daimler has created the most thoroughly-researched, in-depth book about the Other Crowd that I have ever had the privilege to read. This is the sort of book you recommend to everyone, but don't loan to anyone because you know you won't get it back.
KS Thompson, Sidhe Writes

Other Fairy Titles by Morgan Daimler

Fairies
A Guide to the Celtic Fair Folk
978-1-78279-650-3 (paperback)
978-1-78279-696-1 (e-book)

Fairycraft
Following the Path of Fairy Witchcraft
978-1-78535-051-1 (paperback)
978-1-78535-052-8 (e-book)

Fairy Queens
Meeting the Queens of the Otherworld
978-1-78535-833-3 (paperback)
978-1-78535-842-5 (e-book)

Fairy Witchcraft
A Neopagan's Guide to the Celtic Fairy Faith
978-1-78279-343-4 (paperback)
978-1-78279-344-1 (e-book)

Travelling the Fairy Path
Experiencing the myth, magic, and mysticism of Fairy Witchcraft
978-1-78535-752-7 (paperback)
978-1-78535-753-4 (e-book)

A New Dictionary of Faries

A 21st Century Exploration of Celtic and Related Western European Fairies

A New Dictionary of Faries

A 21st Century Exploration of Celtic and Related Western European Fairies

Morgan Daimler

Winchester, UK
Washington, USA

JOHN HUNT PUBLISHING

First published by Moon Books, 2020
Moon Books is an imprint of John Hunt Publishing Ltd., No. 3 East Street, Alresford
Hampshire SO24 9EE, UK
office@jhpbooks.com
www.johnhuntpublishing.com
www.moon-books.net

For distributor details and how to order please visit the 'Ordering' section on our website.

ISBN: 978 1 78904 036 4
978 1 78904 037 1 (ebook)
Library of Congress Control Number: 2019938084

A CIP catalogue record for this book is available from the British Library.

Design: Stuart Davies

UK: Printed and bound by CPI Group (UK) Ltd, Croydon, CR0 4YY
US: Printed and bound by Thomson-Shore, 7300 West Joy Road, Dexter, MI 48130

Contents

Do mo rúnsearc agus an Banríon Chraig Liath

Foreword

"Hey Lora", says Daimler to me, by text one fine day. "I was wondering if there's any way you might be willing to consider writing a foreword for my new book. I've never had a foreword in a book before, but I think for this one maybe it would be good."

"I'd love to", says I. And after I'd seen the first draft... "Your Dictionary is fantastic, mo chara."

So, here we are.

I met Morgan Daimler in person at my first Pantheacon event in California, in 2015, though we'd been aware of each other and moving in the same online communities for a few years before that. They were presenting in one of the Druid suites off-programme that evening, and I showed up, sitting front and centre, as I was eager to hear them speak in person and soak up all the wonderful knowledge. Apparently, that was a little intimidating, as Morgan was an admirer of my work too, and knew well how fierce I am about protecting my native Irish culture and heritage and making sure it's presented in an authentic and non-appropriative way... I was oblivious to their concerns, loved every bit of what they said, and it wasn't until we chatted after that it even occurred to me that they may have been a little nervous with me sitting right there.

We've been slightly intimidating and hugely inspiring each other ever since, I think, in both our professional lives and subsequent personal friendship. It's great.

If you've no idea who I am, and why I'm here at the front of this wonderful work, allow me to introduce myself? Lora O'Brien is ainm dom, and I'm a Draoí; a practitioner of the magic and indigenous spirituality of Ireland. My Irish Paganism work, both personally and as I teach it, centres on what I call Coibhneas Cóir - being in 'right relationship' with the land, the Gods and Ungods (our ancestors, Aos Sí, heroes and warriors... and all the rest), and the sovereign spirit of Ireland herself. This begins with learning as much as I can about those things, and making sure my practice is grounded in the reality of my culture and heritage as a strong, firm foundation.

That's what you have in this book. A strong firm foundation from which to learn the real deal about what the ancestors believed and did, and on which you can base a healthy, respectful, and aware Pagan practice... if that's your thing. And this is not just the lore of Na Daoine Maithe (the Good People) of Ireland - Morgan has spread a broad net and explored Fairy belief and ideology worldwide, though there is a particular love for the Celtic cultures that shines through.

Daimler's scholarship is second to none. With the benefit of translation skills in Old Irish, they have been studying this mythology and lore at source for many years, as well as being drawn deeper into a personal Coibhneas Cóir with the Other Crowd here. But I'll let them tell you more about that themselves if they will, for it's not my place at all. That's between Morgan and the Aos Sí (People of the Mounds) and I, for one, would not be getting in the middle of that in any way.

In short, you absolutely will not find a more thorough, genuine, self-aware, respectful, or knowledgeable writer and educator on Fairy Lore than Morgan Daimler. And this book is their best and most comprehensive work yet.

I look forward to many more years of being intimidated and inspired by my friend, and to continuing our 'Right Relationship' for as long as we both walk these worlds.

This *New Dictionary of Fairies* is a book we all need. I'm absolutely delighted to be a part of that, in some small way, and that you are taking the time to begin or continue your own relationship with the Fairies - whatever that may look like - from such a strong, firm foundation.

Go n-éirí an t-ádh leat… Good Luck!

Lora O'Brien, Waterford, Ireland, 2019.

Introduction

"Nothing is more certain than that there are fairies."
Anonymous interviewee, *'Fairy Faith in Celtic Countries'*, page 67

Throughout the written history of the Celtic language speaking peoples and up through the post-modern era you will find stories of fairies. Enigmatic, sometimes helpful and often dangerous, these beings exist in a complex and symbiotic relationship with humanity. Stories of them and of their interactions with humans both for good and ill are found in all the Celtic language speaking areas as well as in related cultures like the Anglo-Saxon and Norse, with some interweaving of related beliefs over time. The Irish Aos Sidhe may have influenced the Icelandic beliefs of the Huldufolk, and the Anglo-Saxon Aelfe shaped later views of Elves. The Scottish concept of the Seelie and Unseelie Courts have spread to other areas and even into modern fiction. Fairy beliefs are as alive and viable today as they have always been and just as richly diverse, although ironically, the advent of social media and the internet has done traditional beliefs no favours having a tendency instead to narrow beliefs and simplify concepts. Nonetheless, just as the living cultures persist so too does the so-called 'Fairy Faith' albeit evolved and adapted as we move into the 21st century.

In 1976 eminent folklorist Katherine Briggs published her book *'A Dictionary of Fairies'*, a comprehensive look at a variety of fairylore throughout western Europe. This book has become the cornerstone for many as a reference on the subject, yet in the last 40 years the field of folklore and fairylore has moved on from where it was when Briggs was writing. There have been new ideas advanced and new material covered, and in some cases uncovered, yet there is no work that equals Briggs in its scope and depth on the subject. If one is looking for a single go-to resource on fairylore the 1976 *'A Dictionary of Fairies'* remains, I believe, the best option despite the fact that it is out of print and aging. It was this realization that inspired me to create this book, *'A New Dictionary of Fairies'*, which is intended to be a comprehensive resource on Celtic fairies for the 21st century.

As the subject of fairies has grown more popular over the last several decades the amount of available information and misinformation has grown exponentially, creating an often almost impassable maze of questionable sources for those unfamiliar with the subject. Folklore is freely blended with modern fiction and divorced from both the root cultures and actual belief to create the twee fairies that populate many current media sources, and yet the genuine belief in fairies and the older folk beliefs still remain, found as they have always been in the lives of people and in stories preserved by folklorists – historic and modern. It is important to understand the sweeping nature of these beliefs and that they can simultaneously present an unchanging core as well as an evolving face. Fairylore is a living thing as much as the people who perpetuate it but it is also a long and elaborate history of belief and culture, and the two are inseparable.

Every effort has been made in the following text to gather the available folklore around the subjects for which entries are offered. While this represents as thorough a collection of fairy related folklore and anecdotes as possible it is by its nature limited. The subject itself is so vast and varied that it would prove impossible to provide any single source for all of it; rather, this should serve as a good summary of the subjects covered but also potentially a starting place for deeper research. Anyone seeking to go further on any subject covered in this text should look at the bibliography for additional resources.

Ultimately let me end this introduction to a modern attempt at codifying fairylore with a quote from an early 20th century Irish source in the 'Fairy Faith in Celtic Countries', footnote 44:1, which I think perfectly summarizes this subject *"The gentry do not tell all their secrets, and I do not understand many things about them, nor can I be sure that everything I tell concerning them is exact."*

Adventures of Connla

The oldest Irish story that depicts a fairy is the 'Echtra Condla', or 'Adventures of Connla', likely written in the 9th century but probably dating back in oral tales several centuries earlier (Beveridge, 2014).

This story tells the tale of the king's son Connla who is approached by a woman from Fairy as he and his father along with a group of men are standing on a hill. No one else can see the woman except Connla who begins talking to her. She tells him that she has come from a fairy hill and that her people are the fairy people. She then begins wooing Connla trying to convince him to go with her back to her home, while his father and his father's druid fight to keep him from leaving. For a month he lives on nothing but a fairy apple that the mysterious woman has given him before she returns and he chooses to leave with her.

This story is important for its very early depiction of fairies in Irish mythology. It demonstrates several ideas that are still found over a thousand years later in fairylore, including the danger of eating fairy food, the invisibility of fairies, and the places that they may live.

Aelfe

The word aelf (plural aelfe) comes to us from Old English and is the root of our modern word elf. Etymologically Aelfe, like the later word Elf, is related to a root term from Proto-Indo-European which likely means white. It is possible this connection to white relates to the idea of brightness or shining.

Unlike our modern view of elves, which has been heavily influenced by popular culture and mass media, aelfe were a distinct class of supernatural beings. Tracing them back in Old

English material we find that they were likely originally only male and they appear to be a class of beings seen as seductive and potentially magically dangerous (Hall, 2004). Hall in his '*Elves in Anglo-Saxon England*' discusses the use of Aelfe in compounds combined with geography giving us sea-aelfe, mountain-aelfe, or wood-aelfe for example. These beings would represent a cohesive class of spirits broken down into subtypes based on the geography they are connected to.

Aelfe looked more or less human in the older material although their physicality could vary from solid to more ephemeral in nature. These originally all male beings were androgynous in appearance, despite their overt sexuality, and over the centuries understanding of them slowly shifted into viewing them as male or female or even mostly female to a degree that by the late medieval period the grimoires which included them focused mostly on female Aelfe (Brock & Raiswell, 2018). Even after these beings were viewed as being of both genders, however, their seductiveness and beauty remained a strong factor. Female aelfe were often glossed with nymphs, angels, and particularly beautiful human women were called aelfe (Hall, 2007). Hall does suggest though that it's possible the switch from all male Aelfe to Aelfe of both genders may have partially relied on the existing belief in the amazing beauty of the male Aelfe in earlier periods.

A variety of powers were attributed to Aelfe including the ability to cause illness, take cattle, and potentially possess people. The Anglo-Saxon Leechbooks detail a variety of cures directed at Aelfe which when studied can show the existing beliefs about the abilities of the Aelfe. Aelfe are said to have a particular power or skill, referred to as 'Aelfesīden' which is a kind of magic roughly equivalent to the Norse practice of seidhr (Hall, 2007). This would denote a kind of magic that can affect people's luck, health, and mind. Cures for elf-related disorders indicate usage for symptoms of fevers, nightmares, madness, and possession, indicating that Aelfe were thought to be able to cause these things (Jolly, 1996).

Áine

One of the most famous Fairy Queens of Ireland, Áine has strong ties to the south west. Like most Irish deities Áine has a complex and sometimes contradictory mythology and is considered a human girl taken by the fairies in later folklore as well as a Fairy Queen and member of the Tuatha De Danann in the earlier stories. According to some she is the daughter of Manannán Mac Lir while others say she is the daughter of Manannán's foster son Eogabail, a Druid of the Tuatha de Danann (Beresford Ellis, 1987). In the Cath Maige Mucrama her father is a Fairy King who holds Cnoc Áine before being killed, after which Áine rules there. Her name likely means "brightness" or "splendour" and she is often associated with the sun (O hOgain, 2006; Monaghan, 2004). Not far from Áine's hill is another, Cnoc Gréine, associated with the Fairy Queen Grian (literally "Sun") who is also probably a goddess; some sources consider the two to be sisters and MacKillop suggests Áine and Grian might represent the summer and winter suns respectively (MacKillop, 1998; Monaghan, 2004). There is also a modern trend of describing Áine as a moon goddess, although there is nothing in myth or folklore to support that.

Like many Fairy Queens Áine is reputed to have love affairs with mortals and several Irish families are said to be descended from these unions including the Eoghanachta and the Fitzgeralds. The most well-known of these descendants may be Gearoid Iarla, the third Earl of Desmond. Folk stories say that his father found Áine combing her hair out by the edge of Lough Gur one day and the two became lovers, resulting in Gearoid (Evans-Wentz, 1911). His fame is due in part to the amount of folklore surrounding the end of his mortal life and the potential that he may have returned to his mother or been taken by the Fair Folk. By some accounts Gearoid was taken into Loch Gur and would return one day and in other stories he lives within the lake and can be seen riding beneath the water on a white fairy horse, while still other stories claim that Áine turned him into a goose on the shore of the lake (Berresford Ellis, 1987).

The hill of Cnoc Áine is one of the most well-known places associated with her, said to have been named after her during the settling of Ireland when she used magic to help her father win the area (O hOgain, 2006). Midsummer was her special holy day and up until the 19th century people continued to celebrate her on the eve of Midsummer with a procession around the hill, carrying torches of burning straw in honour of Áine na gClair, Áine of the Wisps (Berresford Ellis, 1987). Áine is also sometimes called Áine Chlair, a word that may relate to wisps or may be an old name for the Kerry or Limerick area (Monaghan, 2004; O hOgain, 2006). On midsummer clumps of straw would be lit on her hill and then scattered through the cultivated fields and cows to propitiate Áine's blessing (O hOgain, 2006). Some of these practices are seeing modern revivals. In County Louth there is a place called Dun Áine where people believe that the weekend after Lughnasa belongs to Áine, and in some folklore she is said to be the consort of Crom Cruach during the three days of Lughnasa (O hOgain, 2006; MacNeill, 1962). Additionally, there is another hill called Cnoc Áine in county Derry, and a third in Donegal (O hOgain, 2006). In Ulster there is a well called Tobar Áine that bears her name.

Whether a goddess or fairy queen Áine has been much loved, even up until fairly recently. Her mythology is convoluted but fascinating and as they say, she is "*the best hearted woman who ever lived*" (O hOgain, 2006).

Álfar

Discussing the Álfar is complicated because they appear in Icelandic and related mythology as both one cohesive grouping and subdivided into more specific groupings. Often in Norse myth we simply see references to the Álfar, often paired with but distinct from the Aesir, giving us phrases like in the Voluspo "*How fare the Aesir? How fare the Álfar*?" and this one from the Lokasenna "*From the Gods and* álfar *who are gathered here...*"[1]. Yet we also find distinct groups mentioned among the Álfar that seem to have their own characteristics and descriptors, the Ljósálfar, Dökkálfar, and Svartálfar. It is possible that these distinct groups are literary conventions, created later to better define different mythic motifs, or to reflect foreign influences. Certainly in modern times we see only the general grouping of Álfar in folklore and the word álf is used in compounds such as land-elf and waterfall-elf, implying that álf has more general connotations.

In the Prose Edda we see Snorri Sturluson mentioning distinct types of Álfar who appear in mythology, the LJOSALFAR and the SVARTALFAR. A third group of álfar, the DOKKALFAR also appear in mythology. Each of these will be discussed in more depth in individual entries. Scholars have different opinions on whether these groupings represent actual beliefs about these beings or were artificial categories created by Snorri in order to mimic a duotheistic system.

The Álfar and the Duergar - elves and dwarves - are also difficult groups to entirely sort out. On one hand there are some good arguments that the two may actually be the same, with Svartálfar and potentially Dökkálfar both simply being alternate names for Duergar. This is supported by three main things: many Duergar have names that incorporate the word 'álf' such as Vindalf and Gandalf; the Svartálfar were said to live in Svartálfheim but the Duergar live there as well; and the Svartálfar and Dökkálfar were said to live beneath the ground or in mounds. However, there is also evidence that might support the argument that the two groups were separate, including that they are occasionally referenced in the same work together as different groups. In verse 25 of Hrafnagaldr Óðins we see the Dökkálfar being grouped together with giants, dead men, and dwarves: "*gýgjur og þursar, náir, dvergar og dökkálfar*" [Giantesses and giants, dead men, dwarves and dark elves]. This would at the least seem to indicate some degree of separation between Duergar and Dökkálfar. In the Alvissmol it is also established that the Álfar and Duergar have different languages and kennings for things, which would also indicate separation of the two groups (Gundarsson, 2007). For the most part the Álfar would seem to be beings closely tied to the Gods, perhaps one step beneath them in power and influence, beings who can influence weather and possess powerful magic that can affect people's health. The Duergar are associated with mining and smithcraft and are not as closely tied to the Gods; when they appear in myth dealing with the Gods they must always be negotiated with or otherwise dealt with in some fashion diplomatically.

They are beings that are both benevolent and dangerous as the mood suits and depending on how they are treated, like the elves found across folklore.

Note

1 For my own opinion I think this is likely referencing the Ljósálfar whose realm would seem by descriptions to be close to the realm of the Aesir, however, as far as I know, the original text does not specify which álfar.

Alice Brand

A poem by Sir Walter Scott written in the 19th century that contains fairylore themes. The poem tells the story of Alice Brand and her lover Richard who are forced to flee as outlaws into the forest after Richard kills Alice's brother. The wood belongs to the fairy folk, however, and the elfin King resents their presence and disruption of his realm. He sends out a being named Urgan to curse Richard, choosing this particular fairy to send because he was once a Christened human and is therefore impervious to Christian signs and prayers. Urgan goes out to do this but is stopped by Alice who questions who he is and why he has come to them. He tells her that he was taken by the King of Fairy when he was dying and of his subsequent life in Fairy and admits that he was once a mortal and could be restored if a brave woman would cross his forehead three times. Alice does this and Urgan's true form is restored, and his identity revealed.

Merry it is in the good greenwood,
When the mavis and merle are singing,
When the deer sweeps by, and the hounds are in cry,
And the hunter's horn is ringing.
"O Alice Brand, my native land
Is lost for love of you;
And we must hold by wood aud wold,
As outlaws wont to do.
"O Alice, 'twas all for thy locks so bright
And 'twas all for thine eyes so blue,
That on the night of our luckless flight
Thy brother bold I slew.
"Now must I teach to hew the beech
The hand that held the glaive,
For leaves to spread our lowly bed,
And stakes to fence our cave.
"And for vest of pall, thy fingers small,
That wont on harp to stray,
A cloak must shear from the slaughter'd deer,
To keep the cold away.
"Richard! if my brother died,
'Twas but a fatal chance;
For darkling was the battle tried,
And fortune sped the lance.
"If pall and vair no more I wear,
Nor thou the crimson sheen,
As warm, we'll say, is the russet grey,
As gay the forest-green.

"And, Richard, if our lot be hard,
And lost thy native land,
Still Alice has her own Richard,
And he his Alice Brand. "
'Tis merry, 'tis merry, in good greenwood,
So blithe Lady Alice is singing;
On the beech's pride, and oak's brown side
Lord Richard's axe is ringing.
Up spoke the moody Elfin King,
Who won'd within the hill
Like wind in the porch of a ruin'd church
His voice was ghostly shrill.
"Why sounds yon stroke on beech and oak,
Our moonlight circle's screen?
Or who comes here to chase the deer,
Beloved of our Elfin Queen?
Or who may dare on wold to wear
The fairies' fatal green?
"Up, Urgan, up! to yon mortal hie,
For thou wert christen'd man;
For cross or sign thou wilt not fly,
For mutter'd word or ban.
"Lay on him the curse of the wither'd heart,
The curse of the sleepless eye;
Till he wish and pray that his life would part,
Nor yet find leave to die."
'Tis merry, 'tis merry, in good greenwood,
Though the birds have still'd their singing;
The evening blaze doth Alice raise,
And Richard is fagots bringing.
Up Urgan starts, that hideous dwarf,
Before Lord Richard stands
And, as he cross'd and bless'd himself,
"I fear not sign," quoth the grisly elf,

"That is made with bloody hands."
But out then spoke she, Alice Brand,
That woman, void of fear,
"And if there's blood upon his hand,
Tis but the blood of deer."
"Now loud thou liest, thou bold of mood!
It cleaves unto his hand
The stain of thine own kindly blood,
The blood of Ethert Brand."
Then forward stepp'd she, Alice Brand,
And made the holy sign,---
"And if there's blood on Richard's hand
A spotless hand is mine."
"And I conjure thee, Demon elf
By Him whom Demons fear,
To show us whence thou art thyself,
And what thine errand here?"
"'Tis merry, 'tis merry, in Fairy-land,
When fairy birds are singing,
When the court doth ride by their monarch's side
With bit and bridle ringing:
"And gaily shines the Fairy-land---
But all is glistening show,
Like the idle gleam that December's beam
Can dart on ice and snow.
"And fading, like that varied gleam,
Is our inconstant shape,
Who now like knight and lady seem,
And now like dwarf and ape.
"It was between the night and day,
When the Fairy King has power
That I sunk down in a sinful fray,
And, 'twixt life and death, was snatch'd away
To the joyless Elfin bower.

"But wist I of a woman bold
Who thrice my brow durst sign,
I might regain my mortal mold,
As fair a form as thine."
She cross'd him once, she cross'd him twice,
That lady was so brave
The fouler grew his goblin hue,
The darker grew the cave.
She cross'd him thrice, that lady bold
He rose beneath her hand
The fairest knight on Scottish mold,
Her brother, Ethert Brand!
Merry it is in good greenwood
When the mavis and merle are singing,
But merrier were they in Dunfermline grey,
When all the bells were ringing.
(Acland, 1998)

The poem contains some common fairylore themes including the power of Christian symbols, green as a fairy colour, transformation into a fairy, and rescue from Fairy. The fairies in 'Alice Brand' are averse to Christian symbols, the implication being that they cannot bear them, and so must send one of their member who is exempt from this aversion due to his previous state as a christened human. There is repeated emphasis on the colour green both in naming of the greenwood and in the wearing of green by the pair being what angers the Elfin King who feels that colour belongs only to the fairies. And there is the idea that a human straddling life and death can be seized by the fairies and taken to join their number with the human's relatives all believing the person died; this idea is, of course, seen as well in 'Tam Lin' and the wider array of changeling lore. The idea of rescuing a person from fairy is presented in a more unique way in 'Alice Brand', seeming closer to an exorcism or breaking of an enchantment than what we might expect of the typical rescue. In this sense it is a significant piece of evidence relating to beliefs around the topic. The interweaving of these themes make this particular poem an important one in the corpus of ballad material, although 'Alice Brand' is not as well-known as others like 'Tam Lin' or 'Thomas the Rhymer'.

Aliens

A question that comes up for those who study fairies and/or folklore is what if any connection might exist between fairies and extra-terrestrials? There is certainly no consensus on the topic with avid Ufologists viewing fairies as a previous understanding of aliens and many fairyologists seeing aliens and UFOs as a modern way to interpret fairies and fairy encounters. This article will take the latter viewpoint.

Fairies have been a part of belief and folklore for as long as we have written stories from the various cultures we find them in[1]. However, as we have moved, culturally, into the modern and post-modern period fairies have largely in the dominant culture of America become relegated to children's stories and nostalgia. This left a contextual void for people having experiences to use to explain what they were experiencing. This void was filled by fiction and film as popculture embraced the idea of extra-terrestrials and our cultural consciousness became saturated by these new stories. The first aliens appear in fiction as early as 1887 in a short story titled '*Les Xipehuz*' and in Hollywood in the silent films of the early 1900's; the idea, however, really bloomed post World War II in both speculative fiction and film. The first UFO sighting in the US is thought to have occurred in 1947; the first reported abduction in 1961. This timeline is roughly synchronous with a shift to viewing fairies in America as twee nature spirits and tending to minimize their potential danger to humans.

When we compare fairylore and alien and UFO lore we see some striking similarities:

- In traditional fairylore fairies are well known to steal people, sometimes permanently sometime temporarily. In cases where people are returned they may have terrifying stories of their experience and may have physical marks. In turn alien abduction stories also feature aliens stealing people sometimes for benign purposes, or obscure ones, sometimes for cruel reasons. The people are returned with nightmarish memories and sometimes physical marks. The Slua Sidhe are noted to lift people up into the sky and they as well as some other types of fairies were said to carry people across the sky or fly with them, returning them later; modern UFO encounters sometimes include people being taken up into alien crafts and carried away only to be returned to earth. The reason for taking people, including forced reproduction, are also consistent between both fairy stories and alien abductions although how the two play out historically versus currently vary.
- Time is often noted to move differently in the world of Fairy; so too those who describe alien abductions often talk about weird issues with time. Particularly in Fairy it has been said that what feels like a day there will be much longer amounts of time here and similarly in alien abductions people describe being gone for minutes that were really hours or hours that were really days.
- Some fairy encounters, including those with beings like the Mâran, include sleep paralysis and overwhelming fear that occur to a person in their bed. In the same way alien encounters are sometimes described as happening to a person who is sleeping and wakes to find themselves unable to move and terrified. The descriptions of both types of encounters look almost identical when the type of being isn't mentioned, although the modern alien encounters usually involve abduction as well which the Mâran do not.

- Food can play a role in both fairy encounters and alien encounters. In traditional fairy encounters fairies would often offer food to people, usually with the intent of trapping the person in Fairy so that they could not leave. In some alien encounters the person is offered food of various sorts as well although the intention is unclear. In fairylore when the food was refused there are stories of the fairies trying to force the person to eat the food or drink the liquid, or physically punishing them for refusing; in the same way in some alien abduction stories there have been accounts of people forced to eat or drink substances, in some cases violently.
- Fairies were noted to dance in circles and to leave behind fairy rings in their wake. These could be rings of mushrooms or of darker or lighter grass. UFOs have also been noted to leave circular marks in places they have been seen landing, sometimes flattened grass sometimes burned areas. Similarly, the idea of strange lights being attributed to fairies has a long history in folklore, often associated with danger, while UFOs are described as both lights in the sky as well as strange lights seen through trees. These sites afterwards, of both types, are noted to have strange properties and effects on people.
- Descriptions of alien beings are generally in line with that provided by science fiction and fairylore tells us that the Good People can use glamour to appear however they want - and to make our surroundings appear to us however they want – making it possible that the aliens people are seeing are fairies using glamour. If we expect them to look like what science fiction has taught us aliens will look like it is possible that is exactly what we see during an abduction experience.
- There are people who will say that we see far fewer fairy encounters today and fewer fairy abductions, yet now we

have the phenomena of alien encounters and abductions, which have many of the same hallmarks. One might argue that the fairies are no less active but have simply switched how people are perceiving their activity so that those who believe in or are open to believing in aliens get aliens, while those who believe in fairies continue to have experiences more in line with older folklore. Fairies used to be feared and that fear had power; aliens still are feared as an unknown and technologically superior factor.

For further on this subject I suggest reading 'Passport to Magonia' and 'Trojan Feast' both of which discuss fairies and aliens as an interwoven subject.

Note

1 There is, of course, no way to know how long they have existed in oral cultures.

Allison Gross

A ballad that tells the story of a man transformed into a worm after rejecting the amorous advances of a witch. He is cursed to circle around a tree until one Halloween when the SEELIE COURT rides by and the FAIRY QUEEN takes pity on him and returns him to his true form

Oh, Allison Gross, that lives in yon tower
The ugliest witch in the north country
Has trysted me one day up in her bower
And many fair speeches she made to me
She stroked my head and she combed my hair
And she set me down softly on her knee
Says, "If you will be my sweetheart so true
So many good things I would give you'"
She showed me a mantle of red scarlet
With golden flowers and fringes fine

Says, "If you will be my sweetheart so true
This goodly gift it shall be yours"
"Away, away, you ugly witch
Hold far away and let me be
I never will be your sweetheart so true
And I wish I were out of your company"
She next brought me a shirt of the softest silk
Well wrought with pearls about the band
Says, "If you will be my one true love
This goodly gift you shall command"
She showed me a cup of the good red gold
Well set with jewels so fair to see
Says, "If you will be my sweetheart so true
This goodly gift I will give you'"
"Away, away, you ugly witch
Hold far away and let me be
For I wouldn't once kiss your ugly mouth
For all the gifts that you could give'"
She's turned her right and round about
And thrice she blew on a grass-green horn
And she swore by the moon and the stars above
That she would make me rue the day I was born
Then out she has taken a silver wand
And she's turned her three times round and round
She's muttered such words till my strength it failed
And I fell down senseless upon the ground
She's turned me into an ugly worm
And made me toddle around the tree
And aye, on every Saturday night
My sister Maisry came to me
With silver basin and silver comb
To comb my head upon her knee
Before I had kissed her ugly mouth
I'd rather have toddled about the tree

But as it fell out on last Halloween
When the seely court was riding by
The queen lighted down on a rowan bank
Not far from the tree where I was wont to lie
She took me up in her milk white hand
And she's stroked me three times on her knee
She changed me again to my own proper shape
And I no more must toddle about the tree
(Child, 1882)

In this ballad we see the often capricious nature of the fairies illustrated, as the Fairy Queen aids the cursed man apparently on a whim, returning him to his true shape and removing the witch's curse. This also illustrates the greater power possessed by the Queen, who can remove the witch's magic at will simply by touching the cursed man three times while to place the spell the witch needed to use a wand, turn around three times, and speak magical words.

Alp Luachra

Believed by some to be a natural illness described in folklore and by others to be a kind of fairy being; Rev. Kirk equates it to the Scottish Joint-eater. A salamander like creature that sneaks into the open mouth of a sleeping person if they are lying near water and afterwards resides within them. The Alp Luachra consumes the food the person eats so that the person in turn becomes ill and wastes away. Douglas Hyde speaks of it in his book where a person afflicted by one is described this way:

"I tell you again, and believe me, that it's an Alp Luachra you swallowed. Didn't you say yourself that you felt something leaping in your stomach the first day after you being sick? That was the Alp Luachra; and as the place he was in was strange to him at first, he was uneasy in it, moving backwards and forwards, but when he

was a couple of days there, he settled himself, and he found the place comfortable, and that's the reason you're keeping so thin, for every bit you're eating the Alp Luachra is getting the good out of it, and you said yourself that one side of you was swelled; that's the place where the nasty thing is living." (Hyde, 1890)

In Hyde's account the person finds no relief from doctors but is eventually led by a beggar to a more knowledgeable person who has a cure. The ill man is fed a great amount of heavily salted meat and then instructed to lay down by a stream with his mouth open; after waiting for a long time the Alp Luachra (there are more than a dozen), who are thirsty from the salt, are driven out of the person by the smell of the water. This is considered the standard cure for these beings in folklore, as nothing else will get them to depart the person's body willingly (Briggs, 1976).

Also see: JOINT EATER

Aoibheall

Aoibheall is the Fairy Queen of Clare, a powerful being whose folklore goes back to the 11th century in that area of Ireland and who still appears in stories today. Her name comes from older forms of Irish where the word oibell means spark, flame, or heat, and can also be an adjective meaning bright or merry.

Her sister is the Fairy Queen Clíodhna and the two have been rivals at times over human men (MacKillop, 1998). At one point when the two were contesting over a man named Caomh Clíodhna turned Aoibheall into a white cat. Aoibheall is said to possess a harp whose music can kill those who hear it; she can also control the weather. She is said to be the Bean Sidhe of the Dal gCais and by extension the O'Briens; folkloric accounts say that she had one of the sons of Brian Boru as her lover and came to him as to warn him of his fate before the battle of Clontarf in 1014.

Her sí is at Craig Liath [Craglea] which is also called Craig

Aoibheall [Crageevel] (MacKillop, 1998). Nearby there is a well associated with her called Tobhar Aoibill. Her presence is connected to the area of Slieve Bearnagh and more generally around Killaloe. One later bit of folklore says that Aoibheall left the area after the wood around Craig Laith was cut down. She is often called the Fairy Queen of Tuamhain [Thomond] which was a historic territory of the Dál gCais that is now modern day Clare, Limerick, and some of Tipperary.

She appears as the judge in Merriman's 18th century poem An Cúirt an Mhéan Oíche, hearing the complaint of women that men do them wrong in not marrying them and taking advantage of them. In that poem she is called *"the truthful"* and *"all-seeing"*. She sides with the women, ruling that men must marry by 21 or are open to women's reprisals. She also appears in the folk song An Buachaill Caol Dubh where she asks the spirit of alcohol, personified as a *'dark, slim boy'*, to release a person under his sway.

Aos Sí

See: Daoine Sí

Amadán na Bruidhne - The Fairy Fool

The two most dangerous fairies in folklore, arguably, may be the FAIRY QUEEN and the Fairy Fool both of whom are said to bring madness with a touch. The Fairy Queen may be the more well-known, with a good amount of folklore to be found about her under either the title or a specific name while the Fairy Fool is not as well known.

Although usually simply called the Fairy Fool in English in Irish we find at least two distinct types of Fairy Fools, the Amadán na Bruidhne [fool of the fairy hall] and Amadán Mór [great fool]. The Amadán na Bruidhne inspired terror because one touch from him could paralyze a person, drive them mad, or even kill (MacKillop, 1998). There is some debate about whether his touch was the FAIRY STROKE or a different type of power, but since madness, paralysis and death are things that a variety of fairies can cause, it is hard to be certain. Unlike the illnesses caused by other types of fairies, however, the damage caused by the touch of the Fairy Fool was impervious to any magical or herbal cures, which is part of why he was especially feared. In contrast to the Amadán na Bruidhne the Amadán Mór is a more elusive figure who may appear as a king of the fairies or leading the fairy host but was still associated with the fearsome qualities of the Fairy Fool (MacKillop, 1998). It is always risky, of course, to run into any of the fairy folk but the Fairy Fool represented a particular danger, as is related by Yeats, quoting someone he had interviewed, "They, the other sort of people, might be passing you close here and they might touch you. But any that gets the touch of the Amadán-na-Breena [Fairy Fool] is done for." (Yeats, 1962, p 110).

By some accounts every group of fairies counted among their number both a Queen and a fairy fool (Yeats, 1998). The QUEEN OF ELFLAND is discussed elsewhere and established as a very powerful being; along with the Queen, though, we see the fool, described as just as ubiquitous in Fairy and equally powerful in a different way because the fool brings incurable madness to those they touch. The Fairy Fool can be male or female but it's the male fool that is more commonly seen in stories; the male Fool was described appearing in the form of a sheep with a beard or as a half-naked person with great strength and distorted features (Yeats, 1962). Other folklore said that the Fairy Fool was a shapeshifter who changed shape every couple days between a young seeming human form and that of an animal, however, in any form would try to touch a person and drive them mad (Yeats, 1962). Despite these seemingly fluid forms and variety of appearances the Amadán na Bruidhne in folklore seemed to have been easily recognized for what he was by those who saw him, perhaps indicating that he has an aura of Otherworldliness or madness to him that humans could perceive.

Seeing the Fairy Fool in and of itself presents no danger, and there are stories of those who saw the Fool and managed to escape or avert him without being harmed; however, if he did succeed in touching the person they would go mad. Even if they lived for years afterwards there would be no cure for the Fool's touch. When the Amadán na Bruidhne appeared he might be seen by a person travelling alone or by one person among a group even though the rest of the group saw nothing.

Yeats related one story of the Fairy Fool in his book 'Celtic Twilight' told to him by an old woman in the late 19th century:

> *"He was a boy I knew well, and he told me that one night a gentleman came to him, that had been his landlord, and that was dead. And he told him to come along with him, for he wanted him to fight another man. And when he went he found two great troops of them [fairies], and the other troop had a living man with them too, and he was put to fight him. And they had a great fight, and he got the better of the other man, and then the troop on his side gave a great shout, and he was left home again. But about three years after that he was cutting bushes in a wood and he saw the Amadán coming at him. He had a big vessel in his arms, and it was shining, so that the boy could see nothing else; but he put it behind his back then and came running, and the boy said he looked wild and wide, like the side of the hill. And the boy ran, and he threw the vessel after him, and it broke with a great noise, and whatever came out of it, his head was gone there and then. He lived for a while after, and used to tell us many things, but his wits were gone. He thought they mightn't have liked him to beat the other man..."* (Yeats, 1962, pages 110-111)

According to Yeats' sources June was the most dangerous month for fairy encounters because of the activity of the Fairy Fool.

Ann Jeffries

Ann Jeffries was a servant in Cornwall in the late 17th century who fell ill for a period of time, afflicted by what many believed was a fairy induced illness. After recovering from this sickness Ann by all accounts became a devout Protestant but she also afterwards had a power to heal by laying her hands on a person. She would later admit to her employers, who had kept her on and care for her while she was ill, that she had been made sick by the fairies and that they would come to her and tell her things even after she was well again, and Ann attributed her abilities to them (Buccola, 2006). It was also claimed by her employers' son that Ann lived for some six months on nothing but fairy food, eating no human food at all, and that the Good People provided all that she needed from money to supplies for her healing work (Buccola, 2006). Like many others before her Ann eventually fell afoul of the legal system, not for her healing but for prophecies that she began to give although these too she said came from the fairies. She was eventually imprisoned and denied food, with the intent to prove that she was lying about the fairies feeding her, however, she did not seem to suffer for lack of being fed by her jailers and after some time she was released because they could not prove she was lying about this first claim (Buccola, 2006).

Annwn

The Welsh name of the Otherworld, although it is often given in Welsh dictionaries as 'underworld'. In the Mabinogion it is said to be ruled by Arawn while later folklore names Gwyn ap Nudd as its king. In the first branch of the Mabinogion we learn that rule of Annwn is divided between Arawn and his rival Hafgan, who Arawn is unable to defeat until he gains the help of the mortal Pwyll. After Hafgan's death Arawn rules Annwn in its entirety. A variety of beings, such as the Gwragedd Annwn, are specifically associated with this place. It also seems to be the home of both fairies and some Welsh Gods including not only Arawn and Gwyn ap Nudd but also Bran.

Annwn and its inhabitants appear throughout the Mabinogion in various ways, although the exact location of Annwn is unclear, appearing to shift between tales. In the Arthurian poem '*Preiddeu Annwfn*' it seems that Annwn is or includes a group of islands, whereas the Mabinogion describes it more as a cohesive place within Wales. Annwn itself does not seem to be that different from mortal earth although the animals and other creatures within it vary from those that are like mortal beasts to those that are monstrous and dangerous.

Appearance

Fairy appearances can vary widely, to a degree that it becomes almost impossible to say anything definitive about how fairies as a group may look. There are, however, some broad generalizations that can be made within wider categories that may help people grasp exactly how varied this subject can be, and when we look at specific types of fairies we can make clearer statements about appearance.

Size – in folklore we may find fairies such the Muryans who appear as small as ants while other beings like the Jack-in-Irons, Jimmy Squarefoot, and some types of Trolls can be more than 12 feet tall. There are even some folkloric accounts of giants as tall as trees. Most commonly fairies seem to fall into two rough size categories, with many obvious exceptions, and these are those described between 18 inches and 3 feet tall, such as Leprechauns, and those described between 5 and 6 feet tall, for example Baobhan Sithe. The Tylwyth Teg are described in Welsh sources as about the size of children and as looking much like average adult humans (Evans-Wentz, 1911).

Colouring – fairies can be found with a variety of different skin and hair colours, from those that might realistically be found among human populations to more Otherworldly variations such as green. In anecdotal accounts we find human-like fairies described as blonde, brunette, and red-headed (Evans-Wentz, 1911). Similarly, fairy animals may look much like earthly animals or may be distinctly coloured, sometimes white with red ears or sometimes a dark green.

Anthropomorphic – Many fairies are depicted in folklore and anecdotal accounts as appearing very human looking, no matter what their size or colouring may be. The children of Woolpit were said to have green tinted skin but otherwise looked entirely human and indeed the girl grew into a seemingly ordinary human woman. Stories of the Irish Daoine Sidhe usually describe them as very human in appearance, although clearly of an Otherworldly nature, and some shapeshifting fairies are known to take on human-seeming forms including the Púca and Kelpie.

Animalistic – As described above fairies often appear in anthropomorphic forms, however, these are not always entirely human looking. Descriptions of dwarves sometimes mention that their feet are animal-like and goblins may be described sometimes as having very animalistic appearances including the tufted ears, whiskers, and tails we see in Christina Rossetti's poem '*Goblin Market*'. Huldufolk may be described on occasion with cow's tails, Baobhan Sithe with deer's hooves, and Glaistigs are sometimes said to have the hooves and even bodies of goats.

Deformities – Another common feature of fairies is some type of physical deformity which doesn't seem to impede their actions any but which they are at pains to hide in order to pass as human. In Scottish folklore a fairy may have but one nostril or eye, large teeth, or webbed feet (Campbell, 1900). The Huldufolk, besides having tails, were also sometimes said to have hollow backs so that while their fronts would seem to be that of an attractive human being touching their back would reveal a concave space. Dwarves in some stories were described with backwards turned feet and accounts of brownies might mention a lack of noses.

This is only, obviously, a small sample of the huge array of fairies that can be found in folklore. I hope though that this has illustrated the range of descriptions we see, from human-like to monstrous, from tiny to taller, from what we may call beautiful to what we judge as ugly, from entirely human-like to animalistic, with various skin colours including green. As Katherine Briggs says:

> *"The fairy people are good and bad, beautiful and hideous, stately and comical...one of their greatest variations is size"* (Briggs, 1976, page 368).

Hollow backs, back-turned feet, hooves, single eyes and limbs, small, huge, horns, tails, famine-thin and very large, webbed feet or hands, are all descriptions that we find in various folklore for different types of fairy beings.

Arawn

A Welsh mythic figure who appears in the first branch of the Mabinogion and is described as the king of a land called Annwn, which is often equated to the Otherworld.

Arawn is described in the first branch of the Mabinogion wearing grey woollen hunting clothes and riding a grey horse, with red-eared white hunting hounds (Guest, 1877). After the human king Pwyll crosses unknowingly into Arawn's realm and drives his hounds off a deer they had brought down Arawn confronts him, and after some discussion the two agree to switch places for a year, with Pwyll assuming Arawn's throne in order to defeat an enemy that Arawn is unable to successfully fight. The two remain friends after returning to their rightful places.

Arawn in later folklore leads a version of the Wild Hunt

including his hounds, the Cwn Annwn.

Asrai

An English water fairy that lives beneath the surface of bodies of water and is sometimes dredged up by fishermen. In several folktales featuring Asrai the hapless fairy is pulled up by a fisherman, bound by the human who captured her, covered in water plants, but dies and becomes nothing but a puddle of water in the bottom of the boat (Briggs, 1976).

Athach

A word which in Gaidhlig means, among other things, giant and monster Athach is a term for particularly dangerous Scottish fairies. Not a specific type of fairy but like the Scottish Fuathan Athach is a group which includes a variety of types of fairies known to be especially monstrous or dangerous to humans (Briggs, 1976).

Aughisky

Anglicized name for the EACH UISCE

Avalon

Also called the Isle of Apples or the Fortunate Isle, Avalon is an Otherworldly land found in Arthurian lore. Said to be ruled over by nine sisters led by the eldest, Morgan, who is also the wisest (Simpson & Roud, 2000).

B

Bánánach

See: Battlefield fairies

Baobhan Sìth

One of the most intriguing Scottish fairies is the Baobhan Sìth. There are only a few stories preserved in folklore about this spirit, and they are fairly homogeneous in painting a picture of female fairies, usually appearing in groups, who seduce young men and kill them by drinking their blood. They seem to be members of the FUATH - generally dangerous water spirits - and also of the Unseelie Court. Baobhan Sìth are described as beautiful human-looking women, about five feet tall, who wear long green dresses to hide their feet which are the hooves of a deer. It's said they take the form of wolves and crows or ravens.

The name itself is both straightforward and complicated, as is often the case with folklore. Baobhan is given as 'wizard', a wicked woman who curses or does evil to others, and a female spirit 'who haunts rivers' (Dwelly, 1902). In Gaidhlig Sìth is used in the genitive case as a modifier to indicate something is from or has a nature related to Fairy; hence Fear-Sìthe 'Men of the Fairies' i.e. fairies, Ban-Sìth, 'fairy woman' and muime-shìthe 'fairy godmother'. So with Baobhan Sìth we have roughly 'evil fairy woman' or 'fairy woman who curses', or perhaps 'fairy woman who lurks near rivers'.

When we find the Baobhan Sithe in folklore we find a commonly repeated story of four young men out hunting who stay over in the woods one night, finding shelter in a small lean-to or hut. One of the men begins playing music and they find themselves joined by four beautiful women. Three of the four begin dancing with three of the young men while the fourth lingers near the musician. That young man notices something is wrong with his companions, often seeing a trickle of blood on one of their necks and flees into the night, pursued by the fourth woman; he hides among a group of horses whose iron-shoes deter the spirit until dawn. Upon returning to the shelter he finds all three of his friends have been killed in the night, dying of blood loss.

This story can be found with slight variations although all have the same major points. In one it is one of the dancers who notices blood on another dancer, becomes alarmed, and tells the woman he is dancing with that he needs to go out, at which she tried to convince him to stay; once outside he flees and she chases him through the night (Robertson, 1905). Sometimes the number of men varies or their reason for being in the shelter; sometimes one of them wishes for companions before the women appear other times the women show up claiming to be lost. In one variation the musician who was singing for the group as they danced noticed the women had hooves instead of feet and stopped singing in surprise, at which point all his friends fell dead to the floor and he ran from the building (Robertson, 1905). In several versions the Baobhan Sìth whose partner flees grabs his plaid in her hands as he first tries to run and he leaves it behind to escape. Often the man does not return alone to the shelter but instead goes back to his village and returns with a group of people who together find the bloodless bodies of the remaining men (Robertson, 1905).

The young man in the story was saved because he realized the women were actually Baobhan Sìth and ran away, and because he was smart and took shelter among the horses. Some modern articles will say that the Baobhan Sìth have a fear of horses but that is a misunderstanding of the story; it was the horses' iron-shod hooves that held the fairy off not the presence of the animals themselves. Briggs, repeating MacKenzie makes this clear here:

"He took refuge among the horse and she could not get to him, probably because of the iron with which they were shod." (Briggs, 1976, p16).

In folklore the Baobhan Sìth are said to wear green dresses and to have the hooves of deer in place of human feet although they are very beautiful otherwise (MacKenzie, 1935). They use their beauty to seduce and prey upon men, as the above story illustrates by drinking their blood. Except for possibly having hooves they otherwise seem exactly like human women and are mistaken for them until it's too late. Besides their human form they are also able to take on the form of hooded crows or ravens (MacKenzie, 1935). They show many qualities that are common to fairies, including wearing green, having a deformity (in this case deer's hooves) which they try to hide, and being able to shift shape. Their preference for humans as prey, certainly put them in the darker category of the Unseelie Court.

Baobhan, which is also given as Baobh, is closely related to the word Badhbh, and both have the meanings of 'hag, witch, she-spirit' and 'wizard' (Am Faclair Beag, 2017). Badhbh, of course, is also related to the Irish war goddess Badb, who was later associated with the ban-nighe, the fairy women who were seen washing bloody clothes or armor in rivers as omens of death. I believe it is likely that the Baobhan Sìth is another type of fairy that is rooted in the older war goddess, later diminished and distorted in folklore. It is only a supposition but since we see badb in old Irish also appearing as bodb, and we see Badb/ Bodb meaning deadly, dangerous, fatal and in Gaidhlig baobh having connotations of furious, destructive, frightening, I think it is at least possible (eDIL, 2017; Dwelly, 1902). The association between the Baobhan Sìth and female spirits who haunt rivers is also very similar to the ban-nighe who is strongly related to Badb, and like Badb the Baobhan Sìth can take the form of a hooded crow or raven. We can also see some of this connection in some of the compounds formed with Baobhan, like baobhachd which means both the actions of a wicked woman and the sound of crows (Dwelly, 1902).

The Baobhan Sìth are a more obscure but fascinating type of fairy, one of the few vampiric entities we can find in Celtic fairylore. They seem in many ways similar to the deadlier types of Leannán Sí as well as to the closely related Bean Sí, yet they have a distinct lore of their own.

Battlefield Fairies

In Irish mythology, particularly the Ulster cycle we see references to certain groupings of fairies that appear on the battlefield, although they are obscure figures. For example in this passage from the Táin Bó Cúailnge:

> *"Crothais a scíath & cressaigis a slega & bertnaigis a chlaidem, & dobert rém curad asa bragit, co ro recratar bánanaig & boccanaig & geniti glinni & demna aeoír re úathgráin na gáre dos-bertatar ar aird. Co ro mesc ind Neamain (.i. in Badb) forsin t-slóg."*
>
> "He [Cu Chulainn] brandished his shield and he shook his spears and he brandished his sword and gave a warrior's cry from his throat, so that the bánnaig and bocannaig and Otherworldly-woman of the glen and demons of the air answered because of the terrifying cry he had raised on high. So that the Nemain (that is the Badb) came and intoxicated the host". Translation Daimler 2017

In this and similar examples we see these three beings, the Bánánach, Bocánach, and Geniti glini appearing together, sometimes also with the fairy host and sometimes with the 'demons of the air' which is likely also a reference to the fairy host. All three were known to appear shrieking or screaming over or near battlefields.

There's not a lot of available information about these specific spirits, but here is what we do have:

Bánánach - described in the eDIL as a *'preternatural being haunting the field of battle'* (eDIL, 2017). The root of the name is suggested as Bánán which is further suggested as bán in this case probably meaning pale or bloodless, but also possibly meaning 'white'. We may perhaps postulate from this that these spirits appear pale or are clad in white, which would be in line with some other spirits associated with death. MacKillop suggests that the Bánánach is specifically a female spirit. In the Fianaigecht we are told that the Bánánach and Bocánach appeared with the Red-Mouthed Badb, one of the Irish war Goddesses further connecting them to the battlefield. Arguably we know the least about the Bánánach but if we translate the name as 'pale spirits' or 'white spirit-women' we may possibly tie them into other spirits like the White Ladies; although they may equally be connected to the Bean Sí. In some Irish folklore the Bean Sí are said to wear white, to shriek or wail, and to predict death and they are often connected back to the goddess Badb (MacKillop, 1998). This description does seem strikingly similar to the Bánánach, the biggest differences being the Bánánach's association with the battlefield and less explicit associations with death.

Bocánach - loosely described as a goat-like supernatural being, like the Bánánach it is known to haunt battlefields (eDIL, 2017). The name comes from the word Bocán and Boc, both meaning a he-goat. MacKillop considers them a type of goblin. It's possible that they may be similar to or related to the Púca and the Bócan who are both shape-shifting goblin-like fairies associated with goats. In the Cogadh Gaedhel re Gallaibh the Bocánach and the Bánánach appear on the battlefield with the Siabarsluag, the fairy host.

Geniti glini - a supernatural female specter who appears on battlefields, the name literally means 'Otherworldly-woman of the valley' (eDIL, 2017). O'Mulconry's Glossary gives us this about them: "genit glinde .i. ben i nglinn (gen .i. ben, glynnon

> .i. foglaid .i. banfoglaid bid a nglinn)" [Supernatural-women of the valley that is women of the glen (a girl that is a woman, glynnon that is a outlaw that is a female-outlaw living in the valley]. They are also sometimes called gelliti glini, translated as spirit of the valley, possibly due to a confusion between the words genit (supernatural woman) and geilt, a person driven mad in battle or a crazy person living in the wild (eDIL, 2017). These spectral women are strongly associated with shrieking on the battlefield as well as appearing there. Of the three named in this grouping the Geniti glini would seem to be the most obviously dangerous, particularly with O'Mulconry's direct equation of them with outlaws, using a word - foglaid - that also means reavers, plunderers, and later was a general term for an enemy.

Although we don't know too much about these spirits we can make some general associations based on when and how they appear in mythology. They usually seem to show up right before or during battles, and act to create or magnify feelings of battle-rage, frenzy, and madness. They appear sometimes with Nemain or Badb, Irish war Goddesses, who are both also associated with inspiring these things in warriors and armies. I think we can also safely say that they are not limited to the battlefield but are merely drawn to it, the way crows and ravens are drawn to carnage, since they also appear in conjunction with other mass groupings of fairies like the Siabarsluag. Although the information we have on them is obscure they do seem to have some connections to more well-known spirits including the Bean Sí and Púca and it is at least possible that they might be early literary representations of spirits we later came to know by other names.

Bean Nighe

Bean Nighe means 'Washer Woman' in Gaidhlig and she is a kind of fairy found in Scottish and Irish lore. The Bean Nighe is most often found near streams and rivers, in or near the water, washing the clothes of people who will die soon. Like the Bean Sidhe it is unclear whether the Bean Nighe is an omen of death or a cause of it although she tends to have a grim reputation. Those who encounter the Bean Nighe and interrupt her at her work will earn her ire and she will directly attack people who get her attention this way (Briggs, 1976).

The Bean Nighe is described with webbed red feet, wearing a green dress, and may appear young or old (Briggs, 1976; MacKillop, 1998). Some connect this fairy back to the Irish Goddesses Badb and the Morrigan, while others believe they are the spirits of women who died in childbirth. According to this second theory they are doomed to wash the clothes of those about to die until the time the Bean Nighe would have died naturally (Briggs, 1976).

There is a possibility of less dire encounters with this fairy. A person who finds the Bean Nighe away from her stream or river and can successfully keep her from the water will earn three wishes (Briggs, 1976). Someone who is willing to take a greater risk can attempt to seize hold of the Bean Nighe and nurse from her breast, which will make them her foster child and earn her protection and blessing (MacKillop, 1998).

Bean Sídhe

The name Bean Sí simply means 'fairy woman' and is found in a variety of spellings including the anglicized Banshee. The Bean Sí may or may not actually be a fairy, although she is often considered one in both historic and modern folklore.

When we look at exactly what the Bean Sí may be and what her origin is we find there's no simple answer, but multiple options ranging from literary to folk tradition. MacKillop in his Dictionary of Celtic Mythology says that *"In folk etiology the banshee was thought to be the spirit of a woman who died in childbirth, or of a murdered pregnant woman."* (MacKillop, 1998). Lysaght in her very thorough work 'The Banshee: The Irish Death Messenger' has an entire chapter on the topic which elucidates the following possible theories:

- She may be a fairy
- She may be one of the Tuatha Dé Danann
- She may be the child of a fairy and a mortal
- She may be a human woman, living, abducted by the fairies but allowed to return to caoin for her family
- She may be a fallen angel
- She may be the spirit of an unbaptized child
- She may be the ghost of a murdered maiden, killed by a family member
- She may be a human soul working off misdeeds in a fashion like purgatory (specifically the sin of pride which is why according to folk tradition the banshee has long beautiful hair she combs out)
- She may be someone who was a keening woman when she was alive who was negligent in some way and so must pay by continuing to serve as a keening woman in death
- She may be someone who was a woman who lost her family tragically and never stopped mourning them

It is possible that like so many other kinds of fairies the answer to the Bean Sí's origin isn't one or the other but a combination, with these fairies being made up of some who are mortal dead and others who have always been fairies and may be related to Badb of the Tuatha De Danann. There is certainly no reason to expect a single origin or explanation for the Bean Sí when we already know that very few things with the fairies are either simple or straightforward.

The Bean Sí is a female spirit who is known for attaching herself to a particular family and appearing whenever someone in that family is about to die. In one account a Bean Sí attached to a family near Lough Gur came when a woman of the family was dying and both of the woman's sisters heard sad fairy music playing (Evans-Wentz, 1911). Some people say that only those in the family she is attached to can hear her cry (Ballard, 1991). In other stories the Bean Sí may appear on the night of a death wailing or keening in mourning and may be heard by anyone in the area of the dying person. The sound she makes has been described in a variety of ways including like the sound of a crying fox, howling dog, or moaning scream, but most often is heard as a woman keening.

The Bean Sí, particularly in Ireland is often said to be very beautiful, appearing as a young woman, although in other places such as Scotland she may be described as a very old woman (MacKillop, 1998). She is often described as a grey figure or a woman wrapped in a grey cloak, although by other accounts she wears a long grey cloak over a green dress with her eyes deep red from crying (Ballard, 1991; Briggs,1976). Others say that the Bean Sí wears white, or white with red shoes, and has long golden hair (MacKillop, 1998; Logan, 1981). She brushes her hair with a special comb and it is considered very dangerous even today to pick up a stray comb you find laying on the ground, in case it belongs to this spirit. Folklore tells of those who find a silver or gold comb and bring it home only to be confronted at night by horrible wailing and scratching at the windows until they pass the comb out on a pair of tongs which is pulled back in twisted and broken (O hOgain, 2006).

The Bean Sí is particularly associated with several goddesses among the Tuatha Dé Danann, including Badb and Cliodhna. In some areas of Ireland the word badb (pronounced in those dialects as bow) is the name used for the Bean Sí; like that famous war Goddess the Bean Sí is able to take the form of a hooded crow (MacKillop, 1998). Cliodhna is sometimes called the 'Queen of the Banshees' and she acts as the Bean Sí for the McCarthy family, who are said to be her descendants, appearing to cry and announce a death in the family.

Many people today fear the Bean Sí as the cause of deaths, but in most folklore she is clearly not the cause but merely an omen of the inevitable. She would appear just before or at the moment of death to announce the event to the family and others gathered around the ailing person. Over time her appearance in this capacity and association with immanent death seems to have given her a more sinister reputation, although some authors do suggest that she began with a clear association with the Goddess Badb and the battle field and only slowly switched to the more personal and passive death messenger we know today. If this is so then the Bean Sí may be slowly shifting back into her earlier and more actively dangerous persona as modern belief re-imagines her as fearsome and possibly fatal to those who cross her path.

Bessie Dunlop

An accused 17th century Scottish witch, Bessie Dunlop claimed that the Fairy Queen came to her while she was in labour with her child. Later she said that she was sent a fairy familiar spirit named Tom Reid by the Fairy Queen, a man who had been Bessie's relative but who had been taken by the fairies when he was killed in battle (Wilby, 2005).

Biddy Early

The most famous of all wise woman of Ireland may have been Biddy Early of Co. Clare, who is called a bean feasa, a fairy doctor and a witch by many people even today. Biddy Early was born in Co. Clare in 1798 with the given name of Bridget Connors (Locke, 2013). She was a devout Catholic who was orphaned as a young woman and struggled to support herself; at 19 she married her first husband who died shortly after and then she married her stepson (Locke, 2013). From her second marriage she had a son who died of Typhus around age 8 and many believe it was at this time that she gained her special knowledge and powers—some say from the fairies and others say from the spirit of her young son. Either from her son or from the fairies, she came to possess a special glass bottle that she would use for her cures by peering into the opening (Locke, 2013). In her lifetime she was married four times, and all her husbands were believed to have died from alcoholism (Gregory, 1920; Locke, 2013). She was a Catholic and died, so it's said, clutching a rosary and attended by a priest, but her relationship with the local clergy was hostile; in at least one story she was said to curse the horse of a priest who was speaking out against her (Gregory, 1920; Locke, 2013). She was charged with witchcraft in 1856 but the charges were dismissed due to the amount of local support for her (Locke, 2013). The people were as likely to call her a witch as a healer, but many people respected her and went to her for cures (Gregory, 1920). In many ways Biddy Early is the archetypal Irish folk magic practitioner: ambiguous, feared, respected, connected to the fairies, and abiding in that liminal social place which is both accepted within the community and outside its bounds.

Blood

There are some anecdotal accounts which claim fairies have white blood and are averse to or avoid the colour red and by extension human blood. Versions of these anecdotal claims can be found in 'Fairy Faith in Celtic Countries' and 'The Good People'. Lady Wilde also mentions this, saying that *"The Fairies have an aversion to the sight of blood"* (Wilde, 1888). These are late 19th century and 20th century accounts which hinge on the Catholic belief that fairies have white blood because they are not mortal and have been denied Heaven and salvation and they avoid human blood because it represents the afterlife they are barred from.

We do have a multitude of evidence that red is a colour associated with fairies and that many fairies are known to wear red which contradicts the idea that they would avoid that colour.

There is a modern theory suggesting fairies may avoid human blood due to its iron content, however, the iron in human blood, haemoglobin, is not the kind that would ward against fairies by itself. Iron in human blood is found in a very miniscule amount; there's about 4 grams total in a grown man altogether including blood and bone marrow. Also haemoglobin is chemically different from ferrous iron which almost certainly makes a difference. We do see stories of fairies eating red meat, and in some cases humans even the ones who are averse to iron, as well as drinking human blood, so it doesn't seem like blood and forged iron have the same effect.

Bòcan

A term in Scotland for any terrifying night-time apparition. A Bòcan may be a fairy or a human ghost, and while they appear and frighten people they rarely do any real harm (Campbell, 1900). The term is a general one and does not apply only to fairies.

Also see: Bodach

Bocánach

See: Battlefield fairies

Bodach

The name bodach, like elf and goblin, is used for specific fairy beings and is also a generic term for a type of a fairy. Bodachs are found in Scottish folklore where they are usually seen as a type of frightening night-time fairy that may lead people astray or attack people; in some localized folklore the Bodach is an individual being while in other lore it is a general type of being which can create some confusion. As with so many named fairies we see that there is fluidity in the understanding of who and what Bodachs are.

In Gaidhlig the word bodach has a variety of meanings many of which apply to human men, including an old man, an unmarried man, and a rustic but it can also mean a specter or bogeyman (Bauer & MacDhonnchaidh, 2017). Campbell says that the name means *'a carle or old man'* but he also defines them as night spectres who are *'no living wight'* (Campbell, 1900). From this we can perhaps gain a mental image of the Bodach, based on the other meanings of the word, but we can also most certainly conclude that it is an Otherworldly being that appears at night and is frightening. Bodachs are only ever referred to as male in folklore and the term for them is an exclusively male one as well.

Campbell describes a variety among Bodachs and lists them as both a type of Bòcan as well as a type of fairy being on their own. The Bòcan in Scotland are any type of terrifying night being which may include fairies and ghosts which frighten humans but don't necessarily cause any physical harm to them (Campbell, 1900). In some areas the term Bodach is used in the same general way that Bòcan is elsewhere, to mean any and all terrifying night-time spirits while in others the Bodach is viewed as a distinct type of being (Campbell, 1900). When included as one type in the more generalized grouping the Bodach qualifies as one of the Bòcan because of its night-time appearances and habit of frightening people it encounters, although Bodachs may or may not cause physical harm.

The Bodach was often used by parents to frighten children into behaving and to keep them away from dangerous areas. Some Bodachs were described as haunting areas that would be particularly unsafe after dark, trying to lure a person into going where they shouldn't. Bodachs often appear to children, trying to lure them into the darkness or to scare them, sometimes harming them directly sometimes only frightening them. In some stories the Bodach would rush down the chimney and seize children who were misbehaving, taking them away (Briggs, 1976). They were also drawn to children who were being loud or crying after dark, as well as those who disobeyed their parents.

There is also a tradition of named Bodachs who have a

distinct personality, locality and activity associated with them. One type of named Bodach, Bodach an Sméididh [Beckoning Old Man], would be seen standing near the corner of a house and beckoning with his hands for the viewer to follow him (Campbell, 1900). Another named bodach, MacGlumag na mais, oliath tarrang shìoda, burrach mòr [Son of Platter Pool from grey spike, silken spike, great caterpillar] sometimes just called Son of Platter Pool, appears to children at windows, gnashing his teeth loudly and flattening his face against the glass; if the child cries out the Bodach takes them away (Campbell, 1900). Another named Bodach is the Bodach Glas [Dark Man] who appeared as a death omen for a certain Scottish clan; he would appear three times and the third time singled doom (Briggs, 1976). In that case the Bodach seems to play a role similar to the Bean Sí in Irish folklore, being connected to a specific family and acting to foretell death within that family line. There is also at least one named Bodach with a friendly nature: normally described as a type of Brownie the Bodachan Sabhaill [Little Old Man of the Barn] was a helpful fairy who would come at night and thresh the crops in the darkness for tired, old farmers (Briggs, 1976).

While they can look and act frightening Bodachs can only enter a home if they are called or invited in (Campbell, 1900). They also rarely attack a person unless the person first puts themselves in the Bodachs power, be it by choosing to follow the fairy, by acknowledging its presence at the window, or by breaking cultural rules around behaviour. They are known to take children but otherwise their reputation is ambivalent and focuses more on frightening than harming. In some modern Scottish anecdotal fairylore Bodach is the consort or partner of the Cailleach and in a wider sense modern lore places this fairy in the Unseelie court.

Bodachs are a fascinating type of Scottish fairy, running the gamut in folklore from helpful to harmful, consider in some cases

Brownies and most often seen as Bòcans. These little old fairy men appear in the night to frighten children into good behaviour, inhabiting the same darkness as ghosts and apparitions, and the safest way to avoid them is to refuse to acknowledge them. In many ways the folklore around the Bodach seems to blend together more common fairylore with other influences and certainly we see the classic form of the Bogeyman looming large over naughty children in the Bodach's stories.

Boggart

A generic term used for any frightening supernatural creature whether it was a negative non-human entity, human ghost, or fairy (Simpson & Roud, 2000). In fairylore the term is applied to a kind of fairy that may be found outside or in homes and can be mildly annoying, destructive, or genuinely frightening. In at least one story a family trying to flee their resident Boggart found the attempt useless when the fairy followed them, speaking out from among their packed possessions as they left their old house for the new one (Keightly, 1850).

Bogles

Sometimes spelled Boggle these fairies may be viewed as a type of malicious BOGGART or a kind of GOBLIN but in some places their reputation is less fearsome. The name Bogle is related to the words for demon and scarecrow, perhaps reflecting something of the being's perceived nature (Williams, 1991).

One source in Lincolnshire believed that Bogles were human ghosts who remained and acted out much like a poltergeist until their physical bodies had decayed (Simpson & Roud, 2000). In some areas of Scotland Bogles were thought to only attack murderers, oath breakers, and those who robbed widows (Briggs, 1976). Overall their nature is ambiguous and often potentially dangerous.

Borrowed Midwife

See: Midwife to the Fairies

Borrowing

Fairy borrowing is found across a variety of folklore and forms a balance to fairy THEFT.

Borrowing was always repaid but not always in kind and usually more than was taken. An account in the 'Fairy Faith in Celtic Countries' details an account of a person who loaned the fairies some wheat only to be repaid in barley, given back more than they had originally loaned out (Evans-Wentz, 1911). Campbell specifies that they would repay two measures for every one borrowed, and barley for oats, and more, that if this meal was kept carefully without ever pronouncing a Christian blessing over it, revealing the bottom of the container, or questioning it's uncanniness then it would prove inexhaustible (Campbell, 1900).

In some other instances they may borrow physical objects including kitchen wares and hand mills. Items such as kettles or cauldrons might be borrowed for an evening but there was a specific process that must be followed including chanted phrases upon giving and returning in order for the item to be returned (Campbell, 1900).

The fairies are also well-known for borrowing people, most notably midwives although also musicians. In these accounts of human borrowing the person is usually returned unharmed and in a timely manner, although there are a few accounts that do not end as well for the human. Lady Wilde relates a tale of a man who was hosted at a feast by Finnbheara and returned home later

In contrast to the terms they treated humans, however, the Good People always expected to be repaid exactly on time and exactly as much as had been borrowed, refusing to take the smallest amount more.

Another type of fairy borrowing which is less easily understood is their penchant for taking random objects sometimes for extended periods of time and returning the object later when its least expected. An example of this from 19th century Scotland can be found in Campbell's Gaelic Otherworld:

> *"The Elves are also blamed for lifting with them articles mislaid. These are generally restored as mysteriously and unaccountably as they were taken away. Thus, a woman blamed the Elves for taking her thimble. It was placed beside her, and when looked for could not be found. Some time after, she was sitting alone on the hillside and found the thimble in her lap."* (Campbell, 1900, page 18).

This is typical of such accounts, with the object taken usually disappearing after being left in a common or regular place and reappearing later in plain sight or otherwise located somewhere it could not have been for the duration of its disappearance.

Brahan Seer

A Scottish man by the name of Coinneach Odhar more often known as the Brahan Seer who may have lived in the 16th or 17th century. He was reputed to have made a variety of prophecies before running afoul of a Countess who had him killed by being tarred and feathered. He made his prophecies by looking through a special holed stone and by some accounts this stone was given to him by the Good People after he slept on a fairy hill (Tobar an Dualchais, 2018).

Breac Shìth

A malady described by Campbell in 'The Gaelic Otherworld'. The author there says it means *'elfin pox'* although a closer literal translation might be 'fairy spots'. It is a non-specific illness signified by the silent appearance of hives or similar marks on the skin which disappear again, although they may also be associated with whooping cough or other dangerous illnesses (Campbell, 1900).

Bridget Cleary

One of the most famous CHANGELING accounts in Ireland was that of Bridget Cleary. The events around Bridget's life and death occurred in the late 1890's in Tipperary, Ireland and are considered the prime example of a case of a human murdered by relatives due to changeling beliefs (Sneddon, 2015). Later folklore would also cast Bridget as potentially a witch, and a rhyme from Ireland based on the supposed words of her family as they questioned her goes "*Are you a witch or are you a fairy; Or are you the wife of Michael Cleary*" (Duchas, 2018; 275).

Bridget lived with her husband Michael in Ballyvadlea in co. Tipperary and made extra money by selling eggs to the neighbours. As she was coming home one day she fell ill and as her illness grew more serious her husband eventually summoned a doctor. The doctor, Dr. Crean, arrived and diagnosed Bridget with what he described as a "*nervous excitement and slight bronchitis*"; he left her with medicine believing that her life was in no danger (McCarthy, 1901). Later accounts would state that Michael Cleary didn't give Bridget the doctor's medicine, instead getting herbs from a local fairy doctor because he believed that Bridget had been replaced by a changeling. Bridget was made to undergo several days of 'cures' which included being forced to drink these remedies, having liquids thrown on her, and being repeatedly questioned about her true nature, sometimes at the point of a hot brand from the fire. On the third day after the doctor's visit Michael, along with several other relatives of Bridget, questioned her again and this time she was too weak to answer properly; Michael was now convinced she was a fairy and doused her in lamp oil before setting her on fire (McCarthy, 1901).

After Bridget's death Michael and another man buried her but the crime was eventually discovered. All of the people involved were put on trial and it was discovered that Michael had been going to the local fairy hill waiting for his wife to emerge on a white horse (Duchas, 2018, 275). Michael was convicted and given a 20 year sentence for his wife's death.

Brownies

Brownies are a complicated grouping of fairies which can themselves be further broken down into specific types, like Fenodyree and Bodachs, but may also be grouped into larger categories of fairies such as Hobgoblins. The origin of the name for these spirits is obscure but MacKillop theorizes it may be a shortened version of '*little brown man*' (MacKillop, 1998). It should be noted however, that we do see both male and female brownies in folklore so while MacKillop may be on the right track, 'man' shouldn't be interpreted to literally.

Brownies are somewhat unusual among the wider groupings of fairies because they prefer to live with or near humans, either in human homes or in mills, although some have also been connected to bodies of water like ponds (Briggs, 1976). Brownies in mills come out at night and work in the mill, not always in a way that helps the human owners, while Brownies in homes come out while the human inhabitants are sleeping and clean. Overall Brownies have a good reputation as helpful spirits, however, in older folklore they were seen as ambiguous beings and potentially dangerous particularly to those outside their chosen family, although even that family could be on the receiving end of the Brownie's destructive temper if it was angered (Briggs, 1976).

In descriptions Brownies are usually, as the name implies, a nut-brown colour and are said to dress in rags. This style of dress may be a preference as stories tell of the unfortunate results of well-meaning humans offering their resident Brownie a new set of clothes. In best case scenarios the Brownie snatches up the clothing and leaves forever, sometimes singing happily that the new clothes mean that they will not work anymore; worst case scenarios the helpful Brownie is so offended it transforms into a malicious Boggart. This may be because the Brownie is bound to service and can only be released with purposeful payment, or because they are mortally offended by any implication that they are serving humans (Briggs, 1976).

When Brownies appear in folklore the focus is usually on their role around human homes or farms, and secondarily their place at mills. Around a home they are known to do chores while on a farm they will help bring in crops and tend to the livestock. In one story centred on a mill, a human girl goes to grind wheat after dusk only to find the mill occupied by a Brownie who she douses with boiling water when he gets to amorous with her; he flees to his mother[1] but later dies of his burns (Briggs, 1976).

Brownies must be paid surreptitiously for their work, with food being left out for them but never directly given to them. A household with a Brownie would be expected to leave a bowl of milk and small loaf of bread or cake out once a week to show their gratitude for the Brownie's efforts (Briggs, 1976). This food and drink should be left without verbal thanks and not directly as a gift, but placed carefully where the fairy would find it to avoid any chance of offending them. In this we see a juxtaposition of careful preparation and seemingly casual placement, with the housewife ensuring the Brownie's continued effort for the household this way (Briggs, 1976). Dwelly, in 1902, includes this description of a Shetland practice relating to offering to Brownies:

> *"...that not above forty or fifty years ago almost every family had a brownie... which served them, to which they gave a sacrifice for his service; as when they churned their milk, they took a part thereof and sprinkled every corner of the house with it for Brownie's use; likewise, when they brewed, they had a stone which they called*

> *Brownie's Stane, wherein there was a little hole, into which they poured some wort for a sacrifice to Brownie.".*

Besides leaving if given clothes there are a few other things that will force a Brownie to leave a location. Several accounts of Brownies attached to homes describe the fairies being driven off by well-intentioned efforts to baptize them or reading from the Christian Bible in their presence, two things these fairies apparently cannot tolerate. Farm-oriented Brownies will become destructive and leave if the quality of their work is insulted or more generally if a person speaks ill of them (Briggs, 1976).

Note

1 In alternate versions of the story she is his mother. The tale is often titled 'Meg Mollach' after the female Brownie, although in other versions her name may appear as 'Maggie Moulach'.

Bucca

See Púca

Burfex

Burfex may also be called Burfax, Burphax, or Bursex. Micoll, Titam, and Burfex are invoked together in a ritual to provide the magician with a ring of invisibility, during which one of the three is chosen by the magician and is bound by him to provide him with the ring as well as sexual companionship.

Buttery Spirits

A class of fairy that would haunt cellars and storage areas taking the value of any food that was acquired through illegal means or was ill prepared (Briggs, 1976). Making the sign of the cross over the food was believed to protect it, as, of course, would being morally correct in one's dealings around food. This idea of punishing those who humans who digressed from human mores relating to food is widespread with Campbell noting that the fairies also freely stole the substance of any food that was ill spoken of by its owner; MacKillop points out that Buttery Spirits are a folk motif and Briggs addresses them in her work as well.

The name is drawn from the habit these spirits had of living or lurking in the buttery, known today more commonly as a pantry.

Bwcas

A Welsh spirit comparable to the English and Scottish BROWNIE. In one story a Bwca did housework for a girl in exchange for a nightly bowl of cream, bread, or porridge (Briggs, 1976). A Bwca who is angered may become destructive or prone to pranks and there is a story of one who became so dangerous he had to be exorcized, banished by a wise man for 14 generations (Briggs, 1976).

Bwganod

A Welsh being similar to the English BOGGART of a nature that is, in folklore, ambiguously between human ghosts, phantoms, and fairies. Sometimes classed as a type of goblin or hobgoblin they could take a human form or several animal forms, favoured night time, and inspired great fear in people (Evans-Wentz, 1911).

C

Cabbyl Ushtey

The type of water horse found on the Isle of Man, similar to the Scottish EACH UISGE. Described as pale grey. The Cabbyl Ushtey was known to take cows and children, and sometimes to intentionally panic horses causing stampedes, but was considered more benign than its Scottish counterpart (Mackillop, 1998). One account told of a Cabbyl Ushtey which took two calves from a farmer, tearing them to pieces and eating them so that the farmer moved his herd away from the river, after which the fairy horse took the family's only daughter before disappearing (Briggs, 1976).

Caoineag

A member of the Scottish grouping of water fairies known as the FUATH, the Caoineag [Weeper] is roughly equivalent to the Irish BEAN SIDHE although this fairy isn't often seen only heard. There are several variations of the name including caointeag, caoinheag, and caoineachag [little weeper] all with roughly the same meaning of weeper or mourner. Both Carmichael and the Am Faclair Beag refer to the Caoineag as a 'naiad' reinforcing this fairy's close ties to the water, although Carmichael associates her not only with bodies of water but also land areas including hills and glens.

Although rarely seen there are a few physical descriptions of this fairy under the related name of Caointeag or Caointeach. She is said to look like a child or small woman wearing either a green dress and white cap or a green shawl (Briggs, 1976). There are no descriptions of her possible hair colours or other physical traits.

Like the Bean Sidhe the Caoineag is attached to a specific family and will cry for deaths within that family. Families said to have a Caoineag include the MacDonalds, MacMillans, Mathisons, Kellys, Shaws, Curries, MacKays, and MacFarlens

(Briggs, 1976). It is unclear whether like the similar Bean Nighe she will also be heard by those not related to a family she is connected to. Interestingly unlike other related spirits folklore of the Caoineag indicates that if they can be safely given clothing they can be freed from their service to the family, as we see with fairies like the BROWNIE, or perhaps like the PIXIE she is simply driven off by this gift (Briggs, 1976).

The Caoineag is heard wailing near a waterfall before battle deaths and her crying was greatly feared (Carmichael 1900; Briggs, 1976). Those about to engage in any activity that could be potentially involve combat dreaded hearing her cries as did their relatives waiting for their return (Carmichael, 1900). Unlike the Irish spirit the Caoineag is described as an omen of death whose predicted fate can be avoided by those who heed her warning. According to folklore some of the people in Glencoe were saved from the 1692 massacre[1] because they heard a Caoineag wailing for several nights in a row and took that as a warning and fled the area before the killings started.

Part of the dirge she was heard singing is still preserved in the Carmina Gadelica:

"Little caoineachag of the sorrow
Is pouring the tears of her eyes,
Weeping and wailing the fate of Clan Donald.
Alas my grief! that ye did not heed her cries.
There is gloom and grief in the mount of mist,
There is weeping and calling in the mount of mist,
There is death and danger, there is maul and murder,
There is blood spilling in the mount of mist."
(Carmichael, 1900, page 245)

Note

1 The Mort Ghlinne Comhann, or Glencoe Massacre, occurred during the 1689-92 Jacobite rebellion and was aimed against

the MacIains a sept of the MacDonalds. For more detailed discussion of that see the BBC article 'The Massacre of Glen Coe' here https://www.bbc.co.uk/history/scottishhistory/union/trails_union_glencoe.shtml

Cat Sidhe

In Irish and Scottish folklore there exist stories about cat sidhe (fairy cats) also called cait sith in Scottish Gaidhlig. Cat sidhe are believed to be large, Otherworldly black cats with a single white spot on the chest. Campbell describes them as *"large as dogs"* and *"[having] arched backs and erect bristles"* (Campbell, 1900, page 17). The descriptions bare some resemblance to Kellas cats, the wild cats of Scotland, which has led some to theorize that sightings of them may have been the origin of the cat sidhe stories (Matthews, 2005).

These cats are generally seen as malevolent and some people believe they are actually shape-changed witches. In particular the witch was believed to be able to transform into a cat 9 times, but legend says on the 9th time the witch would have to remain a cat forever (Old Farmer's Almanac, 2012). Jane Manning has a lovely children's book called 'Cat Nights' based on this legend, about a young witch who has adventures each night as a cat for 8 nights and then has to decide if she wants to stay a person or transform one last time. It is also said by some within the MacGillivray family that the clan motto "Touch not this cat" is based on the family having a cat sidhe among its ancestors, reflecting the idea that the Cat Sidhe could transform into a human-like shape (MacGillivray, 2000).

Others believe that these cats are dangerous fairies that should be avoided. In Scotland it is believed that the cat sidhe can steal the souls of the newly dead and so certain protections must be undertaken while the body was watched until burial (MacGillivray, 2000). Most of these protections depend on doing things to distract the cat sidhe and keep it away from the body, such as sprinkling cat nip about the other rooms, or playing games that would draw the cat sidhe's attention (MacGillivray, 2000).

Certain special days have been associated with the cat sidhe. One source mentions August 17th in connection to the cat sidhe as transformed witches, and says that it was on this night that a witch might make the ninth transformation into permanent cat form (Old Farmer's Almanac, 2012). Another cites the folk belief that on Samhain a saucer of milk should be left out as an offering to the cat sidhe to gain their blessing, while failing to do so could earn a curse on the household (MacGillivray, 2000).

Ceffyl Dwr

A dangerous Welsh water horse found in lakes and rivers.

Changelings

A changeling is a fairy or an enchanted object that is swapped for a living human who is stolen by the fairies. If the changeling was a fairy it was usually said to be an old fairy who wished to be doted on by humans, although in some cases it was said that the changeling was a sickly fairy baby that wasn't wanted by its fairy parents (Evans-Wentz, 1911). If the changeling wasn't a fairy then the alternative was that it would be an inanimate object, often a stick or log, which was made to appear like the missing person using fairy magic. Once the living human had been taken and replaced the changeling would seem to sicken and eventually die, or at least seem to die, and would be buried by the human family who then believed the person had died. An example of this pattern is found in the Cornish tale of SELENA MOOR where the woman Grace Hutchins says that while she lived on after being taken by the fairies her family buried what she assumed was a changeling.

Although the most common belief has been that the person themselves was taken, usually physically, and replaced, there have been a few alternate theories over the last hundred years to explain them. During the Victorian period some occultists came to believe that changelings were not a swapping out of physical beings but rather a type of possession where the human would be overtaken by a fairy spirit (Silver, 1999) In 20th and 21st century anthropology changelings were and still are often viewed as attempts by folklore to explain medical conditions, particularly those that affect behaviour such as autism (Narvaez, 1991). For the Victorians the concept seemed to be rooted in an overarching idea that the person's body remained but their spirit could be taken and replaced creating the changeling phenomena, while for later anthropologists and some folklorists the premise was that fairies did not exist so there must be a physical explanation that caused the belief.

The primary targets for fairy abduction were babies, new brides, and new mothers particularly those with a mild temperament who were considered attractive. Good physical health was also a prerequisite in most cases and there is at least one account of a woman who was being taken by the fairies who was left after she sneezed (Lysaght, 1991). The greatest times of risk for a human were liminal periods such as birth or marriage, with babies and children up to age 8 or 9 being at high risk and women in child-bearing years being in equal danger (Skelbred, 1991; Jenkins, 1991). Other popular targets for abduction included new mothers who might be taken to wet nurse fairy babies, and may or may not be kept permanently or later returned. Not all coveted human were necessarily stolen as we see groups including midwives and musicians borrowed but returned whereas babies, children, and some adults were taken permanently. Those replaced with changelings were those who the Good Folk intended to keep, with the changeling used to deceive the human family into believing the person was dead.

There are many theories as to why fairies take humans but no definitive answers. One of the main theories is that the fairies steal people in order to supplement their own numbers

(Gwyndaf, 1991). This idea usually hinges on the related belief that the Good People reproduce rarely and with difficulty and that they must therefore look to outside sources like humans to strengthen their own population. The tale of Selena Moor would seem to affirm this, where the human captive Grace Hutchins affirms that the Cornish fairies take humans and turn them into fairies but also says that the fairy folk do rarely have their own babies and make much of such births. Human babies then are taken to be made into fairies and human women to be used as breeding stock to produce hybrid children or children who may be turned fully into fairies. This is seen particularly in the variety of stories about stolen brides as well as stories of borrowed midwives where the midwife is taken by a fairy man to the bedside of his wife only to find herself delivering the child of a human girl she recognizes but that everyone thought had died. Another belief was that fairy babies were unusually ugly and so fairies coveted beautiful human babies and would exchange one for the other (Skelbred, 1991). They seem to prefer people who are in some way deviant or have broken societal rules (Jenkins, 1991). This can be seen in both anecdotal evidence where people taken are usually out alone when or where they should not be or have failed to follow the usual protocol for protection, or in ballads and folktales where people are taken while in or near liminal places. On the one hand this can represent one way in which people open themselves up to being taken but it could also represent a deeper underlying motivation, in which perhaps the people are being taken because they have some quality that the Fae folk either admire or need more of themselves. This, of course, is predicated on the idea that changelings are left in place of people taken for some at least nominally positive use, however, it is worth noting that not all theories of fairy abduction are benevolent, by even the most lenient standard. If one favours the idea of the teind to Hell as an actual tithe that occurs and in which humans can be used as substitutes for fairies, then arguably people may be taken to be offered to darker spirits so that the fairies themselves may be spared (Lyle, 1970).

Means of identifying a suspected changeling often involve tricking it into revealing itself. In some cases the changeling was said to be one of the Good People who magically appeared to be the human but usually acted very differently; if it was a baby who had been taken the replacement would typically be sickly, constantly hungry, and impossible to please, while an adult who was taken might display equally dramatic personality changes. A person who had previously been kind and gentle might become cross and cruel, while a child who had before been pleasant and easy tempered would suddenly be mean spirited and demanding. This may be done through careful observation, such as the story of the mother who noted that when she was with her child the baby would cry ceaselessly but when alone in her room the baby would fall silent and the mother outside the room could hear music (Lysaght, 1991). A Scottish story along similar lines involved a changeling infant who was seen playing straw like bagpipes, or in a variant was seen playing a reed for other fairies to dance to (Bruford, 1991; Evans-Wentz, 1911). In older folklore a variety of tricks are suggested including boiling water in an eggshell which in the tales will cause the changeling to sit up and declare that as ancient as it is it has never seen such a thing before; a regional variant involves disposing of ashes in an eggshell (Bruford, 1991). A family could also seek out the advice of a wise person or fairy doctor to assess the suspected changeling and confirm or deny its fairy-nature. Generally if the presence of a changeling was confirmed every attempt was then made to regain the human child; only in very rare cases was the family advised to treat the changeling well and accept it's in their family, with the idea that treating it well would earn good treatment for their own child in Fairy (Briggs, 1976).

There is at least one late 19th century Manx account of a

changeling where the child taken was an older boy and was successfully recovered. The account follows in full:

> "'*Forty to fifty years ago, between St. John's and Foxdale, a boy, with whom I often played, came to our house at nightfall to borrow some candles, and while he was on his way home across the hills he suddenly saw a little boy and a little woman coming after him. If he ran, they ran, and all the time they gained on him. Upon reaching home he was speechless, his hands were altered (turned awry), and his feet also, and his fingernails had grown long in a minute. He remained that way a week. My father went to the boy's mother and told her it wasn't Robby at all that she saw; and when my father was for taking the tongs and burning the boy with a piece of glowing turf [as a changeling test], the boy screamed awfully. Then my father persuaded the mother to send a messenger to a doctor in the north near Ramsey "doing charms", to see if she couldn't get Robby back. As the messenger was returning, the mother stepped out of the house to relieve him, and when she went into the house again her own Robby was there. As soon as Robby came to himself all right, he said a little woman and a little boy had followed him, and that just as he got home he was conscious of being taken away by them, but he didn't know where they came from nor where they took him. He was unable to tell more than this. Robby is alive yet, so far as I know…* (Evans-Wentz, 1911, pages 132 – 133).

This account is of particular interest because the person giving it knew the child who was taken both before and after and was aware of the events as they occurred. It also illustrates the interplay of folklore and belief with the events as they were progressing during the boy's experience.

Because the fear of changelings, and more generally of losing a person to the Good People, was so pervasive there were many protections against it and methods of getting a person back. Looking at protections first we see an array of options, beginning with prohibitions against verbally complementing an infant, lest the words attract the fairies' attention and increase the chance of the child being taken. Although in some contexts red was seen to be a Fairy colour it was also used as a protection against fairies, something we see more generally in the use of red thread (with rowan); there is at least some anecdotal evidence of the use of red flannel pinned to children's clothes as a way to keep them from being taken (Lysaght, 1991). In Wales early baptism was common because of the belief that a Christian baptism would protect and infant from being taken (Gwyndaf; 1991). So widespread that they might be termed ubiquitous were belief in the power of iron (or steel) and particularly of keeping scissors, a knife, a fire poker, or tongs over or near the cradle. Other commonly found protections include burning leather in the room, keeping bread nearby, fire, silver, giving the woman and child milk from a cow who had eaten the herb mothan, and being carefully and perpetually watched (Skelbred, 1991; Evans-Wentz, 1911). In many stories it was a moment's inattention or an adult falling asleep that allowed the changeling swap to happen, compounded by a lack of any other protections in place.

I will warn the reader before we get into this section that often the means of forcing a changeling to leave were brutal and could be fatal to the person on the receiving end. There were just as many methods of forcing a changeling to leave as there were protections against them because the belief was that once the changeling was forced to leave the human child or bride would return. To force a changeling to leave usually involved threatening or harming them, most commonly with iron or fire. Bridget Cleary was a woman in Ireland who died in 1895 when her husband and several family members and neighbours burned her alive after several days of trying to 'cure' her, believing that she was actually a fairy who had taken the real Bridget's place. Before being killed she was forced to drink an herbal concoction, doused in urine, and jabbed repeatedly with a hot iron poker, as well as having a priest come in and say mass over her; after several days of this she was set on fire and eventually died of her burns (Giolláin, 1991). A piece of iron might be thrown at the changeling, or in one of the more benign rituals salt could be placed on a shovel blade, marked with a cross and heated in a fire, with a window left open near the changeling (Gwyndaf, 1991). The changeling might be beaten, pelted with refuse and animal dung, or starved in order to force its own people to take it back, with the idea that only this cruel treatment could motivate the changeling's biological parents to return the human child to spare their own offspring (Skelbred, 1991). Fire often played a significant role in these rituals, with some involving the changeling being thrown into a fire or placed on an object that had been heated in a fire (Briggs, 1976). Another ritual to force a changeling to leave involved taking it to a river and bathing it three times in the water, and related practices involved leaving the infant or child at the edge of a body of water - a liminal space - so that the fairies would take it back and return the mortal child; a less kind version involved throwing the changeling into a river (Silver, 1999; Evans-Wentz, 1911). In cases where the changeling left and the human did not return, or the changeling had already died naturally, attempts could be made to force the return of the human captive by burning grass or trees on the nearest fairy hill (Briggs, 1976).

Changelings are found across Celtic folklore and stories of changelings exist in both folklore and more recent anecdotes. The idea that sometimes the Other Crowd take people and that those people may be saved and returned to the human community with effort or may instead be lost forever to their own kind is a pervasive one. Ultimately the fairies may take people to increase their own numbers or to diversify their own gene pool, to possess the beauty of a particular person or for darker reasons, but the folklore is clear that they take people usually with the intent of keeping them. Those who are rescued or otherwise returned are usually permanently altered by their time among the Good People and most often the hard evidence we have shows that attempts to get people back and force assumed-changelings out results in the death of the changeling.

Christian Church Driving Out the Fairies

There's abundant evidence that some Christian traditions did indeed view the Other Crowd as demonic and classified them as demons; we see as much in witchcraft trial accounts where a person who spoke of fairy familiars and dealing with the Queen of Elfame was described by judges as dealing with devils and Satan. There are many examples where terms like elf or goblin are glossed as imp or incubus, going back at least to the 15th century in England and found in the American colonies from their inception.

Related to this is a pervasive campaign of propaganda saying that priests and other such religious men had driven out the Good People through their faith, despite continuous anecdotes and folklore to the contrary. One can argue that these stories of the religious men forcing out the fairies is another means to try to affect their removal by weakening people's belief in them and removing the power of folkloric stories tying fairies to places, as well as eroding practices designed to honour them.

For example:

Canterbury Tales, 'the Wife of Bath's Tale' 14th century:

> *"In the days of King Arthur, Britain was full of fairies. The elf queen danced in meadows with her companions. This is what I read, anyway. Now, no one sees elves any more, because of the prayers of friars. These friars search all over the land, blessing every building and house, with the result that there are no more fairies. Where elves used to walk, the friar himself now goes at all times of the day, saying his prayers. Women can walk anywhere they want without fearing anyone but the friar, who will only dishonour them, rather than beget demon children upon them."* (Chaucer)

Excerpt from 'Farewell, Rewards, and Fairies' by Bishop Richard Corbet, 16th century:

"By which we note the Fairies
Were of the old Profession.
Their songs were 'Ave Mary's',
Their dances were Procession.
But now, alas, they all are dead;
Or gone beyond the seas;
Or farther for Religion fled;
Or else they take their ease."
(Eliot, 1937)

In Bishop Richard Corbet's 16th century poem 'Farewell, Rewards, and Fairies' he says that the fairies tolerated Catholics well enough but have all fled to other lands to get away from Protestant religion, which is why none can now be found. In a similar vein several anecdotes beginning in the 17th century mention fairies fleeing any area where church bells rang, apparently unable to tolerate the sound (Briggs, 1976).

Perhaps we can still see echoes of this effort today not only in the disenchantment of the world and the places where the spirits have in fact been driven off but also in the wider cultural views that see the world around us as un-inspirited and empty. In the way that the dominant narrative may try to describe all things within their own cosmology only as if there could be no other possible options

Christian Symbols and Prayers

The relationship between the Good People and the sacred objects and words of Christianity are complex. Some fairies are utterly unbothered by the symbols and ritual actions of the new religion, some are very concerned about their own place within Christian cosmology, while others seem to violently abhor anything relating to Christianity.

Some examples:

- Redcaps were known to fear very little, but some of the few things that could ward against them included Christian sacred objects and prayers, specifically the sign of the cross or the sound of bible verse being read aloud.
- In the ballad of Alice Brand the Elf King wants to be rid of two trespassers to his wood but because they are Christians he cannot act against them, so he must send someone under his sway who is not affected by such things. To that end he sends a newly made fairy who was once a baptized Christian man, which conveys some protection to him against the power such symbols would normally have over the fairies.
- There are several accounts of fairies being driven off by the sounds of church bells
- A prayer from the Isle of Man is aimed specifically at driving off the fairies based on the idea that they are a kind of fallen angel:

"...here is their prayer against the fairies:--"Jee saue mee voish cloan ny moyrn" (God preserve me from the children of pride [or ambition])."' (Evans-Wentz, 1911, page 130).

- A brownie who was well known in a particular area was driven off forever when a well-meaning priest attempted to baptize him (Briggs, 1976). The moment the holy water struck the brownie's flesh the fairy shrieked and fled never to be seen again. In another anecdote a brownie was upset by the homeowner reading the Bible.
- In one area of Scotland fisherman at sea would never say the words *"church or manse or minister"* to avoid offending the spirits and possibly endangering themselves (Wilby,

2005).

- In some versions of the ballad of Tam Lin, Tam Lin advises Janet to make a compass [circle] around herself with holy water while she waits for the Fairy Rade on Halloween; this renders her invisible to their sight and senses.
- Signing a cross three times over a fairy captive or human-turned-fairy would release them from Fairy or break any magic holding them.
- In several Manx anecdotal accounts merely saying any name of the Christian trinity is enough to cause the fairies to disappear. An example is given in this story, which also shows the complexity of dealing with fairies:

"'A strange man took a nurse to a place where a baby boy was born. After the birth, the man set out on a table two cakes, one of them broken and the other one whole, and said to the nurse: "Eat, eat; but don't eat of the cake which is broken nor of the cake which is whole." And the nurse said: "What in the name of the Lord am I going to eat?" At that all the fairies in the house disappeared; and the nurse was left out on a mountain-side alone.'" (Evans-Wentz, 1911, page 127).

Wilby suggests in her book that this avoidance of Christian symbols and prayers - which is not universal[1] - is likely rooted in the animosity that the Church itself created with its attempts to demonize the Fair Folk. By this logic it is not any power held by the Christian church or inherent in its symbols or prayers that has an effect but rather an almost atavistic reaction on the part of the older fairies to symbols and prayers connected to the religion which has worked so hard to drive them from their traditional homes. Briggs, for her part, suggests that the cross is actually an older symbol, predating Christianity that represents the liminal space of the crossroads where the fairies have less power and could be used either as a physical object or as a motion to ward them off.

Note

1 There are a variety of fairies who express a deep concern over their own salvation, likely representing a portion of fairies who are themselves former humans.

Circumambulating

The idea that movement in magic has significance is, of course, an old one and can be found in both folk magic and folklore. In witchcraft we see this reflected in the idea of casting a circle and in some forms of modern traditional witchcraft in casting the compass[1], and we also find the idea in references to early modern witchcraft which involve the idea of moving directionally around a space either deiseal [clockwise] or tuathail [counter clockwise]. This same idea is reflected in Irish and Scottish folk practices where sacred spaces such as grave yards or holy wells were first circled three times deiseal before being entered.

Movement in circles is seen for a variety of purposes, including taking oaths, enchantment, breaking spells, and protective magic (Wimberly, 1928). We see the idea in various ballads and stories of a person circling or moving around a place or person in order to cast magic on them. This idea also exists in folk magic, such as we see in the Carmina Gadelica in Caluinn a Bhuilg 63 where the visiting carollers circle the house three times deiseal to drive out negative spirits and Oidhche Challaig 66 where inhospitably treated singers circle the fire tuathail before reciting a curse on the house (Carmichael, 1900).

The idea of a circle being used for protection is also an old one. There are examples from The Ballad of Tam Lin where the variously-named protagonist uses holy water to create a protective circle or compass around herself, apparently to avoid detection by the Fairy Rade:

"There's holy water in her hand,
She casts a compass round,

And presently a fairy band
Comes riding o'er the mound." (Tam Lin 39D)

Generally the protagonist takes this action after being explicitly told to by her fairy lover:

"Ye'll do you down to Mile Course,
Between twall hours and ane,
And full your hands o holy water,
And cast your compass roun'" (Tam-Lin 39G)

Wimberly suggests that the references to holy water in these versions are reflections of the later use of milk or water to rescue Tam Lin by bathing or submerging him, and also that it may represent a later Christianization of the pagan practice of using protective circles or compasses. In either view the act seems to secure a level of protection for both the protagonist and later her lover as well by creating a barrier against the Good Folk (Wimberly, 1928). The ballad also suggests that while within this circle the protagonist was invisible to the Fairy Rade passing by and was only finally seen when she moved to pull her lover down from his horse.

The direction of the movement was important, with circling done in a deiseal way, with the sun [clockwise], being seen as blessing or protective:

"So let me walk the deasil round you, that you may go safe out into the far foreign land, and come safe home." (Scott, 1827)

"...the kindred of the deceased carried the body ashore, and, placing it on a bank long consecrated to the purpose, made the Deasil around the departed." (Scott, 1828)

In some cases this is referred to as *'right and round'* or *'right and around'* (Wimberly, 1928). McNeil wrote that all festivals started with the deiseal circumambulation three times of the site or the specific item like bonfire or holy well (McNeill, 1956). Bullán stones are turned deiseal to work cures or for healing prayers and it was once the common practice for holy wells to be circled deiseal before being entered. The concept behind this magic hinges on the idea that moving deiseal, or towards the right hand side or south, is a naturally positive and beneficial direction which follows the motion of the sun.

In sharp contrast compassing tuathail, or widdershins[2] in the Scots language, was seen as having a very different purpose. It was sometimes referred to as 'wrongwise' or 'contrariwise' and represented going against the natural order, towards the left hand side or north, or against the motion of the sun. It is a direction strongly associated with witchcraft and also with invoking Fairy. In the 'Ballad of Childe Rowland' the protagonist's sister is taken into Fairy after going around a church widdershins, with the implication that this action opened her up to fairy abduction; in the same way to gain entrance to rescue her the protagonist must walk three times round widdershins himself. For a few examples:

> *"Margarat Davidsone quhan scho sa the new moyne scho ran thrys widdersones about"* [Margarat Davidson when she saw the new moon she ran thrice widdershins about] (Cramond, 1903).
>
> *"The wemen maid fyrst thair homage [to the Devil], and nixt the men. The men wer turnit nyne tymes widderschinnes about and the wemen sax tymes"* [The women made first their homage {to the devil} and next the men. The men were turned nine times widdershins about and the women six times](Pitcairn, 1833)
>
> *"Upon the pronouncing of some words, and turning himself about wider-shins, that is turning himself round from the right hand to the left, contrary to the natural course of the sun"* (Miller, 1877).

When bullán stones are used for cursing they are turned tuathail and there are some accounts in folklore of stones being held in the hand and turned tuathail to enact hexes as well.

However, while widdershins does have a particularly strong association with hexing and negative magic today, and is even viewed by some Christians as both unlucky and even blasphemous in relation to sacred sites, it was used for positive ends including healing and its historic association with witchcraft is likely, in my opinion, why in modern terms we view it entirely as negative. Some examples of positive uses:

> *"The said Aliesone past thryse widdershynnis about the said Issobel hir bed muttering out certane charmes in unknawen wordis ... and thairby cureing of the said Issobel of hir diseas"* [The said Alison passed thrice widdershins about the said Isobel's bed muttering out certain charms and unknown words... and thereby curing the said Isobel of her disease] (Gillion & Smith, 1953)
>
> *"In cureing of his wyfe, be causeing ane grit fyre to be put on, and ane hoill to be maid in the north side of the hous, and ane quik hen to be put furth thairat, at thre seuerall tymes, and tane in at the hous-dur widderschynnes "* [In curing his wife, by causing one great fire to be put on, and one hole to be made in the north side of the house, and one quick hen to be put through it, at three separate times, and taken in at the house door widdershins] (Pitcairn, 1833).

In these examples of healing we see widdershins motions being used to remove illnesses and work cures on ill people, resulting in a positive outcome for the patient. As previously mentioned widdershins motions were also associated with entering Fairy as well.

The exact use of the circle and the choice of direction depended on the situation and purpose as discussed above, but the wider concept is a recurring thread in folklore and folk magic. This idea includes everything from walking fully around a location, object, or person, to turning something like a stone in the hand with the direction of the motion having intrinsic significance to the outcome. We still see these concepts today in neopagan witchcraft, although how close or far from the folk practices the modern practices have grown is debatable.

Notes

1 The concepts of casting a circle or casting a compass are effectively synonymous, and in fact the term 'compas' or 'compasse' in Scots means "a round or ring; a circle or circuit" (DSL, 2018). In practice they also seem to have many similarities, particularly the older versions.

2 There are roughly two dozen variant spellings for widdershins in Scots. I'm using what I think is the neopagan standard here as the word has passed into some sort of common use through older neopagan texts. Be aware, however, that in older non-pagan material the word may be found in various spellings including, for example, withershins, wyddyrshins, wouderschinnis.

Clúracán

The Clúracán is a more obscure kind of Irish fairy known to haunt wine cellars and get into the stores there. Popularly Anglicized as Clurichaun the name also appears spelled in Irish as Clúrachán and Clútharachán; the definition is given as a small sprite and the etymology is uncertain (MacKillop, 1998). He is often associated with the Leprechaun but unlike that other fairy the Clúracán eschews work, instead getting up to mischief, drinking, and occasionally riding sheep into exhaustion. He usually dresses in red and is considered a solitary fairy (Briggs, 1976).

Clíodhna

Clíodhna, whose name may have various spellings and may

mean 'territorial one', is both one of the Tuatha Dé Danann and a Fairy Queen in modern folk lore. Her epithet is Ceannfhionn (fair headed or fair haired) and she is sometimes called 'the shapely one' (O hOgain, 2006; MacKillop, 1998). In many stories she is described as an exceptionally beautiful woman. Clíodhna is said to have taken the form of a wren, a bird that may be associated with her, and has three magical birds that eat Otherworldly apples and have the power to lull people to sleep by singing and then heal them (Smyth, 1988; MacKillop, 1998).

She is often associated with the Otherworldly Bean sidhe, either as such a fairy or as their Queen. In other folklore she is more generally the queen of the fairies of Munster, and she is connected to both that area generally and cork in particular, where she her home is at a place called Carraig Chlíona (Clíodhna's rock) (O hOgain, 2006).

Her father is Gebann, the Druid of Manannán mac Lir, and in folklore her sister is the Fairy Queen Aoibheall (Smyth, 1988; MacKillop, 1998). In the mythology we have no further references for her family so we don't know who her mother might be or if she had any other siblings. She was well known for taking mortal lovers and several human family lines trace their ancestry to her including the McCarthy's and O'Keefe's for whom she acts as a bean sidhe.

The tide at Glandore in Cork was called the 'Wave of Clíodhna' and she is more generally associated with the water and waves (O hOgain, 2006). In several of her stories she is drowned at this location after leaving the Otherworld either because she is in love with Aengus mac Óg or because she was trying to elope with a warrior named Ciabhán. She is known for her passionate nature and especially for her love of poets who she is likely in folklore to appear to and try to seduce. More generally she has a reputation for seducing and drowning young men (Smyth, 1988).

Clothing

The clothing that fairies wear can be diverse but seem to largely reflect local human styles. Although we do see some fairies like the Fendoree who may be naked in folklore by and large fairies seem to prefer clothing of some sort. Rev. Kirk explains it this way:

> *"Their Apparel and Speech is like that of the People and Country under which they live: so are they seen to wear Plaids and variegated Garments in the Highlands of Scotland, and Suanochs therefore in Ireland."* (Kirk & Lang, 1893, page 14).

The Fairy Census by Simon Young mentions an anecdotal account[1] of a fairy man dressed in a contemporary if eccentric style, wearing green, indicating that rev. Kirk's 17th century observation still holds true.

Colours of fairy dress vary but do follow a general pattern of what we might call preferred colours. The individual entry on COLOURS discusses this in more depth, but here we will summarize as it relates to clothing. The fairies are known to favour wearing green in particular, sometimes accented with red, with specific kinds of fairies known to wear red exclusively. Crocker describes Irish fairies as favouring *"a black hat, a green suit, white stockings, and red shoes"* (Crocker, 1825, page 162). Trows in the Orkneys wear grey, and various specific types of fairies may wear white or blue exclusively. Scottish fairies have been described wearing plaid and Welsh fairies seen dancing by a couple boys were said to be dressed in many different colours (Kirk & Lang, 1893; Briggs, 1976; Gwyndaf, 1991). Modern anecdotal accounts describe them in clothing that is in line with current fashion or that of the previous generation.

Note

1 I am aware of several other first person anecdotal accounts from people I know directly who have similarly stated they have

seen fairies dressed in reasonably modern human clothing, although one person noted the colours and style were a bit odd and eccentric.

Colours

Colours play a significant role in fairylore with many individual types of fairies associated with particular colours, fairies more generally associated with certain colours, and colour forming a kind of subtle language that indicates something of the nature of a fairy a person is dealing with.

Green – Green is one of the most common colours associated with the Good People. In Scotland it was considered unlucky for a person, especially a woman to wear green and witnesses often described the fairies clad in that colour (Evans-Wentz, 1911; Briggs, 1976). In the Ballad of Alice Brand green is called *'the fairies' fatal green'* and a human couple in the story earn the ire of the resident Fairy King by wearing this colour while in his wood (Acland, 1998). Some fairy animals including the Cu Sidhe may be green in colour and in several ballads including Thomas the Rhymer the Fairy queen appears dressed in green. In folklore and anecdotal accounts the Good People, particularly the Trooping fairies, are often said to wear green sometimes with red shoes or hats (Narvaez, 1991; Briggs, 1976). In one modern account in the Fairy Census, #22, occurring in Cornwall a woman reported seeing a fairy clad in olive green indicating that perhaps this colour is still important (Young, 2018). Briggs suggests that green may be related in Celtic folklore to the colour of death, although Evans-Wentz argues it is a colour of life and renewal.

Red – Another common fairy colour although more ill-omened[1] in its appearance than green is red. There's an anecdote of a red clad fairy who would appear at births as an omen that the baby would die (Ballard, 1991). Another story, this one from Newfoundland, tells of a woman who saw fairies dressed in red who ten shot her with elf shot (Rieti, 1991). It isn't entirely clear cut, however, as not all red dressed fairies were always dangerous: Leprechauns were said to wear red hats in some accounts as were Cluricauns and Fir Darrig, Manx fairies have been described wearing red coats, and the Welsh Tylwyth Teg are said by some to wear primarily red and all of these can be either helpful or dangerous (Evans- Wentz, 1911; Briggs, 1976). In some accounts we are told fairies wear red and green together (Narvaez, 1991; Evans-Wentz, 1911). Some fairies like the Red Cap get their names because of the ubiquitous red associated with them, while others like the Leprechaun used to be more strongly associated[2] with the colour but the association has shifted over time.

White – White can be associated with both benevolent and malevolent fairies, having connotations of goodness and of death. Some sources claim the Welsh Tylwyth Teg usually dress in white, as do the Corrigans of Brittany, and the White Ladies and Silkies of England (Evans-Wentz, 1911; Briggs, 1976). There's an account from Shetland of two battling groups of fairies one dressed in white the other dressed in black (Bruford, 1991). Yeats talks about an anecdotal account he heard from two boys who saw fairies dressed in white circling a tree (Yeats, 1892). Although the Fairy Queen is often described wearing green in Isobel Gowdie's accounts of her encounters with the fairies she says the Queen wore white. Many fairy animals are also said to be white including cattle, hounds, deer and horses. There are also some Irish accounts claiming that fairies have white blood which is sometimes found on the ground after night time battles between different groups (O hOgain, 2006).

Black – Black in fairylore is usually[3] an ill-omened colour often associated with death or harbingers of death. To see a fairy wearing black was an omen of death although perhaps not for the person who saw them as in one anecdotal account where a young woman saw black clad fairies before someone near her died (Ballard, 1991). Many of the more portentous fairy hounds are black and to see them is often a sign of impending personal doom. The class of fairy hounds called Black Dogs were described as shaggy and black with red eyes, and while sometimes helpful they could also be very dangerous (Briggs, 1976). Cat Sidhe were also primarily black and fell into the more dangerous category of fairy beings.

Blue – Blue is not immediately associated with fairies by many people but it does have folkloric associations. In Somerset a Hobgoblin that appears in stories was named Blue Burches for his pants and elsewhere a mine fairy who wore a blue hat was known as Blue Bonnet (Briggs, 1976). There are also several accounts of fairies who were seen to wear blue along with other colours including blue and red, and blue, red, and green (Briggs, 1976).

Grey – Although less well known as a colour associated with fairies grey does have its folkloric connotations. The Orkney Trows are said to wear grey and one name for them in folklore is the Grey Neighbours, demonstrating the strength of the connection between the colour and these fairies (Bruford, 1991; Briggs, 1976). Yeats relates a story of a fairy woman in a grey cloak who regularly appeared to a woman and her mother (Yeats, 1962).

Notes

1 Red appears associated with Otherworldly beings in Irish mythology in several places such as the Togail Bruidne Dá Derga and Táin Bó Regamna and in these instances the beings who dress in red are usually of a dangerous nature. It is a colour that has protective qualities, especially used against witchcraft, and there are some anecdotal accounts of it as a protective colour against fairies, however, the wider pattern seems to connect it to the Good Folk rather than against them. See entry on Blood for further discussion.

2 In older Irish folklore Leprechauns were described wearing

red suits or red pants and shirts; however, in modern folklore they are most well-known for wearing green indicating an interesting shift in colour associations with this particular fairy over the centuries.

3 The bulk of folklore supports black clad fairies as negative, however, there are a few contemporary anecdotal accounts of non-malicious fairies appearing wearing black.

Corrigans

Found in the folklore of French Brittany, Corrigans are roughly comparable to the modern idea of small, mischievous elves. They look like adult humans but are the size of children and are nocturnal, coming out after the sun sets. Like other fairies Corrigans may be helpful to humans, especially around farms or houses, but can also be cruel to them if the human is in their power and are usually not willing to aid humans (Evans-Wentz, 1911). They are also inclined to punish those who violate their privacy, reward humans they like, and to take human children.

Corrigans enjoy dancing and anywhere they dance FAIRY RINGS will appear (Evans-Wentz, 1911). When they are seen it is usually in groups and they always wear white clothing (Evans-Wentz, 1911).

Co-Walker

This concept comes to us from the writings of rev. Robert Kirk who is clear that the Co-walker is a type of fairy being attached to but separate from a human being. Kirk describes the Co-walker as looking identical to a living human and being seen by other humans both during the lifetime of the person they are attached to as well as after the human dies although they eventually return to their own people (Kirk & Lang, 1893). While Kirk doesn't describe the Co-walker as being dangerous, or indeed as doing much more than occasionally being seen by other humans as an omen that the living human would be arriving at that location soon, he does make it clear that people with the Second Sight abstained from eating meat at funerals or banquets to avoid sharing a meal with a Co-walker (Kirk & Lang, 1893). Kirk says that people who are able to see such spirits and distinguish them from living humans saw them among the pallbearers carrying the casket at funerals as well as eating at funerals and feasts, implying perhaps that such spirits used their form to move unnoticed among humans. Kirk himself had no idea why the Co-walkers chose to attach to humans saying:

> *"It accompanied that person so long and frequently, for ends best known to itself, whether to guard him from the secret assaults of some of its own folks, or only as a sportful mimicry to counterfeit all his actions."* (Kirk & Lang, 1893, pages 43 -44 language updated by me).

Crodh Mara

Crodh Mara – sea cattle – are a kind of fairy cow that lives beneath the water in Scottish folklore. Also sometimes called Crodh Sìth [fairy cattle] and said to live on seaweed (Campbell, 1900).

Cu Sidhe

There are many different types of fairy animals, both the shape shifting beings like the púca who can take animal form and animals that are part of fairy, such as the horses of the Tuatha De Danann. One of the more interesting and diverse is the Cu Sidhe which translates literally to fairy hound in English. The Cu Sidhe are found in every Celtic language speaking culture under versions of the same name [fairy hound], Cù Sìth (Scottish), Cwn Annwn (Welsh), and appear under Anglicized names in the Isle of Man. Fairy Hounds are also known to ride with the Wild Hunt and may be called the Gabriel Ratchets, Dandy Dogs, or Hell hounds. They are also sometimes conflated with the ghostly hounds known as the Black Dog, Black Shuck, Hell Hounds, Padfoot, Bogey, Moddey Doo or the Grim, although there is some debate about whether these ghost dogs are truly fairy hounds or a different type of being.

Katherine Briggs divides these supernatural dogs into three categories: supernatural beings, human ghosts in dog form, and ghosts of dogs (Briggs, 1978). For our purposes we will discusses all appearances of Otherworldly dogs, but it is important to understand that the subject is complex and that what appears to be a dog may or may not actually be a dog, and what seems to be a fairy may or may not fall into that loose definition. There are also a variety of more intelligent fairy beings like the aforementioned Púca which can take on the form of a dog, among others, but which would not be considered a Cu Sidhe as that dog form is only of the ones they can take, whereas the true fairy hound is limited to that shape.

The Cu Sidhe may appear as huge shaggy black or dark green dogs, as swift white hounds with red eyes and ears, sometimes missing a limb, or as smaller white dogs. The black and green Cu Sidhe are known by their enormous size, often described as being as large as a calf with huge round eyes (Parkinson, 2013; Campbell, 1900). These spectral dogs may be male or female and may appear alone, in pairs, or in packs (Campbell, 2008). A Cu Sidhe may also appear as a black dog with a white ring around its neck, usually seen on a fairy hill (Evans Wentz, 1911). What unites them as group is their nature as beings of Fairy.

The Cu Sidhe when associated with the Wild Hunt usually frighten people, as the Hunt itself is an omen of war, death, and madness, although it can also bring blessings. Because of this and related folklore the black and dark green Cu Sidhe tend to have dangerous reputations. The black dogs are seen as omens of death, although it is a bit murky as to whether, like the Bean Sidhe, the dog shows up to warn of an impending death or whether the dog causes the death (Parkinson, 2013). However, not all black dogs are bad omens; in at least some cases the appearance of the black dog was protective as in one story from Swancliffe where a man has a black dog appear and accompany him through a dark wood, twice, only to find out later that the dog had saved him from being robbed and killed by highwaymen (Parkinson, 2013).

Fairy Hounds may also appear as guardians of treasure, something they are known for in Scotland (Parkinson, 2013). In Ireland Cu Sidhe are often associated with specific fairy locations where they are known to be seen over the course of multiple generations and are known to sit and watch people, but they are only considered dangerous if they are disturbed, otherwise they will remain peaceful[1] (Lenihan & Green, 2004).

In at least one example a small white fairy dog appeared as an omen of the coming of the Good People to a home, to warn the inhabitants to prepare for the fairies arrival. This anecdote comes from the Isle of Man and shows the diverse nature of fairy hounds:

> *"...all the family were sometimes sitting in the house of a cold winter night, and my great grandmother and her daughters at their wheels spinning, when a little white dog would suddenly appear in the room. Then everyone there would have to drop their work and prepare for the company to come in: they would put down a fire and leave fresh water for them, and hurry off upstairs to bed. They could hear them come, but could never see them, only the dog. The dog was a fairy dog, and a sure sign of their coming."* (Evans Wentz, 1911, page 122).

Fairy dogs may appear with the Daoine Sidhe during fairy rades, or they may appear wandering on their own, guarding fairy hills, or going ahead of the Gentry to warn of their presence. Black dogs seem to be territorial, favouring churchyards, roadways, and crossroads, especially where gallows have been (Parkinson, 2013). In stories they are often associated with a particular area which is considered haunted (Campbell, 2008). Cu sidhe may appear standing motionless on fairy hills or even among mortal dogs on occasion (Evans Wentz, 1911).

Many people assume the cu sidhe and black dogs are ill-omens, and indeed they may be, but not always. While the appearance of such a hound, especially if it is baying or howling, is usually an omen of death the fairy hounds may also appear for other reasons. Sometimes they can be protective, either of a location in which case simply leaving them and the area alone will allow you to walk away unharmed, or of a person. They may also appear for unknown reasons, without directly harming or effecting anyone.

Note

1 I am aware of several people myself who have had modern encounters with what they believe are Cu Sidhe at Neolithic sites associated with the Daoine Sidhe, in one case guiding a person to the site when it couldn't be found and in another accompanying the person inside a cairn. These anecdotal accounts happened in the 21st century.

D

Daoine Sidhe

Daoine sidhe or Aos sidhe simply means 'people of the fairy hills' with sidhe being the older spelling of the modern word sí. The term in Irish has been used for what we would in English term the fairy people since at least the 9th century CE in writing and likely further back than that orally, as we see it used in the oldest written Irish story where the Otherworldly people appear, the Echtra Condla. In that tale a woman of fairy appears to Connla, the son of the king, and tells him that her people live in a great fairy hill (side mór) and that they are called the people of the fairy hill (aes side). As with the word fairy itself sidhe is both a noun for a place, a fairy hill, and also an adjective for things that have a nature of that place.

As with many of the other listings in this text the daoine sidhe are ambiguous beings in folklore who may appear as a cohesive group or as a general category that can include others. For the purposes of this article we will be treating the daoine sidhe as one cohesive group, but it should be kept in mind that the folklore is not entirely clear on the subject. It is just as accurate to see the term as a generic as it is to see it as a specific, and context is essential for deciding which is appropriate at any point.

Physical descriptions of the Daoine Sidhe are consistent with those of fairy beings across Celtic language speaking areas: five to six feet tall, although sometimes described as slightly shorter, blond or brunette, usually wearing green or grey, human-like but with an air of the Otherworld about them that distinguishes them from mortal folk. The most common descriptions of them are of pale, fair-haired, and well-dressed people (O hOgain, 2006). One anecdotal account relayed by Yeats in 'Celtic Twilight' of a fairy woman said she looked much like a human woman, perhaps a bit shorter than average, with brown hair, and dressed in styles that had been seen a generation prior in that area (Yeats, 1962).

When asked who the Aos Sidhe are some sources claim they are the Irish gods, the Tuatha De Danann (Evans-Wentz, 1911). Mythology does agree that when the Tuatha De Danann were defeated by the Gaels they went into the sidhe and folklore would later come to call them the Aos Sidhe; what is less clear is exactly how much crossover exists between the two groups. Many of the Queens and Kings of the Daoine Sidhe are members of the Tuatha De Danann mentioned in mythology, including Áine, Finnbheara, and Manannán. However, it is also clear that not all the Daoine Sidhe are necessarily former Gods, with stolen humans and human dead sometimes seen among their ranks as well. Another main theory is that they are a kind of angel who was cast out from Heaven or left following Lucifer but were trapped between Heaven and Hell[1] leaving them as spirits in the air and earth. By this reckoning they are considered a type of demon but of a less malicious nature than a true demon would be. Another common idea found in anecdotal accounts is that some of the Daoine Sidhe are human dead who have been taken and transformed by already existing Daoine Sidhe, and this is widely supported in folklore.

The Daoine Sidhe are very intertwined with mortal affairs, known to both borrow people they fancy and to steal those they want to add to their own numbers. Those likely to be borrowed and returned are musicians and midwives, while babies, children, and attractive adults may be taken and kept. There are folkloric accounts of people who may join the Fairy People for a night of dancing or celebration and be safely returned but these are outweighed in folklore by accounts of those who were taken and kept permanently. Why the Daoine Sidhe take humans is an open question but the stories we have indicate that these humans fill necessary roles, acting as servants and adding to existing populations. Besides taking humans the Aos Sidhe were also well-known for taking animals, including horses and cows, by making them appear to sicken and die if not taking them directly and also for stealing the milk from cows as well (O hOgain, 2006). When it came to permanently taking humans they might make it seem that the person had died using a variety of means although drowning and sudden illness were common. Use of ELFSHOT also occurs and is a means to take animals as well as humans.

Despite the name the Daoine Sidhe are not restricted to the fairy mounds. They are also often associated in folklore with mystical Otherworldly islands found in the west which could be seen at times but rarely reached (McNeill, 1956). Additionally, in Irish folklore the Daoine Sidhe have been associated the wind and air, lakes and bogs, and trees and islands, with fairy trees being of special note (O hOgain, 2006). Although there are stories which would seem to indicate that the Daoine Sidhe do live within the physical edifice itself[2] there are also many accounts that indicate the physical location is merely a gateway between this world and the Otherworld. The lands described in these Otherworldly realms are beautiful, peaceful, without death from age, and without sickness, often described as being perpetually in fruit.

Folklore attributes specific fairy hills to different groups of fairies or to certain fairy Queens or Kings, although it's also clear that these beings had a transitory nature that wasn't tied to any single location. Both Irish and Scottish folklore talk about migrations of the fairies from one hill to another, often in the form of FAIRY RADES (McNeill, 1956; Briggs, 1976). The Daoine Sidhe are also known in stories to occasionally enjoy attending mortal fairs and celebrations, such as we see in stories of Finnbheara enjoying going to horse races or of Áine mingling with mortals during midsummer bonfires on her hill. In many versions of the FAIRY MIDWIFE story the midwife sees the fairy man again, after delivering the fairy child, when she runs into him at a mortal fair or market where he is acquiring items for himself indicating that the Fair Folk did go to human trade places.

Despite this occasional transience of habitation the Daoine Sidhe are known to be fiercely protective of places they consider theirs and it is a long-held belief that no one should damage fairy hills or locations. A person who damaged a fairy tree or dug into a fairy hill was likely to quickly suffer from ill-luck, ill-health, or even death for this offense[3] (O hOgain, 2006).

Although they are discussed here as a cohesive group the Daoine Sidhe in folklore are more often said to live in regional groupings[4] which do not always get on with their neighbours. MacNeill discusses this in her book 'Festival of Lughnasa' where she mentions several folkloric and anecdotal accounts of groups of Aos Sidhe from adjoining provinces in Ireland who acted as rivals with each other over the harvest every year. The Sluigh Dhuinn [Host of Donn] from the south-west would fight against fairy men from other provinces and sometimes engage in hurling competitions with fairies from Cnoc Áine with the winner taking the best of the losing area's crop (MacNeill, 1962). Similarly, the Good people of Connacht and Ulster are known to fight, particularly over the harvest (MacNeill, 1962). This rivalry is not limited to the harvest and we also see accounts of fairies fighting during the night near fairy trees leaving traces of their white blood on the ground which can be seen the next morning (O hOgain, 2006).

The Daoine Sidhe have a monarchy with Kings and Queens but besides the nobility there are also other classes of fairies, and it is likely that humans more often interact with these members of the fairy folk than with the nobility (O hOgain, 2006). This idea also reflects one seen in several places in mythology where we are told the Tuatha De Danann – one possible source or portion of the Daoine Sidhe – include both 'deithe ocus andeithe' [gods and not-gods]. Although this phrase has been explained in various ways by later commentators the longer version in the Coir Anmann supports O hOgain's assertion about class divisions among the Aos Sidhe, saying:

> "*dée in t-áes dána ocus andeé in t-áes trebhtha*" [gods the people of art and not-gods the people of the populous] (Stokes & Windisch, 1897; Daimler 2015).

The Daoine Sidhe are known to keep a variety of animals with mythology and folklore specifically mentioning cattle, pigs, dogs, and horses. The hounds, CU SIDHE, are known to accompany the Daoine Sidhe as they travel and also to appear as guardians of places that belong to the Good People. The horses of the Daoine Sidhe, like those of the Tuatha De Danann, are exceptional animals (Wilde, 1888). In stories these animals can be any colour a mortal horse might be although white and black are often mentioned.

There are particular times when the fairy folk are more likely to be active, including twilight and midnight, and these require extra caution. Additionally, several of the quarter days are periods of notably increased activity, including Samhain, Bealtaine, and Lughnasa. On Samhain the Daoine Sidhe are out on the fairy paths, moving from their summer to winter homes (Estyn Evans, 1957). Bealtaine is a time when the Good Neighbours may show up at a person's door, disguised as a stranger, asking for the loan of milk or fire with the intention of stealing the household's luck for the year if the item was given to them (Wilde, 1888). Lughnasa, as was touched on above, is a period when the Good People are active and involved with the human harvest. The Gentry were owed a tithe of the harvest according to folk belief and their fighting during Lughnasa would decide the fate of an area's crops for good or ill (MacNeill, 1962). Of all the times of year Samhain and Bealtaine were considered the most fraught with risk in relation to the Daoine Sidhe, likely because these are times when they are the most likely to be encountered abroad (O hOgain, 2006).

Beliefs about the Daoine Sidhe can be traced back in Ireland to almost the beginning of the written period, with references to people of the fairy mounds appearing in the Ulster Cycle and 9th century stories like the Echtra Condla, and have persisted until the present day. The forms and expressions of the beliefs change but the themes within the beliefs are consistent and vast in what they encompass.

Notes

1 See the section 'ORIGINS' for a deeper discussion of the folklore relating to this topic. Here we are only touching on the main ideas specifically relating to the Daoine Sidhe.

2 Examples would include a variety of myths and stories where a person who has been taken by one of the Daoine Sidhe is released after a human digs into the fairy hill, refusing to stop until they release their captive. In the Tochmarc Etaine we see this happening when Etain's human husband is trying to force her return from her fairy husband Midhir, and there are similar accounts in the stories around Finnbheara's love of mortal women and fondness for taking them. In at least one story of Finnbheara it is said that his home at Cnoc Meadha was dug into and the hole salted so that he would release a human captive.

3 There are stories, as cited in end note 2 of people who dug into fairy hills to recover those who had been taken by the Daoine Sidhe, however, it is worth noting that this is an extreme action and was generally only done as a last resort. Even then it was still a great risk to take.

We can find a multitude of stories of people who died or suffered for interfering with fairy trees or hills, even into the 21st century, and the belief remains strong enough that roads have been rerouted within the last 20 years – see; Deegan '*Fairy Bush Survives The Motorway Planners*'. This belief is mirrored in Iceland where a similar idea is held about the Huldufolk and Álfar which has also affected road construction, see; Memmot '*Highway May Be Side-tracked By Elves*'.

4 It is also true, however, that the Dagda is said to be the King over all the Sidhe in Ireland, indicating that as with everything else relating to the Daoine Sidhe this is not a simple subject.

Days of the Week

Just as certain times of year are significant as periods of higher activity for the fairy folk, there are also such tides within the week itself, with Friday often referenced particularly in Scottish lore. It was thought unlucky to even call Friday by its name on the day itself, lest the fairies hear a person speaking of it and become angry and so just as the fairies themselves were referred to with euphemisms so was Friday (Campbell, 1900). Related folk belief in Scotland says that on Fridays fairies can enter houses as they want to, coming from the west, and their influence extends to getting into whatever food might be cooking on the hearth (Campbell, 1900). Lady Wilde also affirms Friday as a day of great fairy influence and believed it to be the day that they were most likely to abduct humans (Wilde, 1888). Briggs calls Friday "*the fairies Sunday*" and says that it is the day on which the fairies have the greatest power (Briggs, 1967). There is no certainty on why there is this emphasis on Friday, although it's possible that it relates to Christian cosmology and Friday being the day of the crucifixion, and potentially the day when God's power is weakest on earth.

Some folklore claims that it is on Wednesday that the fairies have the most power rather than Fridays (Briggs, 1967). On Saturdays the fairies might also be active and could come into a home at night to use the spinning wheel unless the band was taken from it (Campbell, 1900). It should be kept in mind that, just as the fairies may be more active on the quarter days but are still present at other times, while they may have more influence on certain days of the week according to tradition they are not entirely absent at any point.

There are a couple days when they are said to have less or minimal influence, however, again based on Christian cosmology. In Scottish folklore some believed that the fairies were not allowed to be out on Thursdays because that was Saint Columba's Day so Thursday was the time when a person was safest from fairy interference (McNeill, 1956). In the Highlands all the days between Thursday and Sunday are seen as having minimal fairy influence, and it's said that on Thursday the fairies cannot hear anything said about them (Briggs, 1967). Generally the fairies seemed to dislike Sundays and even the mere mention of it displeased them (Briggs, 1967). Again this likely ties into Christian theology and the belief that Sunday is a particularly sacred day.

'Dead, Mad, or a Poet'

This phrase has become somewhat common today in relation to people who sleep on fairy hills or go to the fairy folk for gifts. The exact quote is from Robert Graves' 1948 book The White Goddess. Page 19:

> *"There is a stone seat at the top of Cader Idris , 'the Chair of Idris', where, according to the local legend, whoever spends the night is found in the morning either dead, mad, or a poet."*

Graves has a reputation for being quite inventive with the source material, creating whole cloth the 'Druidic goddess' Druantia and the Druidic tree calendar for example, however, in this case, he is perpetuating genuine material in his own words. There is an 1874 entry discussing Cader Idris in the 1884 book 'Bye-Gones, Relating to Wales and the Border Countries'which says:

> *"There is a popular Welsh tradition that on the summit of Cader Idris is an excavation in the rock resembling a couch and that*

> *whoever should pass a night in that seat would be found in the morning either dead, raving mad, or endowed with supernatural genius."*

It would seem likely from the similarity in wording that this or another identical such source from Welsh folklore influenced Graves' later writing.

There's a lot of folklore backing up the wider concept of going to a sacred place, often one associated with the Good People, and sleeping there to acquire inspiration or to be driven mad for one's hubris. We see this in some versions of the story of the Brahan Seer, Coinneach Odhar, a Scottish seer who may have been given his gift after sleeping on a fairy howe and waking to find a holed stone resting on his chest. In the same way Turlough O'Carolan, a famous blind Irish musician of the 17th century, was supposed to have gained his skill and many of his songs by sleeping on a fairy hill.

In the folktale of Lus Mór [Foxglove] the eponymous main character was a man with a hunched back who fell asleep on a fairy hill and woke to hear the inhabitants of the hill signing; when he joined the song at the exact right moment with a new line for the song the delighted Fair Folk healed his back. However, when another man with a similar hunched back tried the same thing but interrupted the song rudely mid-verse he was punished by having his back twisted twice as badly. These are only a few examples of the substance behind the concept, the idea that risking everything by being vulnerable in the Good People's places can bring either great reward or great danger, sometimes both. I might suggest, from my own perspective, that there seem to be potential hints here of what could be initiatory rites relating to the practice of sleeping on or going into the sí, but that's a topic that would take a whole other article to unpack.

The same text mentions that this idea was not unique to Cader Idris but was found in other areas of Wales as well, and offers the example of Maen Du Yr Arddu [black stone of Arddu] where it was said if two people slept on the eponymous stone one would go mad and the other become a poet. The Maen Du Yr Arddu example is particularly interesting to me, because while Cader Idris offers three possibilities for a single person Maen Du Yr Arddu implies that two people must go in and one is guaranteed inspiration and the other madness. The Welsh material differs from the above mentioned Scottish and Irish folklore only in that there is no explicit connection with the fairies there, however, if we look elsewhere in Welsh folklore we do find that Cader Idris was known as a habitation of the fairies and Maen Du Yr Arddu is near a lake, Llyn Du Yr Arddu [Black lake of Arddu] associated with the Tylwyth Teg [Fair Family aka fairies].

The Dearg Due

The Dearg Due is the closest to a classic vampire that can be found in Irish folklore. There are not any references to this being in older folklore texts or mythology. The only sources in which the Dearg Due is mentioned were more modern works and mostly ones that focused on vampires specifically. This has left me a bit sceptical of the Dearg Due's true origins, nonetheless, what is available will be related here.

First a bit about the name. Many sources will explain this name as meaning 'red blood sucker' but I think this unlikely. Dearg does indeed mean red, but Due is a more difficult word to interpret. In Old Irish the name may mean 'red owing' or 'red place', but I think it's more likely the name comes from modern Irish 'Dearg Dú'[1] which could be read as 'red evil' or 'red darkness'. As far as I can tell the words blood and sucker aren't involved.

So, the story then. As it goes around the internet and in the vampire books: Long ago in Ireland there lived a beautiful maiden, the daughter of a rich and greedy father. Many men came from across the land to try to win her hand in marriage but the girl had fallen in love with a local peasant and refused all others. Her father wouldn't allow this and forced her into a loveless marriage with an older man who was terribly cruel to her. Eventually, when she realized her true love wasn't going to rescue her, the girl killed herself. Before dying the girl renounced all that was good in the world, cursed God and those who had made her suffer in life, and swore she would get her revenge. And so it was that after she was buried she rose again from her grave as the Dearg Due; some say that she hunts and kills those who are guilty of hurting others, while others say she seeks out the innocent, especially children and young men to be her victims.

Like traditional Western European vampires the Dearg Due is a human being who died and was buried, and rose from the dead to torment the living. Like those other vampires she roams the night seeking to steal the life force from the living. Unlike other vampires the Dearg Due is not a type of being but a specific individual, and it is said her grave still exists in county Waterford. She only rises from her grave once a year on the anniversary of her death and she can be held in check if stones are kept piled on her grave.

It's hard to pin down how old these stories are or whether they are truly rooted in older mythology or represent a blending of newer thoughts. Certainly they lack the overt fairy folklore we see in the stories of beings like the Baobhan Sithe of Scotland which are also vampiric in nature, or even the more bloodsucking types of Leannán Sidhe found across Celtic speaking countries. But the stories of the Dearg Due are interesting and at the least represent an evolution in folklore as different cultural influences came into play.

Note

1 dú in this case is a form of dubh, literally meaning black.

Deer

Deer are associated with fairies in two ways: there are the white deer which may appear to guide people or lead them to a specific place, and there are mortal deer that are used by the fairies for their milk as cattle would be. Campbell notes in 'The Gaelic Otherworld' a particular association with the red deer of Scotland and this second use by fairies.

Diminutive Fairies

There are accounts of some fairies who are very small in stature, contrasting with descriptions of larger, taller fairies. LEPRECHAUNS and MURYANS are two examples of folkloric fairies whose smallness seems to be an inherent part of their nature. There is also another thread of belief which scholars believe was influenced by Christianity's efforts to disempower the fairies by physically reducing them.

We see this idea reflected in some of the later euphemisms used for the fairies such as Little People, Wee People, and on the Isle of Man Little Fellows and Little Boys (Evans-Wentz, 1911).

Dökkálfar

The Dökkálfar are referenced in a few places in Norse mythology. The name itself means 'dark elves' and Snorri describes them as living in the earth. Grimm calls them 'Genii obscuri' or spirits of the dark and suggests a connection between them and nâir, spirits of the dead, even going so far as to place them living "in hel, the heathen hades" (Grimm, 1888, p446). Grimm also questions whether the Dökkálfar should be separated from the nâir or whether "[t]he dusky elves are souls of dead men..." (Grimm, 1888, p 447). There is some strong evidence that the Dökkálfar were the mound dead or male ancestors and the Dökkálfar are sometimes called Mound Elves; it is not certain, however, and it may be that some Dökkálfar are human dead but others are not[1].

See ALFAR for more on Icelandic elves

Note

1 The idea of some dead joining the elves after death is something we see as well in the Irish, indicating that this may be a wider concept.

Donn

Donn is a complicated figure in Irish mythology who has roles as one of the invaders of Ireland in the Mythic cycle, as a God of the Dead, and as a Fairy King.

Folklore tells us that Tech Duinn is a place where the dead go, but not necessarily their final destination. Some believe that the house of Donn is where the dead go before moving on to the Otherworld (Berresford Ellis, 1987). In the 8th to 10th centuries Tech Duinn was seen as an assembly place of the dead, and a place that the dead both went to and left from (O hOgain, 2006). Besides Tech Duinn (present day Bull Rock, County Cork) Donn is also connected to Cnoc Firinne in county Limerick and Dumhcha in county Clare.

The Donn of Cnoc Firinne had strong aspects of a lord of the aos sidhe, being called Donn Firinne and said to kidnap people into his hill who had been thought to have died (O hOgain, 2006). Like many other Irish deities belief in Donn seems to have survived conversion to Christianity by shifting him from God to Good Neighbour, albeit a very powerful one. In county Clare Donn was Donn na Duimhche, Donn of the Dune, and was believed to ride out as a fairy horseman with his army (O hOgain, 2006).

Dullahan

A Headless spirit which may be a ghost or otherwise may be a fairy. MacKillop suggests the name comes from dubh-luchrachan 'dark puny creature' but I would suggests instead the older Irish dubh laoch or laech 'dark warrior'. The Dullahan appears as a headless phantom riding a horse or in a coach; sometimes the horses are also headless (MacKillop, 1998). He carries his head which appears to be rotting and has enormous eyes and he tosses his head around like a ball. His horse or horses are black with flaming red eyes. Humans who stop to look at the Dullahan with have their eyes put out by his whip and those who open their door out of curiosity at the sound of his passage will be drenched in blood (MacKillop, 1998).

The Dullahan is considered an omen of death.

Each Uisge

The name is Gaidhlig and means water horse; in Irish it's Each Uisce and it has been anglicized to Aughisky. Campbell suggest an alternate name for it of each sìth [fairy horse] as well. We can find variations of these beings across Celtic and Norse folklore under different names and with slightly different stories but the broad strokes are usually the same. A water horse is a fairy that primarily takes the form of a predatory horse which lures humans to ride it only to leap into a body of water and drown them. The Each Uisge can take the form of a human or a large bird, but the most usual form seen is that of horse, either white or black (Briggs, 1976). Irish folklore of the Each Uisce mentions that they are most often on land in November and if a person manages to catch, saddle, and bridle one it can make a fine riding horse but only if it never gets the scent of salt water (Briggs, 1976). The Each Uisge will devour both humans and cattle if given the opportunity, but never eats the liver which will often be the only sign left of the victim.

There may be a very fine line between folklore of the KELPIE and the Each Uisge as both are reputed to be a kind of intelligent fairy that shapeshifts between horse and human forms, with the Each Uisge also having a bird form, and both trick riders into mounting in order to rush to a body of water and drown and eat them. The Each Uisge is also, like the Kelpie in some stories, said to have skin with an adhesive quality that means once a human gets on they cannot let go to get off again.

Each Uisge are very difficult to kill but there is a story in Highland folklore that describes a blacksmith who took revenge on an Each Uisge who had killed his daughter. The smith and his son created several large iron hooks and then lured the water horse onto shore with a roasted lamb, stabbing the fairy with the hooks until it finally died (McKay, 1940). The body dissolved by the next day.

Elf Locks

Also called fairy-locks or witches-locks, Elf Locks are inexplicable[1] tangles or mats in a person's hair that appear overnight while the person is sleeping and are believed to be caused by the fairies or in some cases witches. They also happen to animals, particularly horses. Although some modern stories try to give them a twee backstory of fairies playing in the hair older folklore attributes them to either the person or animal being ridden at night by the fairies or else intentional knotting by fairies apparently as a punishment of some sort, possibly for laziness or dirtiness. As Shakespeare put it when describing the activity of Queen Mab:

> *"That plaits the manes of horses in the night; And bakes the elflocks in foul sluttish [slovenly] hairs".*

An essay in The Good People: New Fairylore Essays discusses an anecdote wherein a man talks about the LUTIN harassing his mare by tangling her mane at night, tangles he could not undo no matter how he tried. People who had elf-locks might be viewed as having been fairy ridden the night before, especially if they woke up exhausted or aching, or as being influenced by the fairies in dangerous ways. In King Lear Shakespeare alludes to an association between elf-locks and madness, and there is a wider view that did connect the two.

Shakespeare is the oldest English language reference to elf-locks and his use of the term implies hair that is ill-kept and possible a person of questionable sanity. In King Lear the character Edward, after being declared an outlaw and fleeing to the woods, says, *"My face I'll grime with filth; Blanket my loins; Elf my hair in knots"*, planning to pass as a madman while in hiding. A footnote in Shakespeare's Works, volume 5 which defines elflocks as matted or knotted hair that is the result of neglect or disease also quotes a 1596 work by Lodge which says, *"His hairs are curled and full of elves' locks, and nitty for want of combing"*. Both of these reinforce the connection between elf-locks and lack of grooming as well as possible madness, something which itself was often attributed to fairies' displeasure with a person.

A sign of supernatural attention, it was very unlucky to have elf-locks but also unlucky to untangle them. There are some divided opinions about whether it was bad luck to brush them out but allowable to work them out with the fingers. Most often they must be cut out, as they could be both painful and distracting. People experiencing elf-locks are usually advised to sleep with protective measures, particularly iron, at hand to ward off the fairies and prevent further such attention.

In other European cultures, such as Italian, the prohibition about removing elf locks remains in place but rather than being seen as sign of ill luck or negative attention hair knotted by fairies is seen as positive in various ways and even a sign of blessing.

Note

1 As always medical and physical explanations should be ruled out before looking to Otherworldly ones.

Elfland

Also Elfhame, Elphame, Elfame, see FAIRY

Elfin Knight, The[1]

This ballad is more familiar to most people in its later song form as 'Scarborough Fair' but in this older ballad the context is clearly supernatural. Later versions slowly lose this aspect and become a simpler song: in one example, variant I, about a woman trying to avoid marriage to an older man, and in others of one lover asking a person to remind another of them and ask them to complete impossible tasks. In the older versions the supernatural is clearly on display, telling the tale of a woman who wishes for an Elf Knight as her true love, and he responds by giving her a series of seemingly impossible tasks to complete to win him. She in turn gives him a series of equally impossible tasks to earn her as his wife. Below is a full version believed to be one of the oldest versions which dates to 1670 (Caffrey, 2002). In the following text some of the key variants will be excerpted and discussed.

The Elfin Knight Version 2B
1My plaid[2] *away, my plaid away*
And over the hills and far away
And far away to Norway,
My plaid shall not be blown away.
The Elfin knight stands on yonder hill,
Refrain: Ba, ba, ba, lillie ba
He blows his horn both loud and shrill.
Refrain: The wind has blown my plaid away
2He blows it east, he blows it west
He blows it where he likes it best
3 'I wish that horn were in my chest,
Yes and the Knight in my arms next!
4 She had no sooner these words said
Than the Knight came to her bed.
5 'You are too young a girl', he said
'Married with me that you would be.'
6 'I have a sister younger than I
And she was married yesterday'
7 'Married with me if you would be
A courtesy you must do for me.
8 'It's you must make a shirt for me,
Without any cut or seem', said he.
9 'And you must shape it knife- and sheerless,
And also sow it needle and threadless.'
10 'If that piece of courtesy I do for you

Another you must do for me.
11 'I have an acre of good untilled land,
Which lays low by yonder sea shore.
12 'It's you must till it with your blowing horn,
And you must sow it with pepper corn.
13 'And you must harrow with a thorn
And have your work done before the morning.'
14 'And you must shear it with your knife
And not lose a stack of it for your life.'
15 'And you must stack it in a mouse hole
And you must thresh it in your shoe-sole.'
16 'And you must prepare it in the palm of your hand
And also stack it in your glove
17 'And you must bring it over the sea
Fair and dry and clean to me.'
18 'And when you've done, and finished your work,
You'll come to me, and you'll get your shirt.'
19 'I'll not abandon my plaid for my life;
It covers my seven children and my wife.'
20 'My maidenhead I'll then keep still
Let the Elfin Knight do what he will.'
(Modified from Child, 1898)

This is a complex ballad and one that stands in stark contrast to others like Tam Lin and Lady Isabel and the Elf Knight. Like the latter though we see this one beginning with a young woman hearing an Elfin Knight blowing his horn and wishing aloud that she had him for her own, and like 'Lady Isabel' the elf seems compelled to immediately respond by going her. He does not seem to want to do this and we can gather his reluctance since his first comment is that she is too young for him, which she counters by saying that her younger sister was just married. In most versions the girl's age is unspecified although she does seem to at least be of marriageable age; only in version D is her age given as the very young 9 years old and we may interpret his challenge to her there as a way to put her off until she's older[3]. In version A the Elf Knight says not only that she is too young but that *'married with me you ill would be'* and in version C he asks her 'Are you not over young a maid; with only young men down to lay?' (Child, 1898). When she insists despite his concern over her age that she is acceptable – by referring to the marriage of her younger sister – he issues her a challenge, more kindly worded in version B above and more bluntly said in C *'married with me you shall never be; until you make me a shirt without a seam* [etc.,]'.

Looking at this section several things are clear. The Elf Knight seems to have no choice in responding to the young woman when she hears his horn and wishes for his company. He also seems unable to simply refuse her advances when she expresses a desire to marry him, or at the least to have sex with him. Instead he responds to her insistence by giving her a list of things she must do to earn him as a spouse, in all versions this seems to include making a shirt that is not sown or cut, and not touched by iron. In several alternate version there are additional requirements including:

D: *'…wash it in yonder well,*
Where the dew never wet, nor the rain ever fell
And you must dry it on a thorn
That never budded since Adam was born.'

Or alternately from version C:
'And you must wash it in yonder cistern
Where water never stood nor ran
And you must dry it on yonder Hawthorn
Where the sun never shone since man was born.'

In both of these we see the key to the additions being the idea of washing the shirt in water that is not ordinary water and drying it on an ancient thorn tree that has either never flowered or never seen the sun for as long as humans have existed.

The girl responds to these challenges with a set of her own which in most versions are more complex than what she has been asked to do and involve plowing, planting, harvesting and preparing an acre of land in ways that are just as impossible as the shirt she has been asked to make. In some versions the land is said to *'lay low by yonder sea strand'* but in some others it is specifically *'between the sea and the sand'* (Child, 1898). We may perhaps assume the challenges are more difficult and numerous because the Elfin Knight is assumed to have a greater ability to achieve the impossible tasks than the girl is.

In the later variations the ballad ends with the young woman telling the Knight that when he has completed his task and is ready to present the literal fruit (or at least grain) of his labour he can return for his shirt. However, in the two earlier versions, A and B, the woman responding with challenges of her own seems to free the elf of the compulsion he was under (or at least a portion of it), as he replies to her telling him when to come for the shirt by saying he won't *'abandon his plaid for his life; it covers his seven children and his wife'*. In other words he doesn't want to give up his own bed and family for this young woman. She at least has the good grace then to reply that she will keep her virginity and he can do as he will, certainly setting him completely free at that point.

There are also variations of the refrain which is presented here in the oldest form of *'ba ba ba lillie ba; the wind has blown my plaid away'* which is found in variants A and B; versions C, D and E are fairly similar with the second line saying 'and the wind has blown my plaid away' but the first line varies from *'over the hills and far away'* to *'blow, blow, blow wind blow'* except version E which uses the opening line of the refrain from versions A and B. the refrain for version F is *'sober and grave grows merry in time; once she was a true love of mine'* and marks the first version with no mention of the Elfin Knight. G introduces the famous lines *'Parsley, sage, rosemary, and thyme; and you shall be a true lover of mine'* and H blends the previous two giving us *'every rose grows merrier with thyme; and then you will be a true lover of mine'*. I returns to the older version with *'Hee ba and balou ba'* as the beginning but the reference to the wind blowing away the plaid to finish; J uses nonsense words. K's refrain is *'Sing ivy, sing ivy; sing holly, go whistle and ivy'* while L uses the variant *'Sing ivy, sing ivy; sing green bush, ivy and holly'*; finally M returns to a version of *'Every rose springs merry in its time; and she longed to be a true lover of mine'*. It is likely that the earliest refrains which rely on references to the wind blowing away the plaid are symbolic and that the plaid in this case was meant to represent either a loss of innocence or security. Caffrey in his article 'The Elfin Knight Child #2: Impossible Tasks and Impossible Love' suggests that the plaid is meant to have sexual connotations and that is certainly likely throughout the ballad. The other versions of the refrain include a selection of herbs: ivy, holly, rose, parsley, sage, rosemary, and thyme. Ivy was used in love magic and had protective qualities; holly is favoured by fairies and also has protective qualities but interestingly was known as a plant that protected the heart against love (MacCoitir, 2006; MacCoitir, 2003). Rose not surprisingly has a long history as a symbol of love and also of beauty. Parsley is associated with lust and fertility; sage for fulfilling wishes; rosemary for love and lust; and thyme for love and attraction (Cunningham, 1985). All of these plants then have significance relating to the meaning of the ballad itself and may have been understood for that symbolism within the original context.

Notes

1 An earlier version of this article appears in my previous book 'Travelling the Fairy Path'.

2 A plaid is a length of cloth that can be worn as mantle but

also serves as a bedcovering. In this context I might suggest the bedcovering meaning is intended although one might also see it as applying to a mantle being worn.

3 In this version as well note that she does not claim that she has a younger sister who is already married but that she 'has a sister eleven years old; and she to the young men's bed has made bold'. This does not seem to be a persuasive argument for the Elf Knight, however, who continues to put her off.

Elfshot

'Elfshot' or 'elf arrows' appear in both Irish and Scottish fairylore as a type of small weapon used against people and livestock by the fairies, and in Scotland also by witches. One of the most common weapons of the fairies, elfshot had various negative effects on those struck by them. The arrows do tangibly exist and can be found as small, Neolithic flint arrowheads. When someone found a flint arrowhead or anything similar looking they would usually believe they had found a fairy arrow (O hOgain, 1995). If the arrow was dull then it was believed it had been used already to bring harm to a human or animal (Campbell, 1900). However, when they are used by the fairies they are invisible and so are the wounds they cause, requiring a special practitioner to be brought in to identify the site of the impact.

Called 'saighead sith' [fairy arrows] in Gaidhlig it was thought to be very lucky to find one on the ground (McNeill, 1956). Although some believed a found elf arrow should be thrown in water or buried to avoid drawing dangerous Otherworldly attention, others believed such an arrow was a powerful talisman which had to be kept covered from sunlight and not allowed to touch the ground again to retain its power (Black, 1894; Wilde, 1888; Evans, 1957). While being struck by one that was cast by a fairy or witch could be deadly the beliefs surrounding the found physical arrows was very different and they were often kept as talismans. Scottish folk belief said that a person could not find an elf arrow by searching for one but only by accident and often with the arrow appearing in an unexpected manner (Black, 1894). There are a variety of ways these arrows might show up, including being found in a person's clothing, possessions, or shoe without the person having knowingly put it there. Lady Wilde, however, mentions the Irish belief that 'fairy stones' were often found near sí [fairy hills] lying on the ground, and ads no particular prohibition against intentionally looking for them. Simply having such an arrow was lucky but they also had magical properties and could be used both herbal charms and in cures for sick cattle (Wilde, 1888; Evans, 1957). Multiple examples can be found in Scotland of elfshot that have been set in silver and were worn as protective pendants.

When used as weapons by the Other Crowd elfshot was thought to be one possible cause of elf-stroke or FAIRY STROKE. Fairy Stroke could take the form of a sudden seizure or paralysis, cramping, pain, bruising, wasting sicknesses, and even death (Briggs, 1976). The most distinctive type of elfshot injury was a sudden, internal shooting pain, without any clear explanation (Hall, 2007). The similarity in symptoms may explain why elfshot was sometimes seen to cause or be related to the fairy stroke, although they were also seen as distinct from each other.

The fairies might use elfshot for a variety of purposes, including punishing humans for slight offenses, tormenting them over greater violations, and stealing humans and livestock into Fairy. If the purpose was a minor punishment the effect might be minor and only last for a short time while if they were truly angry it might involve great pain and suffering indefinitely or even result in the person's death. There are also accounts of the fairies using elfshot to paralyze a person in order to switch the person with a changeling and take the person for their own (Briggs, 1976). If they wanted to take cattle a similar procedure was used, where the animal was shot and would seemingly waste away and die, so the fairies could take it (O hOgain, 1995).

Fairies were also known to give elfshot to witches who would then use it, sometimes at the direction of the Good People. Isobel Gowdie in her trial confession said she had seen elfshot arrows being made when she was visiting among the fairies, and confessed witches[1] in Scotland admitted to using elfshot against other humans (Briggs, 1976). According to Gowdie she had gone with the fairies and on at least one occasion seen the Devil making the arrows and handing them to 'elf boys' who sharpened and prepared them. She claimed that they, along with a short chant, were then given to the mortal witches to be used with details of how to aim and shoot the arrows effectively (Black, 1894; Briggs, 1976).

Because of the widespread belief in elfshot many different cures and treatments for it existed. The 9th and 10th century Anglo-Saxon Leechbooks contain a selection of drinks, salves, and charms to treat humans afflicted with the symptoms of elfshot. Usually a person would be diagnosed with an elf-related ailment, often involving sudden internal pain or an illness that was traditionally attributed to elves, then a cure would be prepared and given in conjunction with a chanted or spoken charm or prayer (Hall, 2007; Jolly; 1996). The Leechbook also offers possible cures for horses suffering from elfshot which involve a combination of actions, including shedding the animal's blood and spoken charms (Jolly, 1996). One 20th century Irish method of diagnosing if a cow had been elfshot was to measure the cow from nose to tail tip three times using the persons arm; if the measure was the same each time it was a normal illness but if the measure differed any time it was a sign of fairy illness (Duchas, 2019). For cattle the animal can be rubbed with an elf arrow which was found previously because it has curative powers over health issues, rubbed with salt water then given some to drink, or given water that has both salt and silver in it (Black, 1894). In Ireland one folk cure was to spill a bit of the cow's blood in a ceremony dedicating the animal to

Saint Martin (Evans, 1957). Often a specialist like a fairy doctor or bean feasa [wise woman] would be called in first to verify that a person or animal had been elfshot and to work the cure if needed (Jenkins, 1991). Sometimes the effect of the shot was deemed permanent and could not be cured at all or the cure applied would not be strong enough to be effective. In some cases, tragically especially in relation to suspected changelings, the cure itself would prove fatal.

Elfshot has gone by names across Ireland, Scotland, and England - elf arrows, fairy arrows, fairy darts, fairy stones, saighead sith – but the beliefs are fairly cohesive across all the areas where they are found. Bringing a variety of painful ailments and allowing the Good People to potentially take a person or animal they desire, elfshot is one of their most dangerous weapons. The effects can be transitory or permanent and may be mitigated with magical charms and herbal cures, and ironically the same exact shot that causes the injury can be used to cure it when wielded by a well-intentioned human hand.

Note

1 It must be remembered, however, that trial confessions, with few exceptions, were obtained under extreme duress and while worth considering for their reflection of contemporary beliefs should not be taken without scepticism of their objective truth.

Ellyllon

Ellyllon are Welsh fairy beings (singular Ellyll) that can most closely be equated to the English and Scottish concept of elves, although the Ellyll tend to be viewed as smaller and more generally benevolent. Ellyllon are associated with forests and similar areas although they may also encroach on human habitations (Sikes, 1880). In stories they are described as small figures but good natured and cheerful.

Elves

The English word elf has a convoluted history. It can be traced back etymologically to Old English and Anglo-Saxon 'alf', and the aelfe are not only the predecessors of the later elves but also cognate to them. Further back the word is likely from the Proto-Germanic 'albiz' and before that the Proto-Indo-European 'albho' which may have meant white (Harper, 2017). In its older forms it was glossed with a variety of Otherworldly and supernatural beings, including fairies, sprites, goblins, and incubi, showing the range of associations that elves had within the Anglo-Saxon and Germanic cultures (Douglas, 2017). By the 16th century elf was used to both describe a malicious creature, often used interchangeably with incubus and goblin, as well as more generically to describe any Otherworldly being (Williams, 1991). The fluidity of the usage of the word is an indication of the wide range of applications it was given.

Understanding Elves present a unique difficulty because this long use to gloss several words in other languages and its long use as a generic. Because of this we end up with a range of beings that fall under the label 'elf' but are very different in nature and description. We may perhaps divide them into two main groupings, the taller elves and the small elves. The latter are generally described as about a foot tall and can appear as old and wizened or younger. The former group are often described as more human in appearance, although they are clearly supernatural in their abilities and are averse to iron. Grimm suggest a division in Germanic mythology of taller elves into three main groups, the Ljósálfar, dökkálfar, and Svartálfar, each living in different domains and having slightly different appearances; Ljósálfar means 'light elves', dökkálfar 'dark elves', and Svartálfar 'black elves'. Snorri writing about Norse mythology described only Ljósálfar and Svartálfar. In Scottish and Germanic sources the taller elves may be described as beautiful and the word elf was sometimes glossed with incubus.

However, in other Germanic sources elves were explicitly called ugly and were said to have long or crooked noses.

The Scottish view of elves may have been strongly influenced by the Norse, and we find the use of the word elf as a generic for Otherworldly beings in use there much as fairy is used elsewhere. This is carried through to the terms related to these beings as well, so that the world of Fairy becomes Elfhame [elf home] or Elfland and the Queen of Fairy becomes the Queen of Elfland or Elfhame. This Norse influence in Scotland may have affected both the terminology as well as the imagery around the Scottish elves who strongly resemble the Norse Álfar (Briggs, 1976).

Elves in folklore are described as difficult to see or invisible beings who can wield ELFSHOT and cause great harm to humans and livestock (Hall, 2007). They were regularly compared to or glossed with incubi because of their habit of seducing mortal women and it was believed, as with the Norse Álfar, that children could be produced by these unions.

Erlkönig

In 1782 Johann Wolfgang von Goethe wrote a poem, 'Der Erlkönig', based on a folksong 'Erlkönigs Tochter' which in turn had been based on a Danish folk story called Elveskud [elf-shot]. In the original story a man meets with several elf-maids while out riding and one of them invites him to join them; he refuses and is either magically sickened or physically attacked, and makes it back home before dying (Jamieson, 1806; Keightley, 1850). In von Goethe's version a father is riding at night with his son and the son is attacked by the Erlkönig, who wants to take the son back with him. Von Goethe's poem was later adapted into English by sir Walter Scott in the 18th century, who made the boy younger and made the Erl-king's intent more clearly to take him to be a kind of adopted child, whereas in von Goethe's the intent of the Elf-king is more ambivalent.

The name 'Erlkönig' literally means Alder King, perhaps linking this being to that type of tree, although it is also possible that erl is a mistranslation of the Danish elle or elf. In the original Danish version it is given as 'ellekoneg', or elf king, with the elfmaid who tries to seduce the man specified as the elf king's daughter (Syv, 1695).

The text of the original Goethe poem, translated by me[1], is as follows:

Who rides, so late, through night and wind?
It is the father with his child.
He has the boy well in his arm
He holds him safely, he keeps him warm.

"My son, why do you hide your face in fear?"
"Father, see you not the Elf-king?
The Elf-king with crown and cape?"
"My son, it's a streak of fog."

"You dear child, come, go with me!
Very beautiful games I play with you;
Many colorful flowers are on the beach,
My mother has many a golden robe."

"My father, my father, and hear you not
What the Elf-king quietly promises me?"
"Be calm, stay calm, my child;
Through rough dry leaves sighs the wind."

"Do you, fine boy, want to go with me?
My daughters shall wait on you finely;
My daughters lead the nightly dance,
And rock and dance and sing to bring you in."

"My father, my father, and see you not there
The Elf-king's daughters in the gloomy place?"
"My son, my son, I see it clearly:
There shimmer the old willows so grey."

"I love you, your beauty tempts me;
And if you're not willing, then I will use force."
"My father, my father, now he's touching me!
The Elf-king has done me harm!"

It horrifies the father; he swiftly rides on,
He holds in his arms the moaning child,
Reaches the farm with trouble and hardship;
In his arms, the child was dead

Sir Walter Scott's Version:

The Erl King
O who rides by night thro' the woodland so wild?
It is the fond father embracing his child;
And close the boy nestles within his loved arm,
To hold himself fast, and to keep himself warm.

"O father, see yonder! see yonder!" he says;
"My boy, upon what dost thou fearfully gaze?"
"O, 'tis the Erl-King with his crown and his shroud."
"No, my son, it is but a dark wreath of the cloud."

The Erl-King Speaks
"O come and go with me, thou loveliest child;
By many a gay sport shall thy time be beguiled;
My mother keeps for thee many a fair toy,
And many a fine flower shall she pluck for my boy."

"O father, my father, and did you not hear
The Erl-King whisper so low in my ear?"
"Be still, my heart's darling--my child, be at ease;
It was but the wild blast as it sung thro' the trees."

Erl-King
"O wilt thou go with me, thou loveliest boy?
My daughter shall tend thee with care and with joy;
She shall bear thee so lightly thro' wet and thro' wild,
And press thee, and kiss thee, and sing to my child."

"O father, my father, and saw you not plain
The Erl-King's pale daughter glide past thro' the rain?"
"Oh yes, my loved treasure, I knew it full soon;
It was the grey willow that danced to the moon."

Erl-King
"O come and go with me, no longer delay,
Or else, silly child, I will drag thee away."
"O father! O father! now, now, keep your hold,
The Erl-King has seized me--his grasp is so cold!"

Sore trembled the father; he spurr'd thro' the wild,
Clasping close to his bosom his shuddering child;
He reaches his dwelling in doubt and in dread,
But, clasp'd to his bosom, the infant was dead.

This poem has several interesting aspects to it, but in it we can clearly see reflections of the Changeling lore found across Celtic countries. As in the story of Connla and the Fairy Woman, we see in this tale a boy who can see and hear the Good People while his father cannot. The boy - whose age is never specified - sees the Elf King pursuing them and hears him trying to convince him to go; the father sees and hears only natural phenomena. In the end the boy says the Elf King has touched him and the father arrives at his destination to find that the boy has died, possibly reflecting the idea that the boy has actually been taken by the Elf King.

Literary critics have suggested that the story is the tale of a seriously ill boy, feverish and delusional, who is hallucinating, and that the father is trying to comfort him while they ride seeking a doctor by explaining the real things the boy is confusing for supernatural ones. This is certainly one possible interpretation of events, however, there is nothing directly in the poem that indicates the boy is ill. This conclusion is generally drawn from the fact that the pair are out riding so late without any reason given for the journey.

From a fairylore perspective the poem does fit classic patterns. The Elf King says that he wants the boy because he is beautiful, something that we know the Fair Folk often prize in those they steal; boys were also a common target to be taken as changelings2. He mentions that his daughters will care for the boy, and promises that the boy will be treated well, but when the boy refuses to come voluntarily he takes him by force. This is similar to the older Danish version where the (adult) man is first tempted by the elf maids and then attacked by them when he refuses their offer. It also reflects other changeling lore where a person might initially be lured, but if they resist might be physically abducted.

Ultimately the Erlkönig is a good example of the way that fairylore changes and adapts over time, showing us the way that a folk story moves from one culture to another. In the Danish it is an adult man that the Elf king's daughter fancies and kills; in von Goethe's poem it is a 'boy' of indeterminate age that the Elf king has set his sights on; in Walter Scott's version it is young child. Some things remain constant between all versions, however, as in all three the person is first lured with pretty words and then eventually physically touched in some way, resulting ultimately in their death. It would seem that what the Elf king wants, he ultimately gets.

Notes

1 You can find a professional translation for the von Goethe free online.
2 This was so ingrained in some areas of Ireland's fairy belief that young boys would be dressed as girls to protect them, because girls were thought to be less likely to be taken.

Escape from Fairies

There are a variety of methods that appear in folklore which a person may utilize to escape if they are taken by the fairies, although these methods only work if the person hasn't eaten or drunk anything given to them by the Fey folk, or broken any other taboos. One of the most common ones referred to is turning one's coat or gloves inside out, which seems to have the effect of dispelling any fairy GLAMOUR and thereby causing the fairies to flee. In one Cornish account a man pulled his gloves from his pocket, reversed them, placed a small stone in one and threw them among the fairies in order to free himself (Bottrell, 1873). Another method to escape fairies is to cross running water, which was believed to stop both fairies and ghosts from pursuing a person (Evans-Wentz, 1911). Those tempted to enter into open fairy hills, especially lured by the sounds of fairy music or light glowing from within, are advised to place iron or rowan at the entrance to keep it open otherwise the fairies might close the way behind the person trapping them within.

Generally people who were taken by fairies and escaped did so with the help of others, either still living humans who rescued them or people who had previously been taken and gave saving advice to the person. Lady Wilde tells a story of a girl brought to a fairy banquet who was warned by another captive: "*Eat no food, and drink no wine, or you will never see your home again*" and thanks to this advice manages to successfully escape later

(Wilde, 1888). We see examples of this in an Irish anecdote where a midwife to the fairies is invited to rest and eat after the birth only to hear a woman by the hearth softly singing in Irish warning her to neither eat nor drink or she'd be trapped there; the midwife politely declined and was taken back to her home safely (Narvaez, 1991). One of Yeats' more well-known stories of a stolen bride tells of how her groom stumbled across her among a group of Fair Folk and was urged to join them but she, unrecognized, led him away from the food and drink to a game being played by the older men; he only recognized her when she was led away by a younger fairy man and when he cried out they all disappeared. There is also an anecdote from Ireland of a man whose wife died in childbed while he was away travelling but he was told by a man of the fairies that she had actually been taken by them and so he sat up with her body when he arrived home waiting for her to come visit her new-born; when she did so he threw a magical charm at her and held her until she was returned to her rightful body (Evans-Wentz, 1911). In this case the woman was rescued because her husband had been warned about what was actually occurring and was able to magically intervene.

We also see examples of people being asked to complete tasks, sometimes time dependant, sometimes of a more impossible nature, in order to earn their freedom. In the 'Queen of Elfin's Nourice' the human woman who has been taken to nurse the fairy Queen's child is promised her freedom when the child in question is weaned. In an anecdote from Scotland a woman who is taken by the fairies after violating fairy etiquette is told she can leave when she eats all of a pile of ground meal and spins all of a pile of wool, only to find that neither ever gets smaller; she succeeds only with the help of another captive who gives her advice on how to complete the task[1] (Evans-Wentz, 1911)

Other anecdotes relate accounts of people who were taken by the Good People and later appeared to relatives with instructions on how they could be rescued if the living person did a certain thing at a certain time; often the person failed to act as instructed and the kidnapped person could not be saved. Folklore around Robert Kirk relates such a story saying that:

> *"...the form of the Rev. Robert Kirk appeared to a relation, and commanded him to go to Grahame of Duchray. 'Say to Duchray, who is my cousin as well as your own, that I am not dead, but a captive in Fairyland; and only one chance remains for my liberation. When the posthumous child, of which my wife has been delivered since my disappearance, shall be brought to baptism, I will appear in the room, when, if Duchray shall throw over my head the knife or dirk which he holds in his hand, I may be restored to society; but if this is neglected, I am lost for ever.'" True to his tryst, Mr Kirk did appear at the christening and "was visibly seen" but Duchray was so astonished that he did not throw his dirk over the head of the appearance, and to society Mr Kirk has not yet been restored."* (Kirk & Lang, 1893, pages xii – xiii).

A similar account from Ireland tells of a bride who was taken and later appeared to her groom to let him know she was among the fairies and could be recovered if he went to a specific place and grabbed her when she went past with the fairy troop, however, when he went to the place and saw her passing he found himself paralyzed (Evans-Wentz, 1911).

Note

1 The woman had asked for a drink while crossing a fairy hill and a fairy woman appeared and offered her one, which the woman then refused. At this offense the woman was promptly imprisoned within the hill and given an impossible task to earn her freedom. Despairing of ever succeeding she asked the advice of an old man who had been imprisoned for a long time and he told her to dab some of her own spit on her left eye each

morning before attempting to eat the meal or spin the wool. While the woman earned her freedom the fairy woman who had taken her swore she would never release the man because he had helped her. See page 97 in the Fairy Faith in Celtic Countries for the original story.

Etiquette

Like anything else on this subject for every rule or guideline there's an exception but this offers the broad strokes. It's important to keep in mind that the Fair Folk in general are not humans and are not like humans; as Yeats would have it they have few unmixed emotions and are beings of extremes, both good and bad. Often what they do seems perplexing to humans, as they act sometimes capricious and sometimes cruel. We cannot approach this subject expecting them to be or do what humans would in any circumstance but we must look at the system they operate in as a guideline to understand their etiquette which is distinct from our own. For example, the Good People have no compunction at all about stealing from humans or harming humans, although we see in folklore that they do have some strict rules about humans doing those same things to them - it is not an equal playing board but one on which they have different sets of rules for themselves and for mortals. This must be understood to understand anything else about them.

This encompasses some basic folkloric rules for humans dealing with the Fair Folk:

Honesty – In folklore and anecdotes the Good People don't lie but always speak the truth. This may be why we see examples of stories such as the tale of Meg Mollach where the girl tells the brownie in the mill her name is 'mise' [myself][1] and he believes her without question. In the same vein this may be why in tales where fairies are in a home and must be tricked out of it we see the protagonists saying something along the lines of 'the fairy hill is on fire' and the fairies believe it immediately and rush out.

Because they do not tell verbal lies they seem not to expect them from humans in stories either. This does not in any way keep them from tricking humans by speaking the truth in ways that get a human to assume a conclusion that is not true. Semantics is an art form of which they are masters.

Keep your word - Building off that last one, should you ever be in the position to make a promise or take an oath to a member of the Other Crowd under no circumstances should you break your word. They don't grade on a curve for this one - a promise is a promise and an oath is an oath. Do what you say you will do.

Hospitality – hospitality is a key aspect to fairy etiquette and caution is needed both in accepting it when it's offered by the Good Folk and offering it to them. The obligation of hospitality and its reciprocation appears in many stories to a human's benefit or detriment.

Lending and Borrowing - It happens that the Good Neighbours do sometimes ask the loan of things from us, and it usually wise to give it. This can range from food to grain to items (usually household items or farm equipment). They always repay their debts, most often with interest but not always in kind; for example there is a well-known anecdote about a man who lent the fairies wheat and was repaid with more than he gave but in barley. There are also stories of fairy mothers who ask a nursing human mother to let a fairy baby nurse just once from them in trade for a blessing; again this is considered good to do. Humans may also borrow from the Gentry but slightly more caution is required as folklore tells us that a deadline for re-payment is always set and must not be missed.

The Issue of Wash Water - This one is a bit complex, but generally speaking, one should not throw dirty water on the ground without an audible warning first, to alert the fairies, and one should not pour such water out over a large rock, lest it be the abode of fairies. Fairies abhor filth and seem to have an especial hatred of dirty water and urine (both of which can be used as protection against them). There is also the matter of having dirty water standing in the home, something that was more common in the past when people would come in and wash their feet; this 'foot water' depending on the area of belief would either drive fairies away or conversely allow them entry into an otherwise protected home.

Gifts - If offered a gift it is wise to accept it and to offer something in return; however, fairy gifts are rarely what they seem. That which seems valuable initially often turns out to be worthless and that which seems like nothing at first is often revealed to be quite valuable. In many stories a handful of leaves or wood shavings is later revealed to be gold, while what may seem like gold later turns to worthless leaves or gingerbread. We see an example of the first in a story told by Grimm in 'Teutonic Mythology', where a man stops to help a mythic figure fix the axle on her cart and she pays him with wood shavings. He eschews this seemingly worthless payment but some of the shavings fall into his boot. The next morning he finds the wood shavings in his boot have turned to gold and regrets tossing the rest away so hastily. In contrast an Irish tale of a fairy who took pity on a man being evicted goes the other way. In that story the man was weeping by a lake when a stranger approached him and asked what was wrong. On finding the man was to be evicted because he couldn't pay his rent the stranger gave him enough gold to pay but advised the man to get a receipt; heeding this advice the man did as he was told and returned home afterwards to celebrate his great luck. The rent collector meanwhile woke the next day to find the gold he'd been paid had become nothing but leaves.

Fairy gifts are also, as often as not, traps, and so great caution should be used with them. In many stories we see something given as a gift that does indeed bring luck or happiness to the person who receives it, but in others the item - particularly if it is food or drink - may act to trap the person or bind them to Fairy.

Gifts are rarely straightforward.

Nothing is Free - Related to the subjects of lending/borrowing and gifts, try to keep in mind that nothing is free. Even gifts that are given as true gifts without hidden traps still come with obligations. Fairy is a very feudal system in that respect, everything is tied together through debts and obligations and what's owed to who. If you give to them then they owe you in return, even if that owing is paid back simply by not causing you mischief. If they give you gifts then gifts are expected in return. We see this played out repeatedly in stories of fairies, such as one anecdotal account from Ireland where a fairy woman appeared to a woman and asked that particular tree not be cut down as the fairies made use of it; the woman was then approached two more times by the fairy woman who first asked for some food but didn't take any ground meal that was offered, then asked for a place to stay but didn't stay (Evans-Wentz, 1911). After this third encounter the woman found the chest she stored her ground meal in overflowing, the storyteller assumed as a thank you from the fairies for leaving the tree alone. In this story we see the human's willingness to aid the Good People and then further generosity repaid in a tangible way, demonstrating the fairies desire to balance the scales of any debt.

Never Say Thank You - It is a widespread belief, although not ubiquitous, that one shouldn't say thank you to the fairies. I have heard one theory behind this, that it implies a debt to them, a blank check if you will, that would allow them to decide how you repay them. Another theory suggests it is dismissive and implies you feel superior to them. Whatever is the case you should try to avoid saying it. Offering a gift in exchange for something you feel you've received can be a good idea, or saying something else along the lines of expressing gratitude for what happened without saying thank you directly, such as 'I am so happy with ---' or 'I really appreciate ---'.

Silence - it is possible for a person to have the favor of the

Other Crowd and to gain by it. However, the fairies have a strict rule about a person not speaking of experiences or blessing they get from the Good People. I think this is why we have more negative stories than positive and why we have more stories of single encounters than multiple ones. A person can sometimes get permission to speak or to reveal things, but the general rule is that to keep their favor you must stay silent about their activity in your life. Those who brag about fairy blessings or gifts almost always lose them and the future possibility of them.

Privacy - Fairies really, really do not like being spied on or having their privacy invaded. Many stories in folklore involve a person who stumbles across the Good People doing their normal thing, is seen watching, and punished severely - in only a few cases does the person manage to talk their way out of any repercussions. It's a good idea to respect their places and to trust your instincts when you feel like you should or shouldn't go somewhere. If you do happen upon fairies it is probably best to stay quiet and hidden, and wait for them to move on, unless they make it clear from the start they know you are there.

Note

1 This, of course, is key to her escape from his vengeful mother after she kills him, because when asked for the name of his attacker he can only repeat 'myself, myself'.

Euphemisms

The use of euphemisms for fairies is widespread across Celtic language speaking countries and can be traced back for at least 500 years[1] in written sources. The general belief is that any time you speak of them it is possible they might overhear you, for although they are not omniscient they are known to travel invisibly and one may never be certain when they are or are not around, and that should they hear you speaking of them you should do so with terms that remind them of their potential goodness. According to folklore the use of some names, including fairy or elf, would anger them but they were more inclined to react well to names that evoked their own potential better nature. This mid-19th century Scots poem illustrates the idea succinctly:

"Gin ye ca' me imp or elf
I rede ye look weel to yourself;
Gin ye call me fairy
I'll work ye muckle tarrie;
Gind guid neibour ye ca' me
Then guid neibour I will be;
But gin ye ca' me seelie wicht
I'll be your freend baith day and nicht."
- Chambers, 1842
[If you call me imp or elf
I counsel you, look well to yourself;
If you call me fairy
I'll work you great misery;
If good neighbour you call me
Then good neighbour I will be;
But if you call me seelie wight
I'll be your friend both day and night].

Below is a list of some common euphemisms for the fairies:

People of Peace or Peaceable People (Scotland)
Seelie wights or Seelie wichts (Scotland)
Guid Wichts [good spirits] (Scotland)
Daoine Sí, Aos Sí – People of the Fairy hills (Ireland)
Daoine Uaisle – Noble People (Ireland)
Daoine Maithe – Good People (Ireland)
Daoine Eile – Other Crowd or Other people (Ireland)
Tylwyth Teg – Fair Family (Welsh)
Fair Folk

Gentle Folk
Gentry
Good Neighbours
Honest Folk
Hill Folk
Forgetful People
Still Folk
Silently Moving People[2]
Themselves

There are also a selection of euphemisms specifically aimed at the diminutive fairies or at diminishing the power of the fairies in their naming. These include:

Little People
Wee People
Daoine beaga [little people] (Scotland)
Guillyn Veggey [Little Boys] (Isle of Man)
Little Fellows (Isle of Man)

We also see some euphemisms based on colours, with the idea that these are the primary colours associated with these fairies. These include:

Greenies
Greencoaties
The Grey Neighbours
Daoine Beaga Ruadh [little red men] (Scotland)

Notes

1 The term Fair Folk, for example, appears in a 1513 work by Gavin Douglas and Good Neighbours, under various Scots spellings, can be found in works by James IV and Montgomery in the late 1500's and early 1600's, as well as in the witchcraft

trial transcripts of the mid and late 1500's.

2 Both Still Folk and Silently Moving People are suggested as euphemisms by Campbell, who also argues that sìth means 'peace' rather than 'fairy hill' and that these euphemistic terms then come from the idea of the fairies as the People of Peace who move silently and invisibly. In both Irish and Scottish Gaidhlig sidhe [fairy hill] and sidhe [peace] are homonyms which has created confusion in terms before and there are in-depth academic papers discussing the possible etymological roots of sidhe and deeper meanings of the word in relation to the fairy folk. I will only say here that the use of the term in older forms of Irish (which are the root of the Gaidhlig) go back to at least the 9th century in writing with the 'fairy hills' meaning indicating the complexity of this issue.

Exorcism

Although exorcisms are often most strongly associated with demonic beings we do also see the concept associated with fairies, who were known to have the power to possess people. There are examples of spells and charms to exorcize fairies from a person found in the Anglo-Saxon Leechbooks and also some examples in Irish folklore.

Of particularly interest is a folk charm in the 1854 'Transactions of the Ossianic Society'. The entry was first in Irish and then translated into English, with some notable variances from the Irish, and dealt with a spoken charm used by a Catholic priest to expel a Leannán Si from a woman named Shighile Tabaois [Sheela Tavish].

This is the English translation from the book:

"Father Conn O'Donnellcomposed this song in order to expel a Leannán Sighe, or incubus, from Sheela Tavish.

The Cross of Christ be upon you, Sheela, against your new incubus,

Let the true Cross of Jesus protect you forever;
From this fairy that lies close to your snow-white bosom,
Who accompanies you at night and gives you hard cuffs.
There is not a fairy that existed since the deluge, even those of the white northern strand,
And of the broad-topped smooth lioses where their hosts assemble,
That I will not satirize by the lays of the old sayings of the sages,
If they will not banish this dull midge from Sheela.
I will write to Aoibheall of the fair northern strand,
The Queen of the Bruighin, and the Familiar (spirit) of hosts;
To inflict vengeance with the wrath of hard cuffs,
Upon this fairy that haunts Sheela, send him away from us.
I suspect he is a fairy that has no place of rest,
And was expelled from the fairy hill of Loran Ruadh;
Or is a genuine imp sent from Aoife of the north,
That was loosed by the expert spells of the surly Tuatha De Dananns.
Let us expel to the fairy hills this sullen midge from us,
Or to the bright waters o the Lee of the rapid currents;
There to be strongly fettered by the Shenad [Shannon's] hosts,
Because he slept with you, Sheela, without your leave."

The English translation is a bit loose from the Irish. For example the two terms given as 'incubus' don't actually mean that. We have stalcaire which can mean a stubborn person or a stalker, and gearrán which is a term for a horse, often a gelding. We see a similar thing with the word being glossed as 'fairy' - síghbharra - which might more accurately read as 'barrow fairy'. That one is worth noting as it specifically identifies this Leannán sí with the barrows, or ancient burial mounds. In the same way when the text calls him 'a pest' or an 'imp' sent by Aoife the Irish term spreas means a 'worthless person'.

This is a really fascinating piece of folk magic, effectively a type of ritual exorcism but what makes it interesting to me is that it calls on both the priest's own God - Jesus - as well as the fairy Queen Aoibheall. It also implicates both Aoife, as another Fairy Queen, and the Tuatha De Danann more generally, for possibly setting this spirit on the woman in question. The chant also includes the claim by the priest that he will not hesitate to satirize any spirits who won't help him to banish this Leannán sí, an unusual suggestion since one might assume that he would usually resort to calling on his own deity for that.

'Exorcism of a Leannán Sí' is only one example of the way that folk magic, fairy belief, and the dominant religion blended into a cohesive system of practice in early modern Ireland. We may look at this approach and say that it is an attempt to cover all the possibilities, as it were, in assuring that a cure is achieved. Or we may see it as reflecting the multiple cultural threads that influenced people, including clergy, even in the 19th century. In any case it is an important piece of evidence and also a useful charm.

There are several accounts in English and Welsh folklore of spirits that had to be exorcized, including a Bwca who was banished by a cunningman. In these cases though the banishment was never permanent but could only be done for a certain length of time; in the above example it was 14 generations. In one story of a troublesome boggart it was trapped for 99 years under a stone by a roadside.

Being rid of fairies, even dangerous ones, was not an easy process and even spells and charms to this effect were uncertain. There are examples of people who tried to flee rather than fight dangerous or problematic fairies but that was also not guaranteed. One Scottish man attempted to be rid of a Leannán Sidhe whose love was too intense for him by fleeing to America, only to find that she had followed him to Nova Scotia (Evans-Wentz, 1911). Similarly a family who was being troubled by a boggart tried to move from their farm to be rid of the fairy only find that he had stowed away in their packed possessions and went with them to their new home (Briggs, 1976).

F

Faerie Oak of Corriewater, The

A later ballad that tells of a woman's attempt to rescue her brother from fairy captivity. Unlike Janet in the Ballad of 'Tam Lin' in this case the young woman is notably unsuccessful. The ballad includes a variety of important pieces of fairylore and gives a fair description of the fairies temperment.

1 The small bird's head is under its wing,
The deep sleeps on the grass;
The moon comes out, and the stars shine down,
The dew gleams like the glass:
There is no sound in the world so wide,
Save the sound of the smitten brass,
With the merry cittern and the pipe
Of the fairies as they pass.
But oh! the fire must burn and burn,
And the hour is gone, and will never return.
2 The green hill cleaves, and forth, with a bound,
Comes elf and elfin steed;
The moon dives down in a golden cloud,
The stars grow dim with dread;
But a light is running along the earth,
So of heaven's they have no need:
Over moor and moss with a shout they pass,
And the word is spur and speed--
But the fire must burn, and I must quake,
And the hour is gone that will never come back.
3 And when they came to Craigyburnwood,
The Queen of the Fairies spoke:
"Come, bind your steeds to the rushes so green,
And dance by the haunted oak:

I found the acorn on Heshbon Hill,
In the nook of a palmer's poke,
A thousand years since; here it grows!"
And they danced till the greenwood shook:
But oh! the fire, the burning fire,
The longer it burns, it but blazes the higher.
4 "I have won me a youth," the Elf Queen said,
"The fairest that earth may see;
This night I have won young Elph Irving
My cupbearer to be.
His service lasts but for seven sweet years,
And his wage is a kiss of me."
And merrily, merrily, laughed the wild elves
Round Corrie's greenwood tree.
But oh! the fire it glows in my brain,
And the hour is gone, and comes not again.
5 The Queen she has whispered a secret word,
"Come hither, my Elphin sweet,
And bring that cup of the charmed wine,
Your lips and mine to wet."
But a brown elf shouted a loud, loud shout,
"Come, leap on your courses fleet,
For here comes the smell of some baptised flesh,
And the sounding of baptised feet."
But oh! the fire that burns, and must burn;
For the time that is gone will never return.
6 On a steed as white as the new-milked milk,
The Elf Queen leaped with a bound,
And young Elphin a steed like December snow
'Neath him at the word he found.
But a maiden came, and her christened arms
She linked her brother around,
And called on God, and the steed with a snort
Sank into the gaping ground.

But the fire must burn, and I must quake,
And the time that is gone will no more come back.
7 And she held her brother, and lo! he grew
A wild bull waked in ire;
And she held her brother, and lo! he changed
To a river roaring higher;
And she held her brother, and he became
A flood of the raging fire;
She shrieked and sank, and the wild elves laughed
Till the mountain rang and mire.
But oh! the fire yet burns in my brain,
And the hour is gone, and comes not again.
8 "O maiden, why waxed your faith so faint,
Your spirit so slack and slaw?
Your courage kept good till the flame waxed wild,
Then your might began to thaw;
Had you kissed him from among us all.
Now bless the fire, the elfin fire,
That made you faint and fall;
Now bless the fire, the elfin fire,
The longer it burns it blazes the higher."
(Douglas, 1901)

Faerie Queene, The

An epic poem written by Edmund Spenser and published starting in 1590. 'The Faerie Queene' is the tale of Arthur and his knights and a variety of adventures and quests they go on, including their interactions with the Fairy realm and the Fairy Queen Gloriana, who is a literary invention of Spenser's. The poem is largely allegorical and possibly intended to reflect the real world politics of the time, with Gloriana acting as a stand in for Queen Elizabeth and Fairy for Elizabethan England (Erickson, 1996).

Fairs

The Good People are known to attend human fairs and also to have fairs of their own.

Fairs held by fairies seem to be much in line with their human counterparts. This account comes which from Keightley's 'Fairy Mythology' is typical in most points:

> *"One time, about fifty years since, a person living at Comb St. Nicholas, a parish lying on one side of that hill, near Chard, was riding towards his home that way, and saw, just before him, on the side of the hill, a great company of people, that seemed to him like country folks assembled as at a fair. There were all sorts of commodities, to his appearance, as at our ordinary fairs; pewterers, shoemakers, pedlars, with all kind of trinkets, fruit, and drinking-booths. He could not remember anything which he had usually seen at fairs but what he saw there. It was once in his thoughts that it might be some fair for Chestonford, there being a considerable one at some time of the year; but then again he considered that it was not the season for it. He was under very great surprise, and admired what the meaning of what he saw should be. At length it came into his mind what he had heard concerning the Fairies on the side of that hill, and it being near the road he was to take, he resolved to ride in amongst them, and see what they were. Accordingly he put on his horse that way, and, though he saw them perfectly all along as he came, yet when he was upon the place where all this had appeared to him, he could discern nothing at all, only seemed to be crowded and thrust, as when one passes through a throng of people. All the rest became invisible to him until he came to a little distance, and then it appeared to him again as at first. He found himself in pain, and so hastened home; where, being arrived, lameness seized him all on one side, which continued on him as long as he lived, which was many years; for he was living in Comb, and gave an account to any that inquired of this accident for more than twenty years afterwards; and this relation I had from a person*

of known honour, who had it from the man himself." (Keightley, 1850, pages 294-295).

A few exceptions can be found, however, with fairs that are overtly dangerous to humans. *The Goblin Market,* described in detail in Rosseti's poem, is a good example of this.

Fairy

The term fairy is actually a complicated one, of obscure origin, which was originally used to describe the Otherworld itself - the world of Fairy - and as an adjective for beings from that world or a type of enchantment (Williams, 1991). The oldest form is the French fay, denoting a being connected to fate, which evolved into the English fay-erie indicating enchantment (Briggs, 1976). Only later would the word shift to indicate an individual being rather than a place or type of magic. In this sense it is strongly reminiscent of the Irish term 'sidhe' which in the same way is a word indicating a place and used as an adjective, but later shifted to indicate the individual beings. Now it is applied as a general term for all Otherworldly beings and to many different groups including ELVES, the DAOINE SIDHE, and the TYLWYTH TEG (Briggs, 1976).

The word has always had an amorphous application that included a range of beings and was equated to other terms like elf or goblin which also had vague connotations. There are multiple accounts across a variety of sources which gloss fairy with elf, goblin, and imp. Campbell mentions the 19th century interchangeability of the terms fairy and elf in Scotland, indicating that the fluidity found between these different names continued until fairly recently (Campbell, 1900). When it comes to the word fairy in early sources, including Chaucer, we see the beings referred to often as elves and their world as Fairy (Williams, 1991). In Milton's epic 17th century poem 'Paradise Lost' we see fairy used as an adjective in line 781 *"or fairy elves,*

Whose midnight revels, by a forest side" (Milton, 1877). This flexible usage of the term continued into modern times in Irish and Scottish Gaidhlig, although it has fallen off in English.

By some modern accounts the word fairy offends them and euphemisms should be used instead. Why this word would offend them may seem less clear to us today, however, just as the words imp and elf had strong associations with evil the word fairy at different points had pejorative uses, including being applied to sexually loose women and later homosexual men, in both cases carrying overtones of sexual impropriety (Briggs, 1967). These associations towards humans only came later, likely because of the word fairy's meaning relating to the Otherworld and enchantment which when used to describe a person implied uncanniness and improper behaviour.

Fairy (Land)

One of the main concepts that exists in modern fairylore and folklore more generally is that of the Otherworld or world of Fairy. This belief tells us that fairy beings may exist in our world but they come from or primarily reside in a distinct world of their own which is known by many names including an Saol Eile, the Otherworld, Fairy, Fairyland, Elfland, and Elfhame. In the Irish material this place can also go by specific names that indicate not an entire world but a particular location there such as Mag Mell or Tír na nÓg. It is worth asking the question: how far back does this concept go?

The biggest problem we have when tracing back the roots of this belief are that we simply hit a point where written records cease and anything prior to that is, by necessity, speculation. There is much that has been written or said based on such speculation but ultimately we can only be certain about that which we can prove. So, with that said, let us look at what evidence we do have.

The oldest Irish story which references the Otherworld is the

Echtra Condla Chaim meic Cuind Chetchathaig which has been dated to the 9th century in writing but is suggested to date back at least another several hundred years orally (Beveridge, 2014). In this story a fairy woman arrives in the mortal world to speak to Connla, son of Conn, and ultimately to convince him to return with her to her own world. When he asks her from whence she comes she replies *"...an immortal land where there is no death or the sin of transgressions. We have our harvest feast without labour; peace cloaks us without strife. We live in the great fairy hill and are called the people of the fairy hill."* (Daimler, 2017). From this we can see that by the 9th century at the latest in Ireland, and likely earlier, there was a belief in an Otherworld beyond or separate from this one which was peopled by fairies, literally áes síde in middle Irish or people of the fairy hill. This concept is carried forward and found throughout later Irish written mythology and folklore as well.

The number of English language terms for the Otherworld may be indicative of both its importance and pervasiveness in belief. In English we see the term fairie entering the lexicon around the 13th century as a term for the land inhabited by Otherworldly beings[1], coming from the 12th century Old French faerie which had the same meaning (Harper, 2018). In Old English the term eldritch may have meant Otherworld and been used to denote beings that were from there or uncanny (Hall, 2007). In Scottish ballads we see the Otherworld referred to as Elfame and Fairyland back to the 16th century. During the periods where we see these words in use in England and Scotland we find stories and ballads that describe an Otherworld similar in many ways to that described by Connla's fairy lover: a place of peace and ease, without death or illness, and to which human beings may be taken.

Its location varies in stories from islands in the west to fairy hills, but these human world spaces seem often to represent gateways into the Otherworld rather than literal physical locations. We see this with Nera's journey into the sidhe in the Echtra Nera or Lusmore's adventures with the fairies where both protagonists enter into a fairy hill and find the inside contains far more than the outside indicates it should be able to encompass. This concept of the Otherworld as a separate place connected to but individual from the human world may be seen as well in the stories where a person must traverse various trials in order to reach it or enact specific rituals. In the 'Ballad of Childe Rowland' the protagonist's sister enters the Otherworld, albeit accidently, by circling a sacred place counter clockwise. In several accounts including the Ballad of Thomas the Rhymer, Reinbrun, and a Welsh anecdote of a midwife brought for a fairy birth, those travelling to Fairy had to pass through things like narrow clefts in rock, total darkness, rivers, and deserts (Acland, 1997; Gwyndaf, 1991).

Fairy itself is described in various ways in different sources but with an overall theme of peace, agelessness, timelessness, and beauty. In the Echtra Condla, when asked from whence she comes the fairy woman responds *"from an immortal land where there is no death or the sin of transgressions. We have our harvest feast without labour; peace cloaks us without strife."* (Daimler, 2017). In the Imram Brain Meic Ferbail, Manannán describes the Otherworld in the same way, as a place of beauty and peace lacking transgression, and this is echoed again in the Echtra Nera where we see the eponymous human protagonist visiting inside a sidhe to find a land with trees constantly in flower and fruit. Tam Lin in the 'Ballad of Tam Lin' describes Fairy as a fair and pleasant place and says that he would happily stay there if he wasn't afraid of being tithed to Hell. Firth Green in 'Elf Queens and Holy Friars' compares the Elfland and Fairy of medieval texts to both Purgatory and Paradise, noting that overall Fairy was described as a place of health, joy, and peace that lacked the unpleasant things of human existence. These textual ideas are reinforced in anecdotal and folkloric accounts with sources in Briggs and Evans-Wentz all talking about Fairy's surpassing beauty and peacefulness, although it should, of course, be noted that the Otherworld was not free of conflict and many tales revolve on such.

Physically Fairy is described very similarly or identically to the human world, differing only in a few details. It has caves and mountains, rivers and lakes, forests and valleys just as the human world does and it is also has the same apparent variety of habitations from lone houses to cities. Things in Fairy are usually described as being of exceptional quality and beauty often in ways that tempt humans who go there. It differs in that there is no sun or moon in fairy according to multiple ballad sources and several anecdotal accounts. The 'Ballad of Thomas the Rhymer' describes the land of Fairy as lacking both moon and sun and also mentions that all the blood shed on earth flows through the rivers and streams of the Otherworld.

It is impossible to know with certainty how far back the idea of the Otherworld goes and there has been much academic speculation about the potential influence of outside religions and cultures on older fairy beliefs. What we can say with certainty is that the earliest written evidence from Irish and Icelandic cultures, dating back at least a thousand years, displays a fairly well-developed Otherworld or land of Fairy. Looking at later evidence we see that this concept despite not fitting into Christian cosmology at all[2] further developed over the last thousand years and has thrived in popular culture and folklore.

Notes

1 Fairie was also used an adjective, much like sidhe, to describe beings with an Otherworldly nature; see the previous entry on Fairy for more on this.

2 The idea of fairies and a separate world of Fairy has long been problematic for Christian theologians and over the centuries has resulted in an array of explanations seeking to fit them in

to a Christian worldview.

Fairies

As Campbell said so well in 'The Gaelic Otherworld':

> "*Of all the beings with which fear or fancy peopled the supernatural, the Fairies were the most intimately associated with men's daily life.*" (Campbell, 1900, page 1).

Indeed throughout written history fairies and all their diverse forms and with their various powers have been intrinsically tied to human life, although defining what exactly a fairy is has often been difficult and fluid. Sometimes viewed as a specific type of being and other times as a wide category that may encompass all beings of the Otherworld to understand who and what fairies are means understanding the layers of contradictions and variety to be found.

Fairies can and do appear in a variety of forms and types and people describe everything from fairy animals, fairies in animal form, small humanoid fairies, and five to six foot tall fairies, and monstrous beings. This array of appearances is explored in greater depth in the section on APPEARANCES. Many attempts are made in source material to categorize fairies in various ways but no one cohesive system exist, instead we find approaches varying by area. In parts of lowland Scotland the fairies may be divided into two courts, the seelie and unseelie, based on their disposition towards humans; in other areas of Scotland we may see fairies divided particularly by those who live in the earth or air; in parts of Ireland we see discussion of fairies of earth, sea, and air; in Wales they may be divided up by tribes or families (Evans-Wentz, 1911).

The exact nature of fairies is uncertain and debated. Many are connected explicitly to the human dead and it is not uncommon in stories to hear a person mention seeing someone among the fairies who they knew as a living human previously. However, there are also fairies who are very clearly said to be inhuman in nature and origins, with sources speculating that they are everything from pagan gods to fallen angels to foreign beings who come from other planets (Evans-Wentz, 1911). In older Anglo-Saxon sources fairies are directly equated to incubi and Puritan American sources would later see them as cognate with imps. Perhaps the most accurate thing that can be said about the fairies was said at the turn of the 20th century by a man in Donegal, who stated that *"Nobody could ever tell their nature exactly"* (Evans-Wentz, 1911, page 73).

In Ireland there are many anecdotal accounts of fairies seen looking and acting much like living humans but clearly of an Otherworldly nature and it was not uncommon for these human-like fairies to have a particular interest in taking living humans to join them, although it was also possible for a human to have a friend among the fairies without being in danger from them. These human-like fairies are described by one source from Sligo thusly:

> *"The folk are the grandest I have ever seen. They are far superior to us, and that is why they are called the gentry. They are not a working class, but a military-aristocratic class, tall and noble-appearing. They are a distinct race between our own and that of spirits, as they have told me….They have a silvery voice, quick and sweet….They are able to appear in different forms. One once appeared to me, and seemed only four feet high, and stoutly built. He said, "I am bigger than I appear to you now. We can make the old young, the big small, the small big.""* (Evans-Wentz, 1911, page 46-47).

Another Irish source discussing the Daoine Sidhe describes them as being of *"majestic appearance and marvellous beauty, in form human, yet in nature divine"* and connects them directly to the old

Irish Gods the Tuatha De Danann (Evans-Wentz, 1911, page 59). Rev. Kirk states that they dress and speak like people in the area which the fairies live in, pointing out that Scottish fairies dress after the local Scottish fashion while Irish fairies of the time were known to dress after the Irish fashion in their own areas. Kirk says they speak in whistles but also that they speak the language of the country they are in and that they may speak more or less clearly at different times. A Manx source described the fairies this way:

> "*...they have seen the fairies hunting with hounds and horses, and on the sea in ships, and under other conditions, and that they have heard their music. They consider the fairies a complete nation or world in themselves, distinct from our world, but having habits and instincts like ours. Social organization among them is said to be similar to that among men, and they have their soldiers and commanders.*" (Evans-Wentz, 1911, page 134).

Multiple sources across all those surveyed including Campbell, Kirk, Briggs, and Yeats repeated that fairies engaged in activities similar to humans, including spinning, weaving, baking, milking, hunting, herding, sailing, fishing, and playing games such as hurling.

Fairies may be visible or invisible as they desire and based on a human's ability to see them. When they travel their passage may sometimes be viewed, particularly if they seem unaware of their human observers, but often the only mark that they are near is the sound of voices or bells or a strange whirling wind on a calm day. The use of euphemisms when speaking of them is based in the idea that they might at any time be near a person but unseen and should not be offended with ill speech. One woman told of how her mother had a friend among the fairies, a woman who was never seen by any men although the woman had seen her when she was young, and this fairy woman would come to her mother with advice and for warnings of danger (Yeats,

1888). A renowned wise woman named Ebhlín Ni Ghuinníola was also said to have a fairy friend who taught her herbal lore and cures, although some asserted he was her Leannán Sidhe; it was claimed that this fairy man was sometimes seen with her as she gathered herbs (O Crualaoich, 2003).

Fairy behaviour and actions towards humans often seem inexplicable because the Good People do not follow the same morality as humans do and have their own system of etiquette. They freely steal from humans yet punish human theft against themselves harshly, and in the same way they can and often do cause harm to humans yet react quite violently to humans who harm fairies or fairy property. An account from the Dúchas collection relates a story where a man sees a group of fairies apparently playing a game of ball who call out to him yet when he responds they attack him and beat him nearly senseless; in contrast the story of Meg Mollach tells of a BROWNIE who is fatally injured by a mortal girl and whose mother spends years seeking revenge for him.

Rev. Kirk published a 17th century treatise on the Scottish fairy folk which has much to say about how they were perceived and understood at that time and in that place. He wrote about the PHYSICALITY of fairies as well as PROTECTIONS against them but he also described in some detail his thoughts on who and what they were, connecting them both to the pagan dead and to spirits of the air. According to Kirk the local fairies "… are distributed in tribes and orders, and have children, nurses, marriages, deaths, and burials, in appearance even as we" (Kirk & Land, 1893 page 8) Although Kirk does suggest that all of this may just be mimicry on the part of the fairies. Both of these assertions – that the fairies live much as humans do and that this life is a degree of mimicry – are supported in other sources and ultimately there is no certainty as to where the truth lies. There is much debate about whether or not fairies are mortal or immortal with some account of fairy deaths and funerals along with others who feel that fairies are decidedly immortal beings and some accounts of fairies telling humans they have spoken to that they "are always kept young" (Evans-Wentz, 1911, page 46).

More generally fairies were often noted to engage in behaviour similar to that of humans. Rev. Kirk talks of them baking and spinning as humans do and in stories such as SELENA MOOR we see them playing music and dancing. In the 'Fairy Faith in Celtic Countries' we can find anecdotes of fairies hunting, playing games of hurling, and fighting each other.

The fairies in Ireland are often said to live in the SIDHE or fairy mounds although even in Ireland it is clear that they are not restricted to these locations. One man living in the Aran Islands around the turn of the 20th century said that the fairies lived there at Dun Aengus but also in the rocks and sea, which is in line with the beliefs found throughout the Celtic speaking world (Evans-Wentz, 1911).

Fairy Brides

See: Fairy Wives

Fairy Courts

It's important to understand that when we talk about fairy courts we may be talking about two distinctly different things. This double meaning and usage comes from the Scots language where the word court means both a group attending on royalty and more generally a group or company. Because much of our fairylore about the courts in a general sense comes from the Scots speaking areas of Scotland this double usage of the word has found its way into modern fairylore, but a lack of understanding of the language means the nuance may be lost.

Firstly the term fairy court is used as a general term to define an entire group of fairy beings, and by that understanding its nature is very broad. When we talk about the Seelie Court (or it's antithesis the Unseelie Court) we are not talking about a specific royal court, but are using the term in that second general sense for all types of beings who may owe allegiance to the monarchy of that court, the Queen of the Seelie Court or Nicnevin who is reputed to be Queen of the Unseelie. However, all beings with such allegiance are no more members of the royal court itself than all people in England are members of the English royal court. When we say they are part of the Seelie court we are using the term very generally, and that is probably the more common usage we find. The idea of this general use of 'Seelie court' started as a euphemism, a way to refer to all fairies in a positive manner which is why it is so intentionally inclusive.

The second way the word can be used, the first definition, relates to the specific group of beings who would attend or serve a Fairy Queen or King; we see this use in ballad material and in some anecdotes. That gets us into what we are going to be addressing in depth here, the Fairy court as a royal court of Fairy. In that case we are talking about a very specific grouping of individuals around and related to the Fairy royalty of a place. With this use of court we swing from overly broad to very particular, as you shall see.

A royal court, fairy or mortal, is set up in roughly the same way and represents - effectively - the royal household. The royal court would include the ruling monarch, their immediate family, royal advisors and counsellors, courtiers1, court officials (such as the chancellor, purser, and chamberlain), entertainers, body servants and some servants more generally, ladies-in-waiting, courtesans, knights, heralds, doorkeepers, cupbearers, ushers, grooms, huntsmen, and clergy (Pattie, 2011; C& MH, 2014). Ladies-in-waiting were usually the wives of nobles attending court (effectively courtiers) or sometimes widows of such nobles who had the task of keeping the Queen company, entertaining her, and keeping her up on the general goings-on at court as well as what was essential gossip. The Queen would also have maidservants or handmaidens who were not nobility and were servants in truth that would handle her personal needs. Defining who was or wasn't in the court could be somewhat nebulous but effectively anyone who was in regular - usually daily or nearly daily - contact with the royal family and made their home at the royal court may be considered a member of the court. How many people a court was comprised of could vary widely from a relatively small number into the thousands depending on the size and power of a kingdom.

Being a member of the court did not mean having rank in it, however. Having rank within a court meant having a specific title and duty within that court, and the system of rank as one may assume was hierarchical. Certain titles implied a great deal more power and influence than others, and some positions, like master huntsman or master falconer, where usually held by members of the nobility (C & MH, 2014). To quote the article 'Officers and Servants in a Medieval Castle':

> *"The presence of servants of noble birth imposed a social hierarchy on the household that went parallel to the hierarchy dictated by function."* (C & MH, 2014).

This is referencing human royal courts, however, it applies equally to courts in Fairy; rank in a court is a matter equally of birth and function within the court itself.

The court would be subdivided into sections by area of function and these in turn would be overseen by one individual and a series of lesser ranking assistants. Lower ranking members may wear the livery of the royal family to indicate specifically who they serve. Sections included the living quarters of the royals, the wardrobe, the stables, the kitchen, and hunting, and each one was then subdivided sometimes into many smaller parts. The kitchen at large for example had a variety of very specific domains including: cooking area; buttery, pantry, confectionery, cellar, larder, spicery, saucery, scalding-house, and poultry (C

& HM, 2014). A scullery maid would not likely interact with the Queen but would report to other lesser kitchen workers who in turn reported to higher ranking kitchen workers and on up the chain of command. Other sections were similarly complex, although how much or little would depend on the overall size of the household and court.

We should note that it is called a court for the same reason our modern legal court bears the name - because the royal court was a place where the Queen or King would make laws and give legal judgements. They would also receive tributes and taxes and generally take any actions to govern their country that was necessary. In this sense a royal court is both a collection of people and a place - it is the sum total of those people closest to the monarch but it is also the place that the monarch rules from. A portion of the officials at court would be people whose jobs would be assisting in overseeing the actual running of the country and implementation of the laws and orders of the monarch. This includes the exercise of military power as well as economic, which would be controlled by the monarch but delegated to court officials to actually handle executing. The location may be one set place, may move between several, or may always be changing. The court is, effectively, the centre of government for any monarchy.

The ruling monarch has a court; the members of their court do not have their own courts because only the ruling monarch has the authority to make governmental decisions, military decisions, and judgements of law. So a Fairy Queen would have her court but her children and other close relatives would not have their own courts unless they are ruling monarchs in their own right of their own territory or have been given specific authority to rule as a representative of the Queen in a different location. In the same way, non-royal nobility do not generally have courts although in some rare cases they might depending on the degree of authority they have over their own territory.

One example of a Fairy court of the type we are discussing comes from the ballad of 'Tam Lin'. When Tam Lin is talking to his lover Janet about how she can rescue him he tells her this:

Then the first company which comes to you
Is published king and queen;
Then next the second company that comes to you,
It is many maidens.
Then next the company that comes to you
Is footmen, grooms and squires;
Then next the company that comes to you
Is knights, and I'll be there.
- Tam Lin 39G (modern English)

What we are seeing described is the Fairy court riding out in procession in groups, with the royalty first, then the queen's ladies-in-waiting, then the more general retinue of servants, then the knights at the rear. This is fully in line with what we might expect of a royal court, although I would imagine other nobles riding along with the king and queen.

When we see fairy courts portrayed in modern fiction they are often greatly simplified or not well explained which may give people a shallow view of what they are. A fairy court, whether that of the Seelie or Unseelie Queen or any of the Irish Fairy monarchs, would be complex and include a variety of beings that were part of the ruler's household, from close family to servants who waited on the royal family, as well as the same range listed above from advisors to huntsmen. These are usually beings who would be in permanent or near permanent attendance on the royal family, with the exception of knights who may be sent out or assigned specific tasks that took them away from the court. Again we can look to Tam Lin as an example of this, as he was a knight within the Queen's court but had been given the task of guarding a specific well in the forest of Carterhaugh. Courtiers, especially nobles, may also spend part of their time away from court, but would generally be expected to spend most of their time attending to the Queen or King.

To understand and appreciate the fairy courts we need an understanding of what they are. Human royalty still exists in some places and still has courts, although largely symbolic now, and there is no indication that fairies do not still operate with a monarchy system which would include royal courts. At the least understand that these courts would include the royal household as well as courtiers, and that rank within a court would be an intersecting matter of birth and function. Everyone in a court has a function which ultimately serves the monarch, and the court itself is both representative of the monarch's power and a tool to exercise that power.

Note

1 Courtiers are almost a topic unto themselves to be honest. A courtier was a person who attended the ruler at court and could include members of the nobility, servants, secretaries, merchants, soldiers, clergy, friends of the ruler, lovers, and entertainers. They may or may not hold actual rank in the court depending on a variety of factors. What defined someone as a courtier was the amount of time they spent hanging around the royal court, whether or not they ever actually even interacted with the ruler.

Fairy Doors

The origin of fairy doors seems to trace to Ann Arbor, Michigan and the early 1990's although they didn't start appearing in random public places until 2005. Originally the idea of illustrator Jonathon Wright the fairy doors began as artwork, although it should be noted that Wright moved on to writing about and hosting a website dedicated to 'urban fairies' and calls himself a fairyologist (NPR, 2006). The initial concept was aimed at children, created by Wright to delight and encourage belief in his wife's preschool students (NPR, 2006). One can now purchase them from a variety of specialty companies as well as mass market catalogues and they also feature in the work of different artists and can be seen in museums and public parks. Some fairy doors open up to tiny rooms, rather like doll house rooms, and the implication is that these are where fairies live. Others are simply doors placed against flat surfaces, meant to replicate the above idea. We even see them now painted onto things, to give the impression of a doorway where none actually is.

Fairy Familiars

Among those people who are known to have regular contact with the fairies there are some who might be said to have a fairy familiar. Unlike the more well-known demonic familiar the fairy familiar was not purely associated with witches but also with cunningfolk, wise women, and some regular people who simply had a reputation for associating with the Fair Folk. In some cases a Leannán Sidhe might act as a fairy familiar (Campbell, 1900).

These familiars were fairy beings, often former humans, who had a connection to the living person and acted as a go between for the human and the fairy beings more generally. A woman named Ketty Rourk in Ireland had such a human-turned-fairy friend, a man who she had known when he was alive and who was thought to have drowned but would come to her among the fairies and give her advice (Evans-Wentz, 1911). Similarly Bessie Dunlop's Fairy Familiar was a former mortal named Tom who was a distant relative of Bessie's (Wilby, 2005).

In appearance a fairy familiar would look like a human being although they were noted to often wear green and sometimes black or white (Wilby, 2005). They were also seen by other people besides the person to whom they were attached, although in some cases, such as Yeats' 'friend of the fairies' there may be specific limitations on who else could see the fairy[1] (Wilby, 2005;

Yeats 1888). These beings were described as tangible, able to give physical objects to humans, and directly influence the human world; those who saw and interacted with them did so, in many instances, during the day and while awake (Wilby, 2005; Davies; 2003; Yeats, 1888; O Crualaoich, 2003).

A person might gain a fairy familiar after being away with the fairies for a period of time, perhaps during an illness, or have such a familiar given to them by a family member or by a more powerful fairy being such as a Queen. These spirits acted as go-betweens for the person and the fairies, gave knowledge of healing skills and acted as guardians for the witch, and in some cases granted the witch special powers of foresight or second sight directly (Pocs, 1999; Davies, 2003; Wilby, 2005). In some case they also acted to punish the human if the person transgressed against the will of the Good People or offended them in some way.

Note

1 Yeats told of a woman he was acquainted with whose mother had a friend among the Good People, a being who may perhaps be categorized as a fairy familiar. This fairy woman was seen by the girl who witnessed the fairy visiting her mother but told Yeats that her mother's fairy friend was never seen by any man only women. It's unclear why this prohibition was in place but the woman recounted how she had once tried to bring her father to see the fairy to prove the fairy woman existed only to have her disappear before he could see her and the fairy woman was quite angry at the attempt (Yeats, 1888).

Fairy Food

1 - Eating Food from Fairy.

One of the main taboos relating to Celtic fairies is that one should never eat any food of Fairy, or drink any drink from it, or the human will be trapped forever in the Otherworld. The general belief is that to eat the food of fairies is to be irreversibly bound to them and their world. We see a wide range of anecdotes centred on this idea, usually featuring a human who has encountered a group of fairies and been invited or inveigled to join them, been offered food or drink, and is then cautioned by a human among the group (often recognized as a recently deceased community member) not to take the offered meal. The warning always includes the explicit message that if the food or drink is accepted the person will not be able to leave and return to the mortal world or their family.

In the 'Ballad of Childe Rowland' the protagonist is advised to eat and drink nothing while in Fairy trying to rescue his sister if he wants to succeed and return again to earth with her:

> *"And what you've not to do is this: bite no bit, and drink no drop, however hungry or thirsty you be; drink a drop, or bite a bit while in Elfland you be and never will you see Middle Earth again."*

One example from a 20th century Irish account of a man who encountered the fairies at night:

> *"I was away with the gentry, and save for a lady I couldn't have been back now. I saw a long hall full of many people. Some of them I knew and some I did not know. The lady saved me by telling me to eat no food there, however enticing it might be."* (Evans-Wentz, 1911, page 68).

This idea that a person would be tempted by food while in Fairy or among the Good People is common in anecdotes appearing even in some versions of the Borrowed Midwife stories[1] and the Stolen Bride[2] stories. Refusing this food is not always as easy it might seem and in at least some cases the fairies seem willing to resort to violent measures to persuade people to eat. Lady Wilde tells a story of a girl taken to a fairy feast and offered food there who was chased out when she refused and told that the next time they took her she would not escape from them (1888). Similarly an account in the Dúchas collection, volume 0274 page 197, tells the story of a fiddler who when he was dying related to his family that he was often among the Good People and had lost the sight in one eye, as he said because *"…the food used to be forced on him; and when he would not eat it a farey [sic] woman struck him in the eye."* (Duchas, 2018).

There are, however, exceptions to this rule, often hinging on obligation or hospitality. There are various accounts of people who were hosted by Fairy Kings or Queens that safely ate food at fairy feasts. There are other examples outside feasting where a person is offered or given food and walks away unharmed. In one anecdote a pair of men was walking and heard fairies inside a sí churning butter; they wished aloud for a drink of the buttermilk and to their surprise it was given to them. One took it and the other refused with the one who refused having bad luck afterwards (Bruford, 1991). Thomas in 'Thomas the Rhymer' is paid by the Fairy Queen with an apple, which he eats and which gives him the ability to speak truly, but the apple does not bind him to Fairy, he is returned to mortal earth after his service is done (Acland, 1997). The difference may be that the men were given food they asked for and Thomas is explicitly given the apple as payment, in exchange for his service to the Queen for 7 years. In the same way we see Isobel Gowdie, a Scottish witch who dealt with the Queen of Elphame, saying that the Queen gave her meat to eat although Isobel was not taken into Fairy but remained on earth. The normal rules of food may not apply when that food is given as part of a clear exchange or payment of a debt owed by the fairy or for services rendered. The Good People are also known to give food as gifts, in which case no debt would be accrued and the person was not bound in any way (Gwyndaf, 1991).

In most of the stories where the food is a kind of trap it is offered to the person when they have done nothing to pay for it; it is simply offered and taken, usually in a social context, or sometimes stolen by the person when they are in Fairy[3]. It is also offered, most often, when the person is either in Fairy or in the company of a larger group of fairies, indicating that this may also be a factor. In the stories where the food is not dangerous to take the circumstances are generally different: the person has asked for food, the person was owed a debt by the fairy, or the person was explicitly in service to a fairy monarch. So it would seem that like so many other things on this subject it is neither simple nor clear cut, that there are some cases when eating fairy food is dangerous and others where it is not.

2 - Giving Food to Fairies.

There is a long standing and deep-seated understanding that fairies were entitled to a portion of the human harvest, including both crops and animals. We see this beginning in Irish mythology where the Dagda negotiates an agreement with the Gaels to give the Gods - who have gone into the sidhe to live - a portion of all their grain and milk in exchange for the Gods allowing the crops to flourish and cows to be in milk. Over time this concept was extended and shifted to the fairies more generally. In the modern period we find examples in MacNeill's book 'Festival of Lughnasa' that discuss the fairies being given a tithe of the crops during the harvest, with an understanding that such a tithe is due to them. While this may not at first seem like a taboo it should be understood in the context of an action that had to be taken in order for humans to prosper.

3 - Fairies Claiming Food.

Related to point #2 is the idea that fairies will claim food they want, under different circumstances; this may be an extension of the idea that they are owed, by longstanding agreement, a portion of what humans' harvest. Evans-Wentz relates anecdotes in 'The Fairy Faith in Celtic Countries' of the belief that if food fell or was dropped it was being claimed by the Good People and should be left to them. Along those lines Campbell in 'The Gaelic Otherworld' and Kirk in 'The Secret Commonwealth' both discuss the fairies removing the substance from food items, either in the fields or on the stove. This theft of the essence of food, rather than its physical presence, is attributed by Campbell to the owner of the item speaking badly of it. Another widespread folk belief in both Ireland and Scotland was that any berries left unpicked after Samhain belonged to the Good Folk and that eating them was unhealthy as they had been either spit on or urinated on by the Púca, as a means of claiming them. Food that had been given to the fairies, or claimed by them, should not be eaten by humans as it was thought to have no value to it, although there are accounts of animals eating it. This falls into the area of a taboo as it was believed that taking what the fairies had claimed for themselves was at best very unlucky.

Notes

1 In 'The Good People: new fairylore essays' edited by Narvaez there is a version of the borrowed midwife tale in which the midwife, after the birth of the baby, is invited to join the household socially before being taken back to her home. She is offered refreshments but a woman sitting near the fire begins singing a song in Irish warning the midwife not to eat or drink or she will never be able to leave. Heading the warning the midwife politely declines and is able to return home safely.

2 Yeats relates a version of the Stolen Bride story in 'Celtic Twilight' in which the stolen bride's human groom stumbles upon her as she is being taken by the Good People and is drawn into their company. She is afraid he will be offered fairy food so she lures him away to play a game with some of the men instead. This is an unusual version, as in most Stolen Bride stories there is no implication that the human groom would

also be taken with the bride but it does reinforce the potential danger of fairy food.

3 The story of Selena Moor is a good example of this, where Grace Hutchins has wandered unawares into Fairy and eats fruit there without permission, in effect stealing from the fairies there, and subsequently finds herself bound to their fate.

Fairy Fool

See: Amadán na Bruidhne

Fairy Hounds

See: Cu Sidhe

Fairy Houses

Fairy houses have a complex history and while they seem to be rooted in the late Victorian period, with its shift to viewing fairies as garden spirits, they draw on the older folklore concepts of giving the fairies of your home and land a place and offerings. Having a fairy house indoors represents offering a space to your house fairies, while having outdoor fairy houses, theoretically is a type of offering to the spirits, the fairies, of that place. These are strongly reminiscent of the Roman household shrines to the Lares Familiaris, shrines which housed objects devoted to household spirits and where offerings could be placed (Connor, 1994).

Like Fairy doors, Fairy houses have taken off as a cultural idea recently and can even be found as public art displays and in museums. They are so popular that books have been written about them and one can easily find instructions for making different kinds of fairy houses online, as well as a wide range of images of them. Fairy houses are limited only by a person's imagination, and while they are certainly often viewed as nothing more than decorative items, they can also have practical uses. A fairy house can serve as a point of connection to your house fairies and yard fairies and also as a place to leave offerings, just as the shrine to the Lares did for the Romans.

Fairy Kings

Less often found in folklore or anecdotes than FAIRY QUEENS there are some stories featuring Fairy Kings. In the ballad of 'Alice Brand' we see a Fairy King referenced and the Scottish witch Isobel Gowdie also mentions a Fairy King. Irish folklore mentions various named Fairy Kings including Finnbheara.

Fairy Paths

A Fairy Path or Fairy Road is the route by which the fairies regularly travel between any two locations. These paths can be found in many places and are invisible to anyone without the Second Sight, unless they happen to catch the Fairy folk unaware. Fairy Paths are often said to stretch between known fairy hills or locations but may also be found in more obscure locations.

It is considered very bad luck to build on a fairy path and those who do so always suffer for it one way or another. In the most benign cases the building will suffer from disturbances, often at night, as the fairies pass through the building following their accustomed route. As one source says:

> *"When the house happens to have been built in a fairy track, the doors on the front and back, or the windows if they are in the line of the track, cannot be kept closed at night, for the fairies must march through."* (Evans-Wentz, 1911).

In other instances attempts at building would be destroyed as soon as they were begun by being knocked down and a noted method of testing for a fairy path by those who could not see them was to put up posts where the building was meant to go and see if they remained standing the next day. In extreme cases the person attempting to build might be killed or suffer extreme misfortune (O hOgain, 2006).

The Welsh Tylwyth Teg have fairy paths as the Irish and Scottish fairies do, although their reputation is more dangerous. As one anecdotal source says:

> *"...the Tylwyth Teg have paths (precisely like those reserved for the Irish good people or for the Breton dead), and that it is death to a mortal while walking in one of these paths to meet the Tylwyth Teg."* (Evans-Wentz, 1911, page 150).

The fairies were known to move their homes at certain times of year, notably on the quarter days, and when they did so they would travel along these fairy paths to get from one hill to another (McNeill, 1956). At any time of year, however, a Fairy Path could be perilous.

Fairy Queens

Fairy Queens are referenced across all types of material as powerful figures and rulers in Fairy. In some accounts they have known first names while in others they are only referred to as the queen of Elfland or Fairy, or as in the Ballad of 'Alison Gross', the Queen of the Seelie Court. They may or may not have a King ruling with them and are known to take human lovers and to favour mortal witches. In ballad and anecdotal accounts the Fairy Queen is described wearing a green or white dress, riding a white horse, and being extremely beautiful, sometimes compared to or confused with the Christian Queen of Heaven. They are also powerful beings who can easily use their magic to influence the human world and people within it.

Fairy Rade

A Fairy Rade is a special type of procession, something like a parade or formal riding out of the Good People, which was known to occur at certain times and along specific FAIRY PATHS. In the ballads of Tam Lin and Alison Gross we are told of Fairy Rades that occurs on Samhain, while 'The Fairy Faith in Celtic Countries' mentions a nightly fairy procession near Tara in Ireland that started just after night fell. Rev. Kirk mentions the Quarter days, which in Scotland would have been 1st February, 1st May, 1st August, 1st and November, as dates when the Good People moved their homes *"so travelling until Doomsday day, being impotent of staying in one Place and finding some Ease by journeying and changing Habitations"* an idea that is echoed several centuries later by the Scottish writer F. Marian McNeil in her book 'The Silver Bough' when she also described the fairies moving home on the quarter days by riding out in procession along fairy roads (Kirk & Lang, 1893, page 7; McNeil, 1956). Two 19th century Scottish sources note the presence of the Fairy Rade on Bealtaine, when the sounds of horses and riders could be heard on the pathways, although they might not always be visible. Another anecdotal account from that same time also on Bealtaine describes the sound of hooves and bridles jangling before the parade of green clad riders appeared (Briggs, 1976). The Fairy Rade is not limited to these dates, however, and we see them riding out at other times as well, noted above; one Scottish source from Barra mentions midnight as a time when the host rides out and when a person is in greater danger of meeting them (Evans-Wentz, 1911).

The Fairy Rade is described in both anecdotal accounts and ballads as a very formal affair with the fairies riding in order and segregated by rank. This is illustrated well in version 39G of the Ballad of Tam Lin:

"Then the first company that comes towards you
Is published king and queen;
The next company that comes towards you,
It is maidens many ones.
The next company that comes towards you
Is footmen, grooms and squires;
The next company that comes towards you

It is knights, and I'll be there."
(Child, 1802; language modernized)

Besides being divided by the rank of the personages there also seems to be a symbolism to the colours of the horses ridden. White is often mentioned with people of high rank, particularly the Queen and those she favours, for example. Besides the colours of the horses they are described as being beautifully outfitted, often with silver bells or even chimes in their manes, and sometimes said to be shod in gold and silver.

Fairy Rings

Fairy rings are also called fairy circles, elf rings, or elf circles. In Welsh they may be known as cylch y Tylwyth Teg [literally 'circle of the Fair Family']. Fairy Rings under various names are found across Celtic language speaking cultures as well as Anglo-Saxon and Germanic cultures. They appear as either as mushrooms growing together in a ring, a dark circle of grass, or sometimes as a circle of dead grass or small stones. The belief is that these rings are created by the fairies' dancing. In 12th century England there was a belief that rings of daisies were caused by elves dancing (Hall, 2007). The fairies love of dancing is well known as is their penchant to take people who disturb their revelry, either as a punishment or through a desire to keep the person in Fairy (Evans-Wentz, 1911).

Fairy rings have no set size and may be anywhere from three feet across to ten times that size (Bennett, 1991; Gwyndaf, 1991). If they were the sort made of darker green within a field then they would be either moss or much darker green grass and were notable because *"no rushes or anything grew on it"* (Gwyndaf, 1991). There is a scientific explanation for fairy rings which are created by the fungus mycelium and can include a variety of mushroom species, both poisonous and edible. This is also the cause of the dark grass circles or less common dead grass rings as the fungus naturally grows upwards and outwards in an expanding circle and effects the nutrient content of the soil (Mushroom Appreciation, 2016). The science and folklore do not contradict but rather exist together in something of a chicken-and-egg paradox. For example, in some folklore it the fairies dancing doesn't causes the circle but it's the circle that draws the fairies to dance there (Bennett, 2001).

A person stumbling across an active fairy circle may or may not see the dancers within it or hear the music which may act as a lure to trick humans into joining in. In traditional cultures people were taught to avoid entering a fairy ring because of the risk the fairies would take the person away or keep them bound in the circle for a hundred years. In one Welsh story preserved in the late 20th century a person was questioned about why they avoided fairy rings and they repeated a story of a boy named Robin Jones who entered a fairy circle one evening; he saw the fairies dancing and after what seemed to him a few hours in their company he asked to leave only to return home to find that a hundred years had passed (Gwyndaf, 1991). Even lingering near an active fairy ring could be dangerous as we see in a Welsh story where a man stopped outside a fairy ring to watch the fairies dance for a few hours and lost fifteen years of time (Gwyndaf, 1991). In many stories a person would dance for what seemed to them like a night or less and then be allowed to leave only to find that a year or more had passed. In some cases the fairy ring seemed to have been used as a kind of trap to take mortals the fairies wanted, particularly children and these desired people were never seen again (Evans-Wentz, 1911). Other times the fairies seemed to treat humans more benevolently. Accounts from Brittany speak of humans who join fairy dances without any harm and are returned without losing any time; only those who offend the fairies while they are in the ring are forced to join the dancing until they collapse form exhaustion or die (Evans-Wentz, 1911).

Once in a fairy ring a person could not leave voluntarily and would dance until the fairies let them go or they were rescued. In one Scottish tale a man fell asleep in the middle of a fairy ring and woke to find himself being carried through the air by the angry fairies who dumped him in a city many miles away (Briggs, 1978). In the above example of Robin Jones robin asked politely to go and was allowed to leave only to find that everyone he knew had died from old age while he danced. In another story a boy was taken into Fairy through a fairy ring and when he wanted to leave the fairies threw him out after pinching him until he was thoroughly bruised and he was returned several years after being taken (Evans-Wentz, 1911).

There are many ways to rescue a person from a fairy ring, although none are without risks. One Welsh method of securing a person's release was to break the boundary of the ring with a stick of rowan (Gwyndaf, 1991). Iron is always an option because of its superlative protective qualities (Hartland, 1891). Any iron object could be used and like the rowan should be placed so that it crossed the edge of the ring or might be tossed into the circle to disrupt the dancing. Certain herbs are also recommended including thyme which could be thrown into the circle (Hartland, 1891). Another method was for someone safely outside the circle to reach in, sometimes by stepping on the perimeter of the ring, and grab the person as they danced past (Briggs, 1978).

Even if a human were successfully rescued though many times the person could not truly be saved. Those who had danced with the fairies in a fairy ring were known to pine away afterwards, unable to fully return to the human world. If they had been taken for years and they might rapidly age or even turn to dust although sometimes they seemed well enough until the truth how much time had passed was related to them by someone else (Brigg, 1978).

Besides the inherent dangers of a fairy ring there was also an aversion to entering them because of the feeling of sacredness around them. Those who accidently damaged a fairy ring would always try to offer some repayment in exchange to avoid the inevitable wrath of the fairies (Bennett, 1991). In both Scotland and Wales there was a folk belief that the fairies would retaliate against those who damaged either the ring or its mushrooms (Bennett, 1991; Gwyndaf, 1991). In an Irish account a farmer who intentionally built a barn on the site of a fairy ring passed out afterwards and had a vision telling him to take down the barn (Wilde, 1888). These spaces were seen as belonging to the Good People and were treated with a degree of the respect paid to the larger sites, such as the sidhe, that belonged to them.

Fairy Stroke

One of the most feared weapons of the fairies was the fairy stroke or poc sí, sometimes also called the fairy blast. There are several modern Irish expressions associated with this term including 'poc aosán' which is a term for a sudden illness, 'poc mearaidh' meaning a touch of madness, and 'buaileadh poc air' meaning to be elfstruck or bewitched (O Donaill, 1977). In Old Irish this might be called poc aosáin [fairy stroke] or áesán [fairy sickness]. Associated with the Slua Sí [fairy host] and the sí gaoithe [fairy wind] the fairy stroke was a sudden and otherwise inexplicable illness marked by a change in behaviour and health. MacKillop suggests that this term is where we get the term stroke from for cerebral haemorrhages or aneurysms (MacKillop, 1996). Yeats described the fairy stroke as the sudden touch of the fairies which caused a tumour or paralysis (Yeats, 1888).

The fairy stroke could afflict both humans and animals but according to some folklore was differentiated from the similar elfshot in its symptoms and method of application. Unlike elfshot which used an arrowhead, sometimes invisible, to injury a person, fairy stroke was caused by a blow from the fairies themselves, or in rare cases being struck by a blunt object they threw. Fairy stroke might manifest as a sudden seizure or else a loss of mental acuity, which may be temporary or permanent

(MacKillop, 1996). Getting the fairy stroke, like many things associated with fairies could be a double edged blade as it cost a person their health and mind but was also believed to convey a special esoteric knowledge (Wedin, 1998). There was also some crossover with changeling folklore as in some cases those who had received the fairy stroke were said to have actually been taken by the fairies while either a glamoured object or decrepit fairy was left behind instead (MacKillop, 1996). This is also true of those afflicted by elfshot indicating that both could be used either to torment people or as a means of taking those humans who the fairies desired.

Those who were struck by the blast might simply be at the wrong place at the wrong time, may have transgressed a fairy rule, or may have failed to adequately protect themselves. One anecdote from Newfoundland tells of a woman struck by the fairy blast because she passed through a crossroads without carrying a bit of protective bread in her pocket while another man received the blast for trying to cut down a tree the fairies didn't want cut (Reiti, 1991). In other examples people were approached by fairies who either offered them items or wanted them to do things and when the people refused the Fey folk threw items at them; wherever the item struck the person was afflicted with pain, sometimes resulting in lifelong debility and other times in madness and eventual death (Reiti, 1991).

Lady Wilde includes this charm for curing the fairy stroke in her book:

> *"There is a very ancient and potent charm which may be tried with great effect in case of a suspected fairy-stroke.*
>
> *Place three rows of salt on a table in three lines, three equal measures to each row. The person performing the spell then encloses the rows of salt with his arm, leaning his head down over them, while he repeats the Lord's Prayer three times over each row--that is, nine times in all. Then he takes the hand of the one who has*

been fairy-struck, and says over it, "By the power of the Father, and of the Son, and of the Holy Spirit, let this disease depart, and the spell of the evil spirits be broken! I adjure, I command you to leave this man [naming him]. In the name of God I pray; in the name of Christ I adjure; in the name of the Spirit of God I command and compel you to go back and leave this man free! Amen! Amen! Amen!" (Wilde, 1888).

Fairy Theft

Fairy theft falls into roughly two categories: theft of people and theft of objects. Theft of people is covered in more depth in the sections on CHANGELINGS and STOLEN BRIDES. Theft of objects mainly tends to encompass food but may also include other items and some animals. The fairies seem to feel entitled to a portion of human possessions (Briggs, 1976). What possessions they take, why, and how are largely situational but seem to relate to the fairies own needs.

Generally when the Good People take an item they will not steal the physical thing outright but rather will either take the essence from it, as they do with FOOD, or as with Changelings they will take the item but leave behind an object that seems identical to the one taken. This duplicate item will eventually reveal it's true but too late for the real item to be retrieved. A main example of this given in folklore is usually cows, which may be stolen and replaced with a variety of things including glamoured objects that may look and act like the cow but provide no milk or edible meat.

There are many ideas as to why the fairies steal from humans, but ultimately no certainty. Rev. Kirk discussed fairy theft of grain, alcohol, and milk and claims that when humans have abundance of food fairies have a lack, indicating a reliance on theft from humans to provide sustenance for themselves. Campbell is more philosophical, stating bluntly that *"the Fairies only take away what a man deserves to lose"* and claiming that should a person speak ill of their own crop or produce the fairies will take its value as a kind of retribution (Campbell, 1900, page 17). In contrast several Irish anecdotal sources like those found in MacNeill's 'Festival of Lughnasa' and Evans-Wentz's 'Fairy Faith in Celtic Countries' believe that the fairies are owed a portion of what humans grow or produce and will take what is not freely given, including food and milk.

This theft from humans, it should be noted, is a norm for fairies and can be considered as fitting into whatever morality fairies have although they punish theft by humans (from fairies) quite harshly.

Fairy Trees

Fairies and trees have had a long connection in mythology and folklore. Today I'd like to take a brief look at a selection of trees and the main fairylore associated with them.

I would note that this folklore can be convoluted as the trees themselves were often reputed to have spirits, much like we might understand dryads in a modern context, but beyond this tree-spirit could also be home to or associated with other fairies. These other fairies may live in or near the particular tree but were not bound to it in the way a tree-spirit would be. If the tree were killed the tree spirit would suffer a similar fate, while the associated fairies would simply move on to another place. There are also many trees that are associated with fairies as either a protection against them or as a tree they prefer to be around.

Birch- In Scotland it's particularly associated with the Ghillie Dhu who was said to lurk in birch groves (Briggs, 1976). The Ghillie Dhu is a solitary fairy who is gentle and helpful but whose appearance often frightens people. In Ireland, however, fairies are thought to dislike birch, which is used to drive out spirits, and avoid this tree (MacCoitir, 2003).

Oak- Oaks have a strong association with spirits and fairies. Most notably there is a kind of fairy called 'oakmen' who live in areas where oaks have been cut and are re-growing; they appear as short, solid looking beings wearing red hats who may dangerous to those who trespass in their woods (Briggs, 1976). There is also the well-known rhyme of 'fairy folk are in old oaks'. Not all oak fairies are dangerous as one entry in the Dindshenchas discusses learning lore from fairy folk in an oak wood (MacCoitir, 2003).

Rowan- Rowan berries by some accounts are the food of the Tuatha De Danann and by extension some people see them as the food of the fairies in general. Rowan is seen as both a protection against magic and also a conduit for magic, appearing in folklore as a charm against fairy magic and witchcraft but also in stories we see rowan wands used to cast enchantments.

Elm- A communal tree it was believed if one elm was cut down the others would die from grief (Briggs, 1976). The spirits of the trees were so tightly bonded that the death of one would doom them all.

Hawthorn- Strongly associated with the Good People it is believed that it's unlucky to bring hawthorn into a home. A lone hawthorn growing in a field is often considered a fairy tree and it is dangerous to bring harm to such a tree because to do so will invite the wrath of Themselves. It's an old custom to leave gifts for the Other Crowd at the base of a lone hawthorn (MacCoitir, 2003).

Blackthorn- Guarded by fairies called Lunantishee who punish anyone who tries to cut blackthorns on Samhain or Bealtaine, going by the old dates which would be Nov 11 or May 11 (Briggs, 1976). MacCoitir suggests that Lunantishee may be an Anglicization of Leannán Sí, connecting the Blackthorn to the concept of fairy lovers. Whether that is true or not the Blackthorn generally had a grim reputation, seen as a dangerous tree that should not be messed with, although like so many others it also had protective qualities.

Ash- Mentioned as a protection against fairies in folklore the Ash was used to reverse or treat maladies caused by fairies (MacCoitir, 2003). These beliefs accorded the tree extra respect, so that it was not burned, some lore relating that any who burned the ash would lose their home to fire (Briggs, 1976). Some stories also mention a person's soul being trapped in an ash or otherwise placed in it.

Willow- It was said that willows walked at night and would follow people travelling alone, and their reputation was overall malevolent (Briggs, 1976). This may connect the Willow more general with water fairies who had a reputation for being dangerous and mercurial like the water itself. Lady Wilde suggests that willows speak in music.

Elder - In England and Scotland the Elder is a protection against witchcraft and evil beings; said to be home to fairies of good intent (Briggs, 1976). In Scotland the sap of the Elder was believed to grant the ability to see the Fairy Rade on Samhain, if the person then stood beneath an Elder (MacCoitir, 2003). In alternate folklore elders are said to be shape changed witches. Elders are another tree that it is generally believed should never be burned or ill luck will follow the person. In Ireland the Elder has a darker reputation, being associated with both ghosts and seen as a wood that invites fairy mischief; in Ireland and the Isle of Man it's believed that fairies ride on Elder twigs and branches (MacCoitir, 2003). In Manx lore the elder is a fairy tree in its own right and disturbing it can bring the same ill luck and harm to a person that we see with the thorn trees elsewhere (Evans-Wentz, 1911).

This is only a small selection of trees and some related fairylore; it is by no means exhaustive. I hope though that it illustrates some of the beliefs we can find associated with different common trees, and the way that fairy beliefs intersect with our everyday lives. Trees are all around us, even when we live in the city they can be found, and where there are trees there is folklore and fairylore.

Fairy Wives

In a reversal of the motif of the STOLEN BRIDE we also see the Fairy Bride that is a woman of Fairy[1] who voluntarily or under compulsion marries a human man. This idea is played out across fairy folklore but particularly in Selkie tales and stories of the Gwragedd Annwn and Tylwyth Teg. The usual pattern with voluntary fairy brides is that a human man comes across a group of fairies or the fairy woman alone,

Having a fairy wife, like anything else involving fairies, is a complex matter and comes with explicit rules. In the case of Selkie wives, who are held by compulsion, they must never find their stolen seal skins or they will immediately leave their human husband. For the Tylwyth Teg or Gwragedd Annwn the rules involved a prohibition that could not be broken or the wife would have no choice but to leave. One Welsh source describes it thusly:

> *"'Occasionally a young man would see the Tylwyth Teg dancing, and, being drawn into the dance, would be taken by them and married to one of their women. There is usually some condition in the marriage contract which becomes broken, and, as a result, the fairy wife disappears--usually into a lake. The marriage contract specifies either that the husband must never touch his fairy wife with iron, or else never beat or strike her three times."* (Evans-Wentz, 1911, pages 146-147)

An example of this is given in this story:

> *"'A young man once caught one of the Tylwyth Teg women, and she agreed to live with him on condition that he should never touch her with iron.*
>
> *One day she went to a field with him to catch a horse, but in catching the horse he threw the bridle in such a way that the bit touched the Tylwyth Teg woman, and all at once she was gone."* (Evans-Wentz, 1911, page 138).

Note

1 There are also accounts of fairy husbands to mortal women but these stories are fewer and do not form their own strata of stories. I will, however, note that what we do have of these stories reflects the same pattern of both voluntary and involuntary pairing.

Fairyology

A term dating back to the Victorian era, a period which showed a noted fascination with fairies and folklore. Fairyology references the study of fairies from what was intended to be a more scientific basis and can be found in print as early as the 1850's. For example a pamphlet was published in 1859 titled 'A Few Fragments of Fairyology Showing its Connection with Natural History' which tries to establish a tie between fairy phenomena and natural phenomena.

Farewell, Rewards, and Fairies

A poem written in the 16th century by a bishop, Richard Corbet, the text laments the lack of fairies in the world and attributes their loss on changing religion. The concept expressed reflects a wider theme seen across the centuries of the RETREAT OF THE FAIRIES from this world.

Farewell, rewards and fairies,
Good housewives now may say,
For now foul sluts in dairies
Do fare as well as they.
And though they sweep their hearths no less
Than maids were wont to do,
Yet who of late for cleanness
Finds sixpence in her shoe?

Lament, lament, old Abbeys,

The Fairies' lost command!
They did but change Priests' babies,
But some have changed your land.
And all your children, sprung from thence,
Are now grown Puritans,
Who live as Changelings ever since
For love of your demains.

At morning and at evening both
You merry were and glad,
So little care of sleep or sloth
These pretty ladies had;
When Tom came home from labour,
Or Cis to milking rose,
Then merrily went their tabor,
And nimbly went their toes.

Witness those rings and roundelays
Of theirs, which yet remain,
Were footed in Queen Mary's days
On many a grassy plain;
But since of late, Elizabeth,
And later, James came in,
They never danced on any heath
As when the time hath been.

By which we note the Fairies
Were of the old Profession.
Their songs were 'Ave Mary's',
Their dances were Procession.
But now, alas, they all are dead;
Or gone beyond the seas;
Or farther for Religion fled;
Or else they take their ease.

A tell-tale in their company
They never could endure!
And whoso kept not secretly
Their mirth, was punished, sure;
It was a just and Christian deed
To pinch such black and blue.
Oh how the commonwealth doth want
Such Justices as you!

Fear Dearg

A fairy whose name means 'Red Man' (plural Fir Dearg) and who is described wearing red clothes and a red hat. Some sources say he is a giant, other that he is human-sized, and others that he stands about 2 feet tall (Briggs, 1976). Crocker mentions that the Fear Dearg has an unusual voice which can sound like a variety of sounds from waves to birds to angelic music.

Yeats claims that he devotes all his time to tricks of a gruesome nature and puts him as part of a group including the Leprechaun and Clúracán. Croker is somewhat kinder in his assessment, comparing the Fear Dearg to the English Puck or Robin Goodfellow and relegating his pranks to mischief.

In contrast to these versions of the Fear Dearg there is another which appears in folklore, named the Fear Dearg not for his clothes but for his red hair. This Fear Dearg is a human man who has been taken by the fairies as a captive and gives aid and useful advice to other captives, sometimes helping them to successfully escape while he remains trapped in Fairy (Briggs, 1976).

Fenodyree

A Manx fairy who is known to be helpful around farms and generally beneficial to humans, although somewhat wild. The Fenodyree would sleep among the sheep when it was cold as he shunned the use of clothing and was terribly offended by any offer it (Evans-Wentz, 1911). Like some other types of fairies any gift of clothing would drive a Fenodyree off and the fairy would never be seen again. If a family were in his good graces, however, he might come out at night and help with the threshing while everyone slept (Evans-Wentz, 1911).

Fetch

A concept in England that is rather obscure in nature the Fetch in folklore is a copy or duplicate of a person which appears as an ill omen, usually of death (Briggs, 1976). Also called a wraith or double the Fetch would be seen by the living person or those who knew them, generally right before they died (Harper, 2018). In more recent material the Fetch has been given many of the qualities and abilities of the Fylgja, although in older folklore it is clear that the Fetch or wraith was only viewed as a death omen. Rev. Kirk suggested the wraith or Fetch was the result of the soul beginning to leave the body shortly before death and being seen by others (Kirk & Lang, 1893).

Fiction

Fairies have appeared in fiction[1] possibly for as long as the genre has existed and have found various niche positions in modern fiction through fantasy, urban fantasy, and paranormal romance. Fairies in fiction have evolved since the time of Shakespeare, when they were not true depictions of folklore but did represent reflections of folk belief, into characters that often reflect pure imagination.

Fairies in older fictional works, including Spenser's 'Faerie Queene', where often used to make political statements and to speak to things that the author could not write directly about. Couching them in terms of the fantastic allowed more leeway in political speech, in the same way that we see outlaws during the 15th and 16th century in England claiming they were embodiments of or servants of the Fairy monarchs. Firth Green discusses this overlap between Fairy and outlaws in his book 'Elf Queens and Holy Friars' and Erickson discusses the literary crossover between politics and Fairy in his 'Mapping the Faerie Queene', both of which are useful for understanding the way that Fairy and fairies have been used as a device to further human messages.

In more modern fiction utilizing fairies they have, in many cases, ceased to be either attached to genuine folklore or a guise for dangerous political views. Instead they have become a device to carry forward human story-telling and a symbol of that which the author envisions as at odds with wider human culture. The diversity of fairy fiction, therefore, is vast and varied. Tolkien's elves function as idealized religious humans as the author envisioned them, or perhaps as Purkiss suggests in 'At the Bottom of the Garden' as Tolkien's dream of a society that represents a paradise and safety from war, even temporarily. In other works fairies might be ecologically conscious – even the voice of the environment urging humans not to ruin the land – or they act as protectors of the world in the face a human civilization that seeks only to destroy and use what can be monetized. In worldviews that see humans as too serious and joyless fairies become symbols of childlike joy or even hedonism; to those who write about humans as magicless and dull fairies become living magic in an ordinary world.

The latter half of the 20th century saw an increase in fairy popularity in fiction with a blend of genuine folklore and invention melding and weaving together throughout different books and series. The fairy courts appear and then change, the folkloric seelie and unseelie courts being poetically renamed to light and dark, summer and winter, and then expanded outward as different authors envisioned new courts and new purviews. The traditional Kings and Queens of Fairy are also changed in modern fiction, sometimes renamed entirely such as we see for example in Laurel K Hamilton's 'Merry Gentry' series and other times with the older names kept the same but the characteristics and lore changed radically. The characterization of the fairies themselves in popular culture has changed as their stories in fiction change, particular influenced with their appearances in children's' stories and young adult urban fantasy. Beings who were formerly dangerous and fearsome become gentle or simply annoying, while others including the Unseelie court more broadly become the stuff of romance.

The beginning of the 21st century has been a divisive one for fairies in fiction with both a continuing of the pattern which emerged in the 1980's and 1990's as well as a counter wave of material coming into print and other media that takes a more traditional view. Genuine folklore and fairylore is finding its way into fiction more often with the idea of frightening fairies and fairies who are truly inhuman in their motivations and actions becoming more common.

Note

1 This segment is specifically looking at works of fiction that were intentionally written as such and excluding mythology and folklore. There is, of course, debate about the subjective nature of the source of myth and folklore but as it has been conveyed forward by people who believe it to be true as opposed to fiction which is written from imagination the two subjects are divided here.

Fideal

One of the Fuath, the Fideal may be a kind of fairy or a specific individual fairy, as there is a story that says the Fideal was killed by a human man who she in turn killed before dying. A seductive being associated with lakes and seducing and drowning men (Briggs, 1976). MacKenzie suggests that the Fideal is the living embodiment of the bog grass and water weeds (Briggs, 1976). This idea is certainly supported by her wider actions of seduction and drowning.

Finnbheara

Finnbheara is one of the Kings of the fairies in Ireland who is known variously as Finvara, Finveara, Fionbheara, Fin Bheara, Fionnbharr or Findbharr. His name may mean 'Fair Haired' in Old Irish; O hOgain, however, suggests the name is an oblique reference to the summit of Cnoc Meadha or the cairn found there. He is said to be the king of the fairies of Connacht, with his home at Cnoc Mheada in county Galway. MacKillop suggests that his popularity in later folklore gave him the title of king of all fairies in Ireland and also of king of the dead[1].

Finnbheara was originally one of the Tuatha De Danann, he is mentioned as such in the Agallamh na Seanoach and is also said to be a brother to Oengus mac ind Óg and youngest son of the Dagda according to the Altram Tige Dá Medar. His mother is not mentioned. In the Altram Tige Dá Medar he is called Finnbarr Meadha and he and Oengus get into a violent disagreement after he disparages one of Oengus's foster daughters while visiting Oengus's home. He is also sometimes said to be a rival of Donn Firinne, another Fairy King, although O hOgain suggests that the two could represent complementary rulers of the year in much the same way other scholars have suggested Áine and Grianne represent the summer and winter suns.

He is generally described as a handsome man, sometimes said to dress in black (Briggs, 1976). We can perhaps assume from his name that he is fair haired. In one story he appears in a coach drawn by four white horses and in another he is riding a black horse (Briggs, 1976). Finnbheara has a strong association with horses in general and with horse racing in specific, and in one tale he appeared to aid Lord Hackett by acting as jockey to his horse in a race before disappearing (O hOgain, 2006).

Finnbheara is married to the Fairy queen Una but he has a reputation for his love of mortal women, and women in general. In the aforementioned Altram Tige Dá Medar he had travelled to visit his brother in order to see Oengus's foster daughters, who had a reputation among the Tuatha De for their beauty and manners. In a story from folklore he abducts a woman named Eithne and keeps her for a year until her husband successfully wins her back from him by digging into Finnbheara's sidhe, salting the earth there, and freeing her from the enchantment she was under by removing a piece of fairy clothing she was wearing (MacKillop, 1998). In the Feis Tighe Chonain he appears as an Otherworldly rival competing with Finn mac Cumhal over a woman (O hOgain, 2006). In many other anecdotal tales he was known as a womanizer and for taking mortal women into his sidhe, even though his own wife was said to be peerlessly beautiful.

A mercurial figure, Finnbheara is well known for abducting people but also for blessing those he favours. He heals a sick woman in exchange for food, and is known for rewarding any blacksmith brave enough to try to shoe his three legged horse (MacKillop, 1998). He is known to appear to mortals and offer them aid of various kinds, but especially aid in horse racing, and then sometimes to invite them into his sidhe. These invitations may be a trap but on other occasions the person would be his guest at a feast, often finding the other guests to be dead people they had known previously, and would return safely to mortal earth the next day (Briggs, 2006). The success of crops in Connacht are also thought in folk belief to rest on both Finnbheara's presence in the area and his favour. In some folklore the crops bloom when Finnbheara and his fairies win at hurling against the fairies of rival provinces (O hOgain, 2006). In one anecdotal tale the fairies of Ulster challenged the fairies of Connacht and the two met and fought as clouds in the sky and *"it was thought that Finnbheara won because there were good crops in Connacht that year."* (MacNeill, 1962, page 593). It was generally believed that there was a standing rivalry between the Good People of Ulster and Finnbheara's people.

Finnbheara is an interesting figure in folklore and one who

has a more complex history than is sometimes appreciated in fairylore. A member of the Tuatha De Danann and also a Fairy King, possibly also ruler of the dead, known to abduct mortals but also to aid them for little or even no recompense. He bridges the space between mythology and folklore, found in myths from the 12th century and also in modern day folklore around Cnoc Meadha. Those who seek to better understand the way that the Tuatha De Danann have merged with and affected our understanding of fairies can learn a lot by studying Finnbheara's stories.

Note

1 The relationship between the fairies and the dead is complicated but we also see this sort of crossover with Donn Firinne, who is called both a Fairy King and a god of the dead.

Finfolk

A particularly Orcadian type of fairy being, Finfolk are sea fairies who have human form but can live easily underwater. Renowned for their magical skill they sometimes travelled among the humans of the Orkneys and the female Finfolk even sought human husbands, in an effort to escape marriage to the unattractive and foul tempered Finmen who would force them to work and earn silver (Towrie, 2019).

Like other types of fairies Finfolk were said to live on a magical Otherworldly island, to steal humans, and to be averse to Christianity.

Food

There has been a long and ongoing debate about whether fairies physically consume food or merely take the essence out of the food. The evidence from folklore supports both being equally true, and whether tangible food is consumed or the essential value of the food is taken may depend on a variety of factors including what type of fairies we are discussing and the circumstances of them taking the food. Rev. Kirk, Campbell, and Evans-Wentz each discuss the idea of fairies taking the essence of food, showing that this idea extends back to at least the 1600's and has continued into the 20th century, and arguably into contemporary belief. All use different terms for what exactly the fairies are taking from the food, with Kirk uses the Scots word 'foyson' which means vitality[1] but when applied to food describes its nourishing power; Campbell refers to it as the toradh which is a Gaidhlig word for fruit but in this case refers to the substance or profit of the food and drink; Evans-Wentz calls it the quintessence. The consensus is that once this substance is taken physically consuming the food has no value and most sources agree that eating food which fairies have consumed first has no value for either humans or animals. There are also anecdotal accounts that describe fairies physically eating food, such as a story Yeats related in Celtic Twilight of a fairy woman who shared a meal with a family where she took a single bite out of each item on her plate.

Looking across folklore we can find a variety of different food preferences attributed to fairies in different areas and to different types of fairies. Below we will take a look at a selection of such preferences:

- Crops: Fairies will steal, and presumably eat, any and all human food and produce if the owner of it speaks badly about it, by taking the 'toradh' out of it so that it gives no value to the humans (Campbell, 1900). Fairies are known to take the 'substance' from such crops as turnips and grain, and will take butter if they can (Evans-Wentz, 1911).
- Wild plants: Some of the smaller fairies are said to eat leaves, weeds, roots, and *'stalks of heather'* although they use their glamour to make these items look like common cooked human foods (Briggs, 1976). It is said that some fairies also eat rowan berries, and rowan berries were said

to have been the food of the Tuatha De Danann by some accounts (McNeill, 1956).

- Vegetarian fairies: It is said that some Irish fairies eat fruits, vegetables, honey, and drink milk, but do not eat meat (Lysaght, 1991). This aversion to meat is explained by an anecdotal source as being rooted in the fairies' alleged aversion to the colour red[2] which is further explained as caused by their jealousy over humans' future salvation through Christian cosmology.
- Beef: The Corrigans and Lutins of Brittany are fond of meat, especially beef, and will steal cows from farmers and butcher them for fairy feasts (Evans-Wentz, 1911). We also see this among the Welsh fairies who were known to eat cows, in at least one account a man witnessed them killing his ox although the animal in question was later magically resurrected (Evans-Wentz, 1911).
- Humans: there are a variety of fairies, including hags and water horses, who are known to eat human flesh and an assortment of the humanoid fairies who do as well. Briggs mentions one fairy court's feast which featured the prepared and cooked body of an old human woman, to the horror of one of the human guests (Briggs, 1976, p 145). Folklore of the hag Black Annis describe her eating human children; kelpies try to trick people into riding them in order to get to a body of water, drown them, and eat them (Briggs, 1976). The Baobhan sidhe drinks human blood, and the welsh form of the Leannán Sidhe, the Lhiannan Shee, is also said by some to have a vampiric nature, while the Gean-cánach feeds on a human's life force (Briggs, 1976).
- Cooked foods: They will also steal quality food from a human hearth while the food is cooking, including meat or vegetables, leaving behind something spoiled or rotten in its place (Wilde, 1920).

- Staple human foods: The Good Neighbours of Orkney and Shetland eat oatmeal, fish, and drink milk (Bruford, 1991). Yeats recounts a tale of one of the Gentry who passed a Halloween with a family and ate with them, a meal of duck and apples, although she had only a single bite from each portion (Yeats, 1962). Scottish fairies as far back as the 17th century were known to eat bread, and to drink milk as well as various kinds of alcohol (Kirk, 1691)
- Dairy products: Milk in general is widely reported to be consumed by fairies, not only cow's milk but also goat's milk and deer's milk (Briggs, 1976). In Wales the fairies are popularly known to eat eggs, butter, and drink milk (Gwyndaf, 1991). Milk and butter are often mentioned in Irish sources as well, with fairies known to take cows into Fairy for their own use milking and also to steal milk from the cows of mortal farmers.

Milk and grain are the most commonly mentioned foods, with the grains prepared as they would seem to be prepared in ways similar to humans; most sources including Briggs and Campbell refer to the fairies using grains ground into meal and porridge is mentioned in different sources as is baking and baked goods. Baking is mentioned as is cooking more generally, and when fairy feasts are mentioned, barring the more macabre ones, they seem to be filled with the same dishes humans would eat. Several types of fairies appear to either be fond of barley or to grow it as their own crop, and to eat it. This widespread love of grain and milk is particularly interesting in folk belief as it echoes much older myth from the De Gabail in t-Sida where the Tuatha De Danann retreat into the sidhe (fairy hills) and cause all the crops to fail and cows to go dry until an agreement is reached whereby they will be given a portion of each harvest, specifically "ith" [grain] and "blicht" [milk].

Besides an emphasis, perhaps, on dairy and baked goods,

generally fairies seem to eat much the same foods humans do, although certain types of fairies are more specific in their diets and some, of course, eat things we would not. While they are often noted to take the essence from foods they are also equally often said to eat the food itself so both seem equally possible.

There is also a belief that food which falls from a person's hands is desired by the fairies and should be given to them. As one Irish Professor explained it:

> *"If you were eating and food fell from you, it was not right to take it back, for the fairies wanted it. Many families are very serious about this even now. The luckiest thing to do in such cases is to pick up the food and eat just a speck of it and then throw the rest away to the fairies."* (Evans-Wentz, 1911, page 70).

By this belief fairies can be very diverse in their diets and may indicate their own preferences based on what they take in any situation.

Notes

1 Interestingly foyson can also be applied to people, in the sense of physical strength or vigour and might perhaps also reflect the energy that fairies like the predatory Leannán Sidhe take from their human victim. In that case if fairies are absorbing or consuming the foyson, the vital force, within any living thing including what remains in food items then we are looking at one principle of feeding applied across all methods of eating, no matter the type of fairy or what – or who – is being fed on.

2 According to Lysaght's source in the article found in 'The Good People' the fairies do not seem to be vegetarians based on any moral compunctions, but because they are averse to the colour red, and therefore cannot stand the sight of red blood or raw meat.

Friends of the Fairies

Throughout the Celtic speaking world we find certain people with a reputation for seeing and interacting with fairies and to whom other people sometimes go for knowledge or advice about them. These people may have culturally specific names but are often known in English as friends of the fairies or for being touched by them.

Yeats and Lady Wilde both mention that Mná Feasa and other cunningfolk, under the name Fairy Doctors, were thought to gain both knowledge and ability from their connection to the Good People. As Yeats describes them:

> *"The most celebrated fairy doctors are sometimes people the fairies loved and carried away, and kept with them for seven years; not that those the fairies' love are always carried off--they may merely grow silent and strange, and take to lonely wanderings in the "gentle" places... Those we speak of have for their friends the trooping fairies--the gay and sociable populace of raths and caves. Great is their knowledge of herbs and spells. These doctors, when the butter will not come on the milk, or the milk will not come from the cow, will be sent for to find out if the cause be in the course of common nature or if there has been witchcraft... The fairies are, of course, visible to them..."* (Yeats, 1888, pages 146-147).

Yeats in his Celtic Twilight talked to several people who could see the Good People and while most of them were not skilled with herbs or sought out for magical knowledge they did all relate to him various accounts of what they could see of the Other Crowd, sometimes as he stood by. This willingness to talk about what was seen varied, and while some who maintained a connection to the Otherworld showed a willingness to share what they experienced, others were notably reluctant to speak of it. As one Welsh source relates:

> *"Only certain people can see fairies, and such people hold communication with them and have dealings with them, but it is difficult to get them to talk about fairies."* (Evans-Wentz, 1911, page 154).

This reluctance to speak may come from the deep-rooted beliefs that the Good People are often inclined to punish a loose tongue and to remove any blessings they have given to those who brag of them.

Generally speaking those who were singled out as fairy friends tended to be eccentric people in various ways. Lady Wilde describes one such friend of the fairies from Sligo, Ireland as someone who didn't eat meat or drink alcohol, paid but didn't eat at communal feasts, and maintained the same style of dress year-round despite any weather (Wilde, 1888). Similarly Ann Jeffries, who was known for her association with the fairies in Cornwall, was described as someone who defied social norms before her affliction by the fairies and also, according to her employers' son, defied gender norms (Buccola, 2006).

Such people were usually first contacted by the Good People, if they were not born with the Second Sight, during times of stress or times associated with crisis. Often these crises would be health related, particularly serious illnesses such as we see with Ann Jeffries, but they would also come to people during liminal times such as childbirth which we see with Bessie Dunlop who was approached by the Fairy Queen while she was in labour with her child.

Fuathan

Fuathan, singular Fuath, are a grouping of water spirits in Scotland. The word in Gaidhlig has several meanings including hatred, aversion, spectre, but when the definitive article 'an' is used it is translated as 'the fairies' (Dwelly, 1902). Carmichael describes the word Fuath thusly:

> *"...a spectre, a kelpie, a demon, a water-fiend frequenting glens, rivers, and waterfalls."* (Carmichael, 1900).

Campbell describes them as dangerous beings who seem to be blend of fairies and ghosts (Campbell, 1900). Many different kinds of fairies fall into the wider category of Fuathan and while they do have a strong water connection it is fair to say that the term is often used the same way the word fairy is in English to encompass all Otherworldly beings.

They are generally described as fair haired and human-like overall in form but with some telling sign, such as a webbed hands and feet, tails, or missing noses (Bunce, 1878). They are often categorized as water fairies, to the point that several sources including the Faclair Beag gloss them as naiads, however, Campbell in 'The Gaelic Otherworld', argues against this saying that this view is based on one over eager folklorist's opinion based on a single story.

Like some other fairies Fuathan are averse to iron and do not like crossing fresh water; they can also be killed by light according to some folklore (Bunce, 1878).

Fylgja

A Norse concept, a fylgja may be an independent protective spirit or a projected part of the person's own soul; when it is the person's own soul it usually takes an animal form. Fylgja can follow family lines and there are examples in Norse myth, such as in Hallfraedarsaga, of Fylgja who were inherited through generations or seemed to be primarily attached to one individual but would also aid family members (Gundarsson, 2007). Fylgja are often compared to or equated to Fetches, but they lack any sense of ill-omen; in contrast the Fylgja was viewed as positive and seen as both protective and luck-bearing. It was common for a person's Fylgja to be of the opposite gender although we should note that in tales this occurs most often with men having female

Fylgja and sexual elements or relationships were not uncommon between a man and his fylgja-woman. Fylgja may mean 'follower' or 'following' and they can act in decisive ways to aid the human they are connected to, providing knowledge as well as physical protection (Gundarsson, 2007). Claude Lecouteux strongly connects the Norse concept of the Fylgja to fairies, arguing that Celtic examples of fairy women who act as tutelary spirits and protectors of family lines as well as those who attach themselves to individual humans are the same beings that the Norse would label as Fylgjas (Lecouteux, 1992). He refers to these spirits as 'Doubles' and points out their many similar characteristics and functions to Fylgja.

G

Gean-Cánach

A dangerously seductive male fairy similar in nature to the predatory female Leannán Sidhe is the Irish Gean-cánach, or 'love talker'. He appears as an attractive young man smoking a pipe, walking in the untamed places, and is quick to seduce women when he can after which they lose the will to live (Briggs, 1967). The Love Talker only lays once with his victim then departs never to be seen again leaving her to waste away. The folklore is unclear whether the woman dies for want of him or perhaps because he has stolen some vital life energy from her, but based on the parallels with the Leannán Sidhe the latter possibility seems likely.

Geniti Glini

See: Battlefield fairies

Gentry, The

Called Daoine Uaisle or Na h-Uaisle in Irish the Gentry are sometimes seen as a distinct class of fairy and other times as part of the Good People more generally. As the name implies they are viewed as the nobility of Fairy, described as quite beautiful and powerful, possibly wearing white (Evans-Wentz, 1911).

Giants

There are a variety of giants to be found in fairylore, beings who can be 7 or 8 feet tall or more. In English folklore these are usually named beings like the Jack-in-Irons or Jimmy Squarefoot. In other cultures these may appear as a type of being in their own right such as the Norse Jotun or Anglo-Saxon Ettin, both names meaning 'giant'. Some of the Celtic Gods like Bran the Blessed and the Cailleach are also described as giants in some folklore. Giants may appear very human but on a larger scale or may be monstrous, such as the aforementioned Jimmy Squarefoot who was part man and part boar, or they may have extra heads or limbs.

Gifts

Fairy gifts are rarely straightforward and even when given out of good will usually come with instructions that must be followed to ensure success and avoid difficulties. Those who find themselves favoured by a fairy friend for example are often bound not to speak of it or else they will lose not only their friend but also any money and worldly goods they have gained through the fairy's intercession.

This portion of a story from 'Fairy Faith in Celtic Countries' may illustrate the idea well, it is a conversation between a fairy man and a young boy whose step mother is cruel to him:

> *"'If I give you a trade will you be inclined to follow it?'*
>
> *I said yes, and the old man then continued, 'How would you like to be a piper by trade?'*
>
> *'I would gladly become a piper,' says I, 'but what am I to do without the bagpipes and the tunes to play?'*
>
> *'I'll supply the bagpipes,' he said, 'and as long as you have them you'll never want for the most delightful tunes.'"* (Evans-Wentz, 1911, pages 103 – 104).

Here we see a gift being given but only after the human has agreed to do as the fairy says, and with the understanding that as long as the fairy's advice is followed all will be well for the boy.

Fairy gifts are rarely straightforward and gifts from the Good People usually have a cost. The MacLeods' on the Isle of Skye possesses a fairy banner, said by some to be a gift from a Leannán Sidhe to one of the MacLeod lords, which ensures victory in battle but it can only be used three times before losing its power and any pregnant woman or cow who comes into its presence, according to folklore, will go into early labour (Campbell, 1900).

This illustrates well the value and risk of fairy gifts. In the Ballad of Thomas the Rhymer Thomas is given the gift of prophecy but also bound to only speaking the truth, something which causes him to try to refuse this gift as he points out it will do him no service among his fellow humans, although the Fairy Queen will not retract it. Another anecdotal account from the 'Fairy Faith in Celtic Countries' mentions a woman who wished for help with her spinning only to have the fairies who answered her become troublesome when the work was finished and she could provide nothing else for them to do. Even more straightforward gifts, like a baby in response to one wished for, might be a baby which was stolen from another human family (Campbell, 1900).

Campbell summarizes fairy gifts thusly:

> *"In every instance, however, the benefit of the gift goes ultimately to the fairies themselves, or, as it is put in the Gaelic expression, 'the fruit of it goes into their own bodies; (thèid an toradh 'nan cuirp fhèin).*" (Campbell, 1900, page 12).

Gillie Dubh

One of the most well-known of the Scottish fairies, the Gillie Dubh is solitary being who is generally reclusive but unlike many solitary fairies is good natured and helpful to humans. The Gillie Dubh is unique in some respects because of how focused his folklore originally was to a very specific area, and how many alleged sightings of him there were for a sustained period of time, which has led some modern authors to suggest that he was, in fact, a human rather than a fairy. Despite this theory the folklore around the Gillie Dubh remains strong and his stories continue to be told and have spread beyond his original home region.

The name 'Gillie Dubh' - sometimes given as Ghillie Du - literally means dark [dubh] lad or servant [gillie] but the 'dark' here refers to hair colour not temperament or nature. Briggs points out that this fairy, who is considered ubiquitously male, was called Gillie Dubh due to his dark hair and not his clothing (Briggs, 1976). This is a reflection of the common practice in both Irish and Gaidhlig of referring to a person's hair colour by calling the person themself by that colour, hence 'dark lad' a dark-haired lad, 'red woman' a red haired woman. The Gillie Dubh is said to dress entirely from forest flora, specifically leaves and moss (Briggs, 1976).

During the 18th century he was commonly known in one area of Scotland, and as one author put it:

> "*...he was seen by very many people and on many occasions over a period of more than forty years in the latter half of the 18th century.*" (MacKenzie, 1921, p234).

He is most strongly associated with the area of Gairloch in what used to be Ross and Cromarty [now Wester Ross] and further north particularly with the area around Loch an Draing (MacKillop, 1998; MacKenzie, 1921). His preferred home is birch groves, of which he is the special guardian, and one might surmise that it is the leaves of this tree that he prefers to dress.

In at least one story he sheltered a lost child in the woods at night and then to have brought her home the next day; this girl is also the only living person the Gillie Dubh is ever known to have spoken to (Briggs, 1976). Some modern folklore suggests that the Gillie Dubh aids lost travellers, likely rooted in this older anecdote. His overriding characteristic, however, is his reclusive nature and reluctance to engage with humans.

By the measure of the Scottish fairy court system the Gillie Dubh would be considered a Seelie court fairy. Despite this there is one story of a group of Scottish lords in the 18th or 19th century who set out to hunt him down (Briggs, 1976; MacKenzie, 1921). Despite thoroughly hunting the woods and loch area they found nothing and left empty handed (MacKenzie, 1921). No reason is given for this decision, as it's clear the fairy wasn't harming or even harassing anyone, and even more oddly the people who did this chose to stay with the woman who had been rescued from the woods by the Gillie Dubh, now a married adult. It seems that after this time the fairy stopped appearing so often or easily to people as he had previously.

Glaistig

Glaistig are complicated Scottish fairies which are known to be protective of children and the elderly but can be very dangerous to men. Campbell suggests the name may be derived from the word glas which he gives as meaning grey, although it's actual meanings are more complex and can relate to green or grey in Gaidhlig; it's possible in this case its related to a form of the word, glas and glais, which specifically relate to paleness and a grey complexion. Since either could apply to the Glaistig who may perhaps have a pale complexion but is also known to wear green it is impossible to be certain. Carmichael argues instead that the name is means 'water imp' and is a combination of the words glas, which can mean water, and stic meaning demon or imp.

The Glaistig may appear as a beautiful woman with slightly damp or dripping hair, as a woman wearing a long green dress to conceal her lower half which is that of a goat, or may appear in the form of a goat. Dwelly describes the Glaistig as "*Supposed she-devil or hag in the shape of a goat*" and "*[a] beautiful female fairy, usually attired in a green robe, seldom seen except at the bank of a stream, and engaged in washing, also known as maighdean uaine [green maiden]*" (Dwelly, 1902). Campbell says she has a '*wan and grey*' face and wears a green dress (Campbell, 1900, page 23). Bunce incudes her among the ranks of the Fuathan, probably because of her association in some stories with water. Carmichael is unremittingly harsh in calling her "*a vicious creature, half woman, half goat, frequenting lonely lakes and rivers. She is much dreaded, and many stories are told of her evil deeds*" (Carmichael, 1900, pages 302-303).

The Glaistig is believed by some to have been a human woman who was taken by the fairies and transformed into one of their own (Briggs, 1976; Campbell, 1900). This may perhaps explain her kindness to children and older humans, although not her antipathy to younger men.

The benevolent tales of Glaistigs describe them as shapeshifters who can appear as young women or as goats and who will help those humans they like by herding their cattle in exchange for some milk (Briggs, 1976; Campbell, 1900). Campbell compares them to Brownies with their focus on specific families or farms and taking on of chores. In the more malevolent tales of Glaistigs they appear to seduce and kill men. In those accounts a Glaistig is described as a beautiful woman with the lower body of a goat which she hides beneath her green dress; she seduces mortal men and once in her thrall she kills them and drains them of blood (MacKillop, 1998).

Like many fairies the Glaistig is averse to iron. In one account a Glaistig was captured by a man named MacUalrig Mor who tried to force the fairy to swear to leave the area and bring no further harm to anyone by swearing on the iron of his plough; upon touching the plough her hand was burned to the bone and she fled (Carmichael, 1900).

Glashtin

A water fairy found in Manx fairylore. The Glashtin is described as being part horse and part cow, although it is also called a 'water-bull' (Evans-Wentz, 1911). Like other water horses he is able to take a human form, although his differs slightly from the Irish and Scottish Each Uisge because while he is said to be very handsome his ears are pointed like a horse's even in his human form. One Manx tale relates how a Glashtin showed up on a girl's door during a storm while she was waiting for her father to return and when she let him in, went to sleep by the fire; she saw his ears and realized what he was only surviving because dawn arrived and the rooster crowing drove the fairy away (Briggs, 1976).

Glamour

Glamour is a special kind of magic that fairies have which they use to deceive the senses. The word itself comes to us from Scots meaning enchantment or magic but with an emphasis on deception. It is believed to be a variant of gramarye, itself from the older English and with the medieval sense of occult learning (Kerr, 2012). In older Scottish accounts glamour was associated with witches, warlocks, and fairies. In modern terms glamour has developed new meanings but it is still associated with fairy magic.

Glamour is often thought of as a purely visual type of illusion but actually the power of this magic goes deeper and is able to fool all of a human being's senses at least for a time. There is an anecdotal account from the Isle of Man that demonstrates this:

> *"'I heard of a man and wife who had no children. One night the man was out on horseback and heard a little baby crying beside the road. He got off his horse to get the baby, and, taking it home, went to give it to his wife, and it was only a block of wood. And then the old fairies were outside yelling at the man: "Eash un oie, s'cheap t'ou mollit!" (Age one night, how easily thou art deceived!).'"* (Evans-Wentz, 1911, page 127).

In this account we see that the fairies' glamour was enough for the man to hear, see, and feel – at least – the baby as real even though it was not.

In many stories fairy glamour plays a part, particularly in fooling or deluding the senses of a human. Often in Stolen Midwife stories the midwife initially believes she has been brought to a fine home, sometimes even a very well off one, only to touch an eye with fairy ointment and realize that she is actually in a cave or some other rough location. Similarly we see stories where a human stumbles across is brought into a fairy feast and sees what seems to be a spread of delicious food before them, only to later have it revealed to be a collection of unpalatable things. And the most well-known example may be the fairy habit of using glamour to make an object like leaves or gingerbread look and feel like money only to have its true nature revealed later.

Green Children, The

A medieval account from Suffolk originally printed in Latin but later translated into English discusses the case of two fairy children who wandered out of their own world and into the human one. The boy and girl were found near a location with various caves and brought to the local knight, likely the highest ranking person nearby, because while they could speak to each other they lacked any language understandable to the local people and both children had skin tinted green. At first the pair refused to eat anything but fresh beans, and within a short time the boy died. However, the girl eventually learned to speak the local language, adapted to eating the food, and was even baptized. She recounted how the two had come from a land without sunlight, but a perpetual twilight, where all the people had green tinged skin; they had followed the sound of bells through a cavern and emerged into the human world only be dazzled by the light of the sun until they were found by the locals. The girl lived out her life afterwards as a human in service to the knight and was apparently as normal as anyone else only noted to have loose morals by the standard of the day.

A full retelling can be found in Keightley's 'Fairy Mythology'.

Grimoires and Fairies

Generally when we look for resources on fairies we look (rightly) to folklore. There is, however, another more obscure source that can provide us some information and this is the later ceremonial magic grimoires. These texts are very different in nature and tone than other sources and we must keep that in mind as we look at them but they do give us a glimpse at a particularly English view of fairies from the 16th and 17th centuries.

The only female beings found in the grimoire material are fairies according to Brock and Raiswell who suggest that all other spirits found in grimoires are explicitly male; even those described as female are referred to as dukes and are only female in illusory form (Brock & Raiswell, 2018, p65). When we look at the Grimoire material we find three main groupings of beings: Fairy Queens, Oberon, and the so-called Seven Sisters. These are all given names although the names vary in different manuscripts. The Seven Sisters can be bound to teach a person about herbs, nature, and provide a ring of invisibility (Harms, Clark, & Peterson, 2015). The queens can be called on for scrying, manifestation, sex magic, knowledge of nature, truth, and may also provide a ring of invisibility (Brock & Raiswell, 2018; Harm, Clark, & Peterson, 2015). All of the names given, however, are somewhat problematic in that they either can be found nowhere else outside the grimoire material or else they closely resemble common names or words.

Goblins[1]

Goblins are an often-mentioned type of fairy, but perhaps a poorly understood one, as they represent as much of a grouping as a specific kind of being. This is, of course, true of several kinds of fairies, especially the more well-known ones. Nonetheless, a great deal can be said about them.

The word goblin is of obscure origin but appears in print back to the 14th century and may come from the Latin Gobelinus, and also to be related to the German word Kobold; the meaning is given as an ugly fairy or devil (Goblin, 2016). Like the words fairy and elf the word goblin originally was used as a generic term rather than a specific to indicate a more general type of being. In Scots, for example, we can see more than a half dozen kinds of fairies which are described as goblins and in later

English folklore the same holds true. Besides being glossed with the names elf and fairy, goblin was used in earlier periods as a synonym for other negative types of fairies, such as Thurs and Shuck, both of which had connotations of maliciousness and evil (Williams, 1991). The prefix 'hob' was added in front of the word goblin, giving us HOBGOBLIN, to indicate a goblin type spirit which was less negative and more benevolent; hobgoblins were inclined to mischief but also known to be helpful to people where goblins were not (Briggs, 1976). MacKillop posits that the word as well as the being were borrowed into Celtic belief from outsiders, likely from Germanic folk belief probably of the Kobold (MacKillop, 1998). The Irish Púca is sometimes described as a goblin, and goblins are often seen as equivalent to bogies. An array of subgroups of fairies are considered goblins or hobgoblins including the aforementioned Púca (and more general Puck), Bogies, the Fuath - themselves a general term inclusive of specific types – Boggarts[2] and Bogles, who are usually considered the eviller sort of goblins, the Welsh Coblynau, and Irish Clauricaun and Dullahan (Briggs, 1976; MacKillop, 1998). Even the usually benevolent Brownie is sometimes considered a goblin, or perhaps more properly a HOBGOBLIN (Briggs, 1976).

When they appear in folklore goblins are generally described as wizened or smaller than the average human and unattractive in their features, ranging from grotesque to animalistic. In Rossetti's poem *'The Goblin Market'* the depiction of the goblins directly relates them to animals describing them with whiskers, tails, and with fur (Rossetti, 1862). Dickens described them as small, with long arms and legs, and rounded bodies (Silver, 1999). These descriptions are typical of those found in older folklore as well where goblins are usually referred to as grotesque and ugly. Generally goblins are male and their physical descriptions reflect ideas closer to imps or devils than the usual fairies who appear fair on the outside no matter how dangerous they may be on the inside. This may reflect a belief that goblins, although a type or kind of fairy, were closer to or on the border of being demonic; this is muddy water at best as there was often a fine line between the Fey and demons in the medieval period particularly among the literati. Briggs suggests that it was particularly the influence of Protestant belief which edged the goblins into the category of the demonic as they directly equated them to *'imps from Hell'* (Briggs, 1967). In fact imp is often given as a synonym for goblin, further confusing the issue. Specific types of goblins, such as the bogies, were known as shapeshifters as well and could alter their appearance at will in order to more easily deceive people. Because of their fearsome reputation many people were afraid of goblins, and even the generally more benevolent hobgoblins (Evans-Wentz, 1911).

Goblins were known to favour specific locations and might set up residence in a home; in one story a bogey takes over a farmer's field and had to be tricked into leaving (Evans-Wentz, 1911; Briggs, 1976). In Rossetti's poem they have their own market and a well-worn path which is taken to and from it each dawn and dusk. Like many Fey goblins are usually considered nocturnal and are most likely to be encountered at night (Evans-Wentz, 1911). Goblins of various sorts might also be associated with wilder locations and with the ruins of former human habitations and were known to lead people astray, either as part of a frustrating but ultimately harmless joke or to the person's eventual death (Briggs, 1967). By modern reckoning goblins fall under the dominion of the Unseelie court and may be either solitary or trooping fairies, depending on what kind of goblin is being discussed (Briggs, 1976). Hobgoblins, however, are harder to be certain of as they are usually seen as more benign and can be associated with helpful spirits like Brownies.

There is at least one well known piece of more modern literature which refers to goblins, Rossetti's poem *'The Goblin Market'*. In the poem the goblins appear in a fairly typical form being deceptive, malicious, and grotesque in appearance.

They play the usual role of a group of fairies trying to trick mortals, in this case by getting them to eat dangerous fruit. In the poem when the person the goblins are seeking to trick resists they become violent, which is also in line with the general temperament normally seen with them. Goblins play a prominent role in the film 'Labyrinth' where they are depicted more as hobgoblins, being somewhat dangerous and set against the story's heroine but overall more mischievous than actually malicious. Goblins also feature in the Harry Potter novels and movies, and while they physical resemble the goblins of folklore in those fictitious depictions they are very different in character from the traditional, being more similar to traditional depictions of dwarves with their focus on money and metalsmithing than folkloric goblins.

Ultimately goblins are a difficult group of fairies to define, being both a specific type of being and also a class of being. The word itself is just as ambiguous, the etymology uncertain beyond the 12th century, and the ultimate root unknown. The term goblin can be used to indicate a specific being which is small, grotesque and malicious or a broader category of beings that were generally described as 'imps' and ran a gamut from devilish to mischievous. When the prefix hob is added it indicates a more benign nature to the creature being discussed; Shakespeare's Puck is referred to as a HOBGOBLIN in the play 'A Midsummer Night's Dream'. However, Protestant influence did add a darker reputation even to the hobgoblin who were considered out-right demonic in some places. The only way to be certain of the usage of goblin or hobgoblin to look at the context of the reference, however, one can safely say that goblins were generally viewed as dangerous and to be feared, whatever sort of goblin was being discussed.

Notes

1 This is a revised version of an article previously printed in my book 'Fairies'.

2 Boggarts may also be angered brownies and there is a somewhat fine semantic line at times between a hobgoblin and a brownie.

Gremlins

The source of the name Gremlin for these fairies is obscure. They evolved in the modern era the Goblin was first noted during WWI when pilots began noticing their malicious antics, specifically mechanical and electrical problems with airplanes and landing strips. Gremlins are described as being anywhere between 6 inches and 2 feet tall, shagged haired, green or grey skinned, and dressed in odd but colourful clothing (Simpson & Roud, 2000). Stories of Gremlins began among Royal Air Force services men and then appear in print in 1929 spreading from there (Simpson & Roud, 1929). Gremlins may be considered a type of Goblin and often seem to enjoy their malicious pranks on humans.

Grogach

An Ulster version of the Scottish GRUAGACH, also sometimes called a Grogan. In most ways similar to its Scottish counterpart, although the Grogach is noted for its nudity. Like other types of fairies they can be driven off with a gift of clothes; in one story a well-meaning farmer's daughter gifts their Grogach a shirt only to have him leave forever because he believes they are trying to be rid of him (Briggs, 1976).

Gruagach

Fairies who is sometimes compared to the BROWNIE although the Gruagach prefers to live in barns or the wild rather than houses and will help with cattle. In older forms of Irish the word Grúacach has meanings including wise and very hairy and is glossed as a goblin. While both meanings may play into understanding this being it is possible that the 'hairy' definition is the root of the name.

The Gruagach may be either male or female, generally human-like in looks, and may appear as young and attractive, or as wizened, old, and very hairy. Highland Gruagachs are often described as blond, with the females favouring green dresses and the males being seen in either green or red (Briggs, 1976). In alternate folklore the Gruagach may be very shaggy, rather than attractive, and shun clothing. The Gruagach may be described sometimes as gigantic or ogre-like but most often is very similar to a human (MacKillop, 1998). There are a few descriptions of female Gruagachs having wet or dripping hair appearing at a household's door asking for a chance to warm up by the fire which MacKenzie suggests – and I agree – are likely a confusion between the Gruagach and Glaistig.

Female Gruagach are known to watch over cattle and were sometimes offered milk; this milk would be poured out into the natural hollow in a stone called a 'Leac na Gruagaich' [stone of the Gruagach] (Evans-Wentz, 1911). In East Bennan there is a place known as Uamh na Gruagaich [cave of the Gruagach] after the famous fairy who lived there and was renowned by the people for caring for their herds; sadly she is said to have died trying to cross the water over to Ireland after the people offended her with a gift of clothing (Carmichael, 1900).

Carmichael favours Gruagach as female but does mention at least one male Gruagach and also at least one possible[1] instance of a human and Gruagach producing a child, the folklore preserved in a song:

"'Inghean oighre Bhaile-cliath,
Cha cheilinn, a thriath nan lann,
Do ghruagach Eilean nan eun
Is ann a rug mi fein mo chlann.'
Daughter am I of the heir of Dublin,
I will not conceal, thou chief of spears,
To the gruagach of the Isle of birds
I myself bore my children."
(Carmichael, 1900, page 308).

Note

1 I will, however, emphasize possible here as the word has had enough other uses that without adequate context to ensure a fairy is being spoken of it is possible the term is being used, even if unusually, for a human.

Gwragedd Annwn

Welsh lake fairies, the name Gwragedd Annwn can be read as 'women of the Otherworld'. The Gwragedd Annwn are fairy women who live in lakes and are almost always associated in stories with fairy cows inhabiting the same bodies of water. The singular would be Gwraig Annwn, woman of the Otherworld.

Gwragedd Annwn appear as young attractive women, often living in lakes and herding cattle in and out of the water. Stories of them often focus on their role as FAIRY WIVES after being won by a mortal man. A fairly typical example of the story tells of a man who wishes to court a beautiful Gwraig Annwn he has seen herding her cattle near a lake by his property. In order to win her he must bake bread which is neither to hard not too soft; once she accepts it the couple may wed and she brings many fairy cows with her as dowry but with the caveat that should he ever strike her three times needlessly she will immediately leave. This he eventually does over the course of several years, giving her a soft hit for things like laughing at a funeral and crying at a birth. As soon as the third blow is struck, no matter its gentleness, the fairy wife immediately leaves taking all her cows with her but not the half-human children she has had during her time with her mortal husband. The most famous example of this type of story may come with the Physicians of Myddfai, recounted in multiple sources, who were said to be the greatest healers in Wales and to have gained their healing knowledge from a Gwraig Annwn ancestress. When married to a human man they are reputed to be good wives and mothers to any children they have, and while they may be compelled to leave they remain connected to these children afterwards, particularly by teaching them (Briggs, 1976).

The Gwragedd Annwn may appear in their own distinct folklore but are also sometimes conflated with the TYLWYTH TEG, and may perhaps simply be female Tylwyth Teg appearing under a specific name. For example, this anecdote appears in 'Fairy Faith in Celtic Countries' and describes the women in the story as Tylwyth Teg yet they fulfil all the characteristics of Gwragedd Annwn:

> *"There is a lake called Llyn y Morwynion, or "Lake of the Maidens ", near Festiniog, where, as the story goes, a farmer one morning found in his field a number of very fine cows such as he had never seen before. Not knowing where they came from, he kept them a long time, when, as it happened, he committed some dishonest act and, as a result, women of the Tylwyth Teg made their appearance in the pasture and, calling the cows by name, led the whole herd into the lake, and with them disappeared beneath its waters."* (Evans-Wentz, 1911, page 144).

Gwyllion

Gwyllion are a kind of female mountain fairy in Wales. Wirt Sikes describes them in his book, 'British Goblins', as dangerous to travellers and eager to lead people astray and harass those who travel alone. They might also sometimes avail themselves of the hospitality of a human home during stormy weather, and it was considered better to let them than to try to drive them out (Briggs, 1976). The surest method to drive off Gwyllion was cold iron, that is a bared iron knife, which would quickly cause them to flee, Sikes refers to this as "exorcism by knife" (Sikes, 1880).

Gwyn ap Nudd

A Welsh mythic and folkloric figure appearing in Arthurian and Mabinogion related lore. He initially appears in writing as a being imprisoned in the Underworld and bound to keep dangerous creatures from getting free and destroying humanity but over time he shifts into the role of a Fairy King (Briggs, 1976). Briggs refers to him as leader of the PLANT ANNWN, who she describes as specifically underworld fairies, while MacKillop credits him as being king of the TYLWYTH TEG more generally.

Gwyn's name means, roughly, 'White (or Blessed) son of Nudd'. He is described as leading a hunt including a pack of red-eared white fairy hounds, and having a face that is blackened (MacKillop, 1998).

In Arthurian stories Arthur commits Gwyn to fighting every Calan Mai [May 1st] for Creiddylad against Gwythyr fab Greidawl. In later folklore some believe that Gwyn supplants Arawn as king of the Welsh fairies.

H

Hags

As discussed here, found largely in English lore, Hags represent one type of dangerous water fairy known to haunt rivers and drown the unwary. Although Hags can be considered a general grouping they most often appear in folklore under specific names, notably Jenny Greenteeth, Peg Powler, and Black Annis.

Hags appear in the form of old women, thin and frightening looking, with long fingers and sharp nails. They are known to lurk in or near rivers and reach out and grab unwary passers by, especially children, and drag them into the water to drown them (Cox, 1904).

Hags are one type of fairy that is not averse to or warded off by iron, and iron will do nothing to protect a person from these beings. At least one Hag, Black Annis, is described with iron claws (Briggs, 1976).

Hagstones

Also called holed stones, holey stones, or witch stones; hagstone is common name for stones with naturally occurring holes that transect the entire stone. The hole in the stone must be natural and cannot be manmade to be effective as a charm. The name hagstone is derived from their use in preventing malicious night time assaults by fairies and witches, sometimes referred to as being 'Hag ridden[1]', and dates back to at least the 18th century as such (Simpson & Roud, 2000). Hagstones are strung on twine or thread and hung over beds or in stables to prevent magical attacks and to keep the fairies from riding a person or animal. They may also be carried by a person for the same effect.

Note

1 See the entry on Måran for more on being hag ridden.

Hares

A form sometimes assumed by fairies, particularly to steal milk from cows in the field.

Hobs

Found in English folklore a Hob is a kind of smaller, hairy fairy that can be associated with either farms or wilderness and which is normally helpful but can be dangerous if angered. Some Hobs are described wearing ragged clothing while others are said to be naked. The name itself, despite modern folk etymologies, has no connections to the word hearth instead being a historic nickname for 'Robin' or 'Robert' that was used as a slang for a foolish country-dweller (Simpson & Roud, 2000). This term came in later centuries to be attributed to supernatural beings, including Hobs, Hobgoblins, and Hobithrusts.

Hobs were known to live in human habitations and like some other fairies could be viewed as more of a general category than a specific; BROWNIES are often considered a type of HOB or a type of HOBGOBLIN, for example. The domestic ones were believed to be lucky to a household, but the ones who lived in more wild areas could be more ambiguous. One Hob who lived in a cave, or 'Hobhole', in Runswick Bay had a reputation for curing Whooping cough and parents would bring their children to the cave and recite a short chant to the Hob asking for this cure (Briggs, 1976; Simpson & Roud, 2000). Another, malicious Hob, near Hurworth named Hob Headless plagued the roadway until he was finally bound beneath a stone near the road for 99 years (Briggs, 1976).

A Hob could become a nuisance if annoyed and it was possible to anger them enough to make them dangerous (Simpson & Roud, 2000). Banishing a troublesome Hob was a difficult proposition and the Hob that was successfully bound into the stone is unusual.

Hobgoblins

Hobgoblins are a type of fairy which, like GOBLINS, are more of a sub-category than a true group themselves. The name 'hobgoblin' is a composite of two words 'hob' and 'goblin'. Goblin has been previously discussed in a separate section. Hob comes from the Old English hobbe which was a nickname for Robin or Robert and was used a synonym for elf with a connotation of trouble making (Harper, 2018). The use of the name Hob goes back to the 13th century, and appear a century later sometimes by itself as the name of a supernatural being (Simpson & Roud, 2000) Hobgoblin is found dating back to at least the 16th century; the name is strongly tied to the character of Robin Goodfellow. Hence a hobgoblin was a fairy who was less malicious than mischievous in nature (Harper, 2018)

Hobgoblins generally occupy a rather grey area being neither trooping fairies nor entirely solitary fairies either, but may move between the two categories. In the same way they are also difficult to clearly define as either Seelie or Unseelie because they are neither clearly benevolent nor overtly malicious towards humans. Their pranks may be generally harmless and they can even be inclined to helpful behaviour yet they may also sometimes be dangerous as well. In the older folklore they are viewed more positively with Shakespeare's Puck in 'A Midsummer Night's Dream' being referred to by a fellow fairy as a hobgoblin, with the statement that:

> *"Those that hobgoblin call you and sweet Puck; You do their work, and they will have good luck."* (Shakespeare, 2004).

This would seem to imply that calling him a hobgoblin is a way to earn his amity, yet later sources, especially in Puritan America, would align hobgoblins with devils and demons (Briggs, 1976). The truth of their nature may lie somewhere in the middle, with the hobgoblin being less malicious than a goblin but more difficult to deal with than some other more clearly benevolent fairies.

Some fairies that fall into the category of Hobgoblins include: Puck, Robin Goodfellow, Púcas, Brownies, Hobithrusts, Lobs, Pixies, Gruagachs, Fenodyrees, Boggarts, and Will'o'the'Wisps (Briggs, 1976). Many of these are overtly trickster fairies known for their ambivalent natures and mercurial antics, which may tell us much about the nature of hobgoblins.

Hospitality

There are certain expectations of hospitality to fairies and which may be assumed to extend from fairies as well.

In one tale from Scotland a woman who asks for a drink while crossing a fairy hill is punished for refusing it:

> *"'Two women were walking toward the Point when one of them, hearing churning going on under a hillock, expressed aloud a wish for some buttermilk. No sooner had she spoken than a very small figure of a woman came out with a bowlful and offered it to her, but the thirsty woman, ignorant of fairy customs and the penalty attending their infringement, declined the kind offer of refreshment, and immediately found herself a prisoner in the hillock. She was led to an apartment containing a chest full of meal and a great bag of wool, and was told by the fairy that when she had eaten all the meal and spun all the wool she would be free to return to her home. The prisoner at once set herself to eating and spinning assiduously, but without apparent result, and despairing of completing the task."* (Evans-Wentz, 1911, page 96).

In a similar story two men are near a fairy hill and hear activity within and one asks for a share of the baking only to see small cakes appear on the hillside. One man eats and the other doesn't because he fears to eat fairy food but the man who eats has great luck afterwards. In these cases it seems that exempts this from the regular rules relating to fairy food is that the human explicitly asked for the food before it was offered.

Some degree of offering hospitality to the fairies is self-defence as well. It is said in Scotland that the fairies can enter homes unless they are well defended and when they do if they do not find water left out for their use they will take blood from the human inhabitants in its place (Campbell, 1900). There are several accounts of fairies that may come seeking a welcome into a home, particularly in bad weather and who it would be bad luck to refuse; these include the Fear Dearg, Gwyllion, Trows, and Glashtin. Several Irish folktales and anecdotal accounts mention the fairies coming into homes at night and expecting a pleasant welcome, including fresh water left out, a bit of food, and a nicely banked fire.

House Fairies

A class of fairy rather than a specific individual being house fairies would be any type of fairy that prefers to live in or closely around human homes. House fairies under various names can be found across not only Celtic language speaking cultures but also in every culture that has beings analogous to fairies. These encounters, descriptions, and offerings given are widely the same across cultures, even those with only tenuous connections to each other, indicating that it is the human home not the spirits dwelling in it which is the significant factor (Lecouteux, 2000).

Like fairies more generally it is difficult to define exactly what a house fairy is, with a wide array of beings including former deities, spirits-of-place, human ancestors, and Otherworldly beings all filling the roles of house fairies in different stories. Significant dates to offer to these beings often fall at the same times as holidays honouring the Gods or the dead, reinforcing this crossover between the groups (Lecouteux, 2000). Folklore and anecdotes about house fairies are more common in rural settings but can also be found in suburban and urban areas.

They are petitioned with food offerings and often with milk

given on a regular basis and are known to become angry or to leave a home if the quality of their work is insulted or they are offered something they find offensive, often including clothing. When they are pleased or are in harmony with the home they live in they will act in the house's best interests and to aid the family living there, cleaning up around the building and caring for livestock as well as helping to bring in the harvest. When angered they become destructive and work against the same things they previously nurtured, damaging the home and destroying crops.

Huldufolk

Meaning 'Hidden folk' an Icelandic term that can indicate a specific type of being, may be used as an equivalent for the ÁLFAR, and may also be used as a general term for all fairy-like beings. Huldufolk are believed to live in a world similar to the Celtic Otherworld, which adjoins ours and which can be travelled to from ours. They often live in stones or boulders which folklore says it is very bad luck to disturb.

Huldra

A kind of Scandinavian fairy that looks like a very beautiful woman but always has some hidden deformity in stories; sometimes a tail, or a hollow back. The Huldrekall (male huldra) is quite ugly with a long nose.

Humans Becoming Fairies

See: Transforming to a fairy.

I

Initiation

For discussion of initiation through or with fairies see: 'DEAD, MAD, OR A POET'.

Invisibility

Although some people today may attribute this ability to newer folklore relating to fairy glamour or even see it as evidence of fairies fading from this world, the idea of fairy invisibility can be traced back over a thousand years in Irish mythology. There is evidence of the concept in Irish myth for as long as we have evidence of the fairy folk themselves in those same stories:

1. *"Síd mór i taam conid de suidib nonn ainmnigther áes síde."*

   "Cía a gillai" ol Cond fria mac acailli. úair ni acca nech in mnaí acht Condla a óenur."

   - Echtra Condla, 11th century material likely dating to the 8th century

   ["We live in the great fairy hill and are called the people of the fairy hill."

   "Who [do you speak to], oh boy?" said Conn to his son. Because no one could see the woman but Connla alone.]

2. *"Oenfer sund chucund innossa a Chucucán", ar Loég...."Acht ni saig nech (fair) & ní saig-som dana for nech, feib nacha n-aicced nech issin dúnud chethri n-ollchóiced hErend"*

   "Is fír aní sin a daltán," for se. "Cia dom chardib Sídchaire-sa..."

   -Tain Bo Cuailigne, 12th century from oral material that dates earlier

   [A single man coming towards us now, oh Cu Chulainn," said Laeg...."But none advance on him and he advances on no one, as if no one saw him in all the camp of the four grand provinces of Ireland."

"The man coming there, oh fosterling," said he, "he is to me a friend from the fairy-troop..."]

In these examples, from texts written about a thousand years ago but generally based on oral material hundreds of years older, we see people of the sidhe coming to interact with people in our world but remaining unseen by those they didn't want to be seen by. Cu Chulainn's friend among the sidhe walks through the encampment of the men of Ireland, the army who at the time was fighting against Cu Chulainn and Ulster, unimpeded and as Laeg relates unseen. Connla's fairy woman, who has come to court him and tempt him to join her in the sidhe, appears next to him and talks to him but only he can see and hear her until she chooses to speak to his father Conn as well[1]. There are other similar stories in other texts, including the appearance of a rider from the fairy mounds to Etain in the 'Tochmarc Etaine' and of the fairy woman Fidelm in the 'Tain Bo Cúailgne'. In the exact same way we find tales in later folklore of people of the fairy hills who appear to specific people but not others or who can choose who sees them in our world.

We find this power to go unseen among the Tuatha Dé Danann as well as the fairy folk, but there is some persuasive evidence that it is an ability that the fairies had first. This power seems to have come to the Tuatha Dé Danann from their connection to the Good Neighbours and particularly from Manannán's gift of the Féth Fiadha. The Féth Fiadha is a magical mist or veil, likely a type of enchantment, which hides those under its power by making them invisible or otherwise deceiving the sight of those who looked at them so they were hidden. We find a discussion of this in the story 'Altram Tige Dá Medar' where the Féth Fiadha is given to the Tuatha Dé Danann by Manannán so that they *"could not be seen"* and he also teaches them *"to carry on their mansions in the manner of the people of the fair-sided Land of Promise and fair Emhain Ablach"* (Dobs, 1929). Manannán is also the one in that version of the story who allocated the sidhe to the Tuatha Dé Danann and decided who would live where. From this we can safely gather that it was Manannán who taught the Tuatha Dé Danann to live among the Fairy folk after they were forced into the sidhe by the Gaels. We may also perhaps conclude that it was the Daoine sidhe, through Manannán, who taught the Tuatha Dé Danann how to move unseen and how to live in the sidhe, not the other way around.

Rev. Kirk in the 17th century wrote about the fairies' ability to pass unseen, saying that they could *"...appear or disappear at pleasure"* (Kirk & Lang, 1893, page 5). This shows both the continuity of the belief as well as the widespread nature of it. In anecdotal accounts from the 18th and 19th century those with the Second Sight are sometimes said to be able to see the Good People and relate their activities to other humans nearby when those others cannot see or perceive the fairies themselves. Modern anecdotes and folklore also relate the ability of the Slua Sidhe specifically and the Good People more generally to pass unseen, sometimes with the sound of voices or bells or with an unusual whirlwind.

Ultimately the evidence we have from Irish mythology shows us that the idea of the Fair Folk going unseen, or being selectively seen, can be traced back in writing at least 1,000 years. If we accept scholars' assertions that the oldest text discussed here, the 'Echtra Condla', can be further backdated based on language to the 7th century[2] then we are looking at a 1,400 year old story of a fairy woman who was seen by one person in a crowd. The ability by the Good People to make themselves invisible is one that is not only deeply ingrained in their mythology and folklore, but even seems to be something they taught to the Irish Gods.

Notes

1 Later in the story Conn's druid is able through magic to temporarily hide her entirely from Connla so that she cannot

keep courting him, but he is apparently unable to force her to reveal herself.

2 Some scholars feel the 8th or 9th century is more likely while others argue for dates as early as the 7th. See Beveridge 'Children into Swans' and Oskamp's 'Echtra Condla' in Etudes Celtiques 14 for further discussion on dating of this manuscript.

Iron

Iron is the most often referenced protection against fairies although it is not ubiquitous. Several types of fairies are or appear to be immune to it and a few others make use of it themselves like the RED CAP which is said to wear iron toed shoes. Despite that iron is known to ward off many kinds of fairy beings as well as human ghosts and some other types of malevolent spirits.

Rev. Kirk asserts that there is nothing that frightens dangerous spirits more than this metal, speculating that it is because iron is found in the earth and by its location reminds these beings of their fate in Hell1 (Kirk & Land, 1893). Even those fairies who are considered helpful or are choosing to be around humans, including some FAIRY WIVES, may be driven off by iron (Evans-Wentz, 1911).

Isobel Gowdie

One of the most famous and controversial of the Scottish witches, Isobel Gowdie lived in the 17th century and was brought to trial for practicing witchcraft. Unlike other accused witches Isobel by some accounts seemed to have confessed voluntarily and certainly did so in great detail, admitting not only to the stereotypical activities expected of European diabolic witches but also of consorting with fairies, feasting with the Queen and King of Elfland, and being given elfshot by the fairies which she was told to use against other humans.

Isobel claimed to have done as much good as harm with her magic, unusual in a time when people brought to trial tended to either defend themselves as helpful cunningfolk or capitulate entirely under torture and confess to doing great harm (Wilby, 2005). Her stories of meeting with the monarchy of Fairy and her descriptions of the Queen and King are in line with wider folklore of the time period.

Jack in Irons

A Yorkshire giant who appears to travellers at night. The Jack in Irons gets his name from his appearance, wrapped in iron chains (Briggs, 1976).

Jimmy Squarefoot

A Manx fairy who can appear as either a giant boar or a man with a pig's head and tusks. Originally Jimmy Squarefoot in his pig form was the steed of an unnamed giant but at some point the giant and his wife left the Isle of Man, and Jimmy remained behind (Gill, 1929). Briggs describes him as having both the form of a black pig and a human-like man and lurking in the area of Glen Rushen (Briggs, 1976). Gill felt Jimmy had some connection to water, although what exactly he could not clarify, and suggested his home might be at a stone circle near Awin Reash.

Although known sometimes to leap out and frighten travellers and to throw stones at his own wife, Jimmy Squarefoot was generally a benign creature.

Joint Eater

An obscure fairy mentioned by rev. Robert Kirk in his seminal work 'The Secret Commonwealth' where it is described as an invisible elf that can exist within a person and consumes the essence or value of any food the person eats. Kirk calls it an Elf, a Joint Eater and a Just Halver and says that it is the attendant of something called a 'Great-Eater', describing it thusly:

> *"...feeding on the pith or quintessence of what the man eats; and that therefore he continues lean like a hawk or heron, notwithstanding his devouring appetite."* (Kirk & Land, 1890, page 71).

Briggs considers the Alp Luachra and Joint Eater to be different names for the same beings and suggest the cure used for the Alp Luachra would apply as well for the Joint Eater that is feeding the afflicted person salted beef and then having them wait with open mouth near water until the creature is lured out (Briggs, 1976).

Kelpies

One type of water horse found in Scotland and Ireland is the Kelpie. Often described in Scottish older sources as a water-demon the Kelpie is a shape shifting fairy who can assume the form of a horse or of a dark-haired person, usually but not always a man. As a horse he is appealing and fine-looking, with a coat that is either very dark or white. As a person he would seem human except that his hair remains damp and may have water weeds in it if one looks closely.

Kelpies are most associated with running water, such as rivers, and with lakes (Allen, 1952; Briggs, 1976). In many stories the Kelpie lurks near their watery home in the form of a horse waiting for a traveller to pass by and then tries to trick the human into riding on the Kelpie's back. Once mounted the person finds they are unable to let go of the magical being and are carried into the water where the Kelpie drowns and then eats them. As 18th century poet Robert Burns puts it:

> *"Then, water-kelpies haunt the foord,*
> *By your direction,*
> *An' nighted trav'llers are allur'd*
> *To their destruction"*
> (Burns, 1786).

Kelpies are known in their human form to take human lovers and sometimes to produce children with them. These human lovers may or may not be willing and the lore surrounding them is complex and sometimes dark. Not all accounts fall along these lines, however, and there is at least one where the Kelpie seems to genuinely love the girl and chooses to give up his Otherworldly life for her. In that story the girl realizes his true nature and traps him with a silver bridle, forcing him to work in his horse form on her father's farm for a year before he is given the choice to give up his fairy nature and marry her (McNeill, 2000).

Also see: Each Uisce

King Orfeo

Also sometimes known as 'Sir Orfeo' a poem that is compiled from three main manuscripts dating between the early 14th and late 15th centuries. The poem itself is an intriguing blend of the Greek myth of Orpheus and a Celtic tale of a man retrieving his wife from the fairies who have stolen her. The following version comes from Childs 19th century ballad collection with the language updated from Norn to modern English.

There lived a king in the east,
Refrain: Early green's the wood
There lived a lady in the west.
Refrain: Where goes the doe yearly
This king he has a hunting gone,
He's left his Lady Isabel alone.
'Oh I wish you'd never gone away,
For at your home is misery and woe.
'For the king of Fairy with his dart,
Has pierced your lady to the heart.'

And after them the king has gone,
But when he came there was a grey stone.
Then he took out his pipes to play,
But sore his heart with misery and woe.
And first he played the notes of grief,
And then he played the notes of joy.
And then he played the good rollicking reel,
That could have made a sick heart healthy.

Now come you into our hall,
And come you in among us all.
Now he's gone into the hall,
And he's gone in among them all.
Then he took out his pipes to play,
But sore his heart with misery and woe.
And first he played the notes of grief,
And then he played the notes of joy.
And then he played the good rollicking reel,
That could have made a sick heart healthy.
'Now tell to us what you will have:
What shall we give you for your play?'
'What I will have I will you tell,
And that's me Lady Isabel.'
'Yes take your lady, an yes go home,
And yes be king over all your own.'
He's taken his lady, and he's gone home,
And now he's king over all his own.
(Child, 1898, language updated)

Knowe

A Scots word, a variant of the English word knoll, indicating a small hill. In folklore something akin to the Irish SIDHE. Often associated with fairies as their homes or entrances to the Otherworld.

L

La Belle Dame sans Merci

A poem by John Keats written in 1819 and then revised in 1820. The poem describes the more dangerous sort of LEANNAN SIDHE, a fairy lover who seduces a human knight and then leaves him to pine away for want of her.

"O what can ail thee, knight-at-arms,
Alone and palely loitering?
The sedge has withered from the lake,
And no birds sing.
O what can ail thee, knight-at-arms,
So haggard and so woe-begone?
The squirrel's granary is full,
And the harvest's done.
I see a lily on thy brow,
With anguish moist and fever-dew,
And on thy cheeks a fading rose
Fast withereth too.
I met a lady in the meads,
Full beautiful—a faery's child,
Her hair was long, her foot was light,
And her eyes were wild.
I made a garland for her head,
And bracelets too, and fragrant zone;
She looked at me as she did love,
And made sweet moan
I set her on my pacing steed,
And nothing else saw all day long,
For sidelong would she bend, and sing
A faery's song.
She found me roots of relish sweet,

And honey wild, and manna-dew,
And sure in language strange she said—
'I love thee true'.
She took me to her Elfin grot,
And there she wept and sighed full sore,
And there I shut her wild wild eyes
With kisses four.
And there she lullèd me asleep,
And there I dreamed—Ah! woe betide!—
The latest dream I ever dreamt
On the cold hill side.
I saw pale kings and princes too,
Pale warriors, death-pale were they all;
They cried—'La Belle Dame sans Merci
Thee hath in thrall!'
I saw their starved lips in the gloam,
With horrid warning gapèd wide,
And I awoke and found me here,
On the cold hill's side.
And this is why I sojourn here,
Alone and palely loitering,
Though the sedge is withered from the lake,
And no birds sing."

Lady Isobel and the Elf Knight

A Ballad about the consequences when a woman wishes for an elven lover.

Fair lady Isabel sits in her bower sewing,
Yes as the daisies grow gay
There she heard an elf-knight blowing his horn.
The first morning in May
'If I had yonder horn that I hear blowing,

And yonder elf-knight to sleep in my bosom.'
This maiden had scarcely these words spoken,
Till in at her window the elf-knight has leapt.
'It's a very strange matter, fair maiden,' said he,
'I cannot blow my horn but you call on me.
'But will you go to yonder greenwood's edge?
If you cannot go, I will cause you to ride.'
He leapt on a horse, and she on another,
And they rode on to the greenwood together.
'Light down, light down, lady Isabel,' said he,
'We are come to the place where you are to die.'
'Have mercy, have mercy, kind sir, on me,
Till once my dear father and mother I see.'
'Seven king's-daughters here have I slain,
And you shall be the eighth of them.'
'0 sit down a while, lay your head on my knee,
That we may have some rest before that I die.'
She stroked him so fast, the nearer he did creep,
With a small charm she lulled him fast asleep.
With his own sword-belt so fast she bound him,
With his own dagger so grievously she struck him.
'If seven king's-daughters here you have slain,
Lie you here, a husband to them all.'

Leannán Sídhe

The Leannán Sídhe appears across several different Celtic language speaking cultures with each culture having its own slight variation. The name in any language translates to 'fairy lover'[1] and there are two similar but different kinds of being to whom the name is applied in folklore. The first is a more straightforward use of the term, where it simply refers to any fairy being who takes a human lover. The second seems to be a more distinct kind of fairy in its own right that preys on humans. Both kinds of Leannán Sidhe can be dangerous to humans in their own ways, however.

The more well-known Leannán Sí was popularized by the writing of WB Yeats and stories of that being can be found across folklore of the 19th and 20th century. The name may be Anglicized to its more phonetic form of 'Leanan Shee' and can be found under various spellings reflecting that. According to Yeats this spirit would seduce humans, especially poets or artists, and inspire their creativity while feeding on their life force. The only way to escape the predatory Leannán Sidhe was to find another person for her to attach herself to, otherwise you would be bound to her even after death (Yeats, 1888). Although a person who had such a Leannán Sidhe would reach great artistic heights and produce amazing works their life would be short and end abruptly, as the fairy would drain them to death while they were still young. Allegedly anyone who was able to resist the seduction of this fairy would find her bound to him instead (Yeats, 1888). In the Isle of Man this fairy is called the Lhiannan-Shee and haunted the areas around springs and wells where she would live unseen except by the man she lured into her affections who she would feed on until his death (Briggs, 1976).

Stories of these predatory Leannán Sídhe focus on an exceptionally beautiful fairy woman who seduces a mortal man and once she has him under her sway drains his life. In the Irish folklore the man is willing to do this for the inspiration he gets in return, while in the Manx lore the only thing the man gets is the Lhiannan-Shee's company. Neither of these beings are literally vampiric although they do appear to feed on human life energy, but we do find something closer to a true vampire in the Scottish Baobhan Sith, which has some similarities to the Leannán Sidhe.

The second type of Leannán Sidhe is straightforward, a fairy who chooses a human lover, but is less often discussed particularly in modern folklore. Campbell in 'The Gaelic Otherworld' describes this type of Leannán Sidhe as a type of familiar spirit and relates it directly to the tradition. Although less popular in modern tales this type of fairy lover is not uncommon in folklore and is seen often enough that Katherine Briggs in her book 'Fairies in Tradition and Literature' devotes an entire chapter to this type of Leannán Sídhe. With this type of fairy lover they may or may not seek to take the human partner out of the mortal world, and may or may not produce offspring with the human partner in stories.

The most well-known example of this type of Leannán Sídhe may be from the Fenian Cycle in Irish mythology, the story of Niamh and Oisin. In this tale Fionn's son Oisin is approached one day by a woman from fairy named Niamh who wants him to go with her into the Otherworld. He chooses to go to Tír na nÓg with her, and the two live happily for a time. Niamh bears Oisin two children but this new family isn't enough to keep him content and eventually he tells her that he wants to visit Ireland and see his family again. Niamh warns him that if he goes he must not get off his horse for any reason or touch the earth. When he reaches Ireland he finds out that everyone he knows has died and his old companions are considered legends among the people now. Before he can return to the Otherworld he sees some men struggling to move a heavy stone which he knows he could easily lift so he leans over in his saddle to help them, only to have the girth come loose and drop him to the ground. As soon as he touches mortal earth he ages quickly, only having time to relate his story before dying.

Other examples can be found in mythology and folklore of these types of beings as well, often blurring the lines between fairies and divine ancestry of family lines. In most cases if a child is produced the family will later trace its decent back to that spirit, such as the Fitzgeralds' tracing their ancestry to the fairy Queen Áine who was a lover of the earl of Desmond. The McCarthy's are said to be descendants of the Fairy Queen Clíodhna, and by some accounts the O'Brien's are connected to the fairy Queen Aoibheall through her love of one of their male ancestors.

Folklore also speaks of fairy lovers who may not necessarily produce children into a human line but become attached enough to it to follow it or watch over it. Some versions of the story of clan MacLeod's Fairy Flag say that it was a gift from a fairy lover. It is not infrequent in stories for a fairy lover to give a family line they are part of a special item or token as a sign of favour. The Fletcher family on the Isle of Man had a cup that had been given to them by a Lhiannan-Shee and they had a custom of drinking from it once a year (Briggs, 1976).

Humans who have a Leannán Sidhe may stay in the mortal world but are changed by their relationship with their fairy lover, usually becoming more secretive and shunning human love. The secrecy may have a good reason behind it, as Leannán Sidhe seem more than other types of fairies to require strict secrecy of those who would keep them, and losing one is has consequences for the mortal.[2] In one tale from Scotland a young woman went mad after losing her Leannán Sidhe, something which happened because she made the mistake of trusting her sister with her secret only to have her sister repeat the story to others (Briggs, 1967).

In other cases the human lover might be taken by the fairy lover into the Otherworld. There is a story from Ireland of a young man who had a fairy lover and was taken by her on Bealtaine; his family hired a fairy doctor who tried for 9 days and nights to secure the youth's return until on the ninth night he appeared and told his family he had married his fairy lover and wanted to stay with her in the sidhe (Briggs, 1967). Often when Leannán Sidhe are involved like this the human partner is simply taken from the mortal world much as other stolen humans are – although voluntarily – seeming to die but actually going to live among the Good People. In the stories where the human partner stays in our world but sees their Leannán Sídhe regularly they are often required to keep their secret or lose them, as mentioned in the above Scottish example. As with all things, however, there are various versions and exceptions to be found.[3]

It is not always the fairy who is courting the human and we do have folklore exploring the other side of the equation. Several folk songs are predicated on the attempts by mortals to win the heart of a fairy lover, including Scarborough Fair, which is based on older folk ballads including The Elfin Knight. In the oldest versions of the Elfin Knight the girl wishes for an elfin knight as a lover or husband and he responds with a list of seemingly impossible tasks she must first accomplish. Just as we see in discussion of fairies courting mortals going badly, however, there are also stories of mortal attempts that go awry. Lady Isabel and the Elf Knight tells the story of a woman who wishes for an elf knight on Bealtaine morning only to have him appear and kidnap her to a greenwood where he tells her that he is going to kill her as he has seven other king's daughters before her. She tricks him into falling asleep, binds him with his own sword belt, and kills him with his own dagger before escaping. In other versions along the same lines there are ballades where a girl wishes for an elfin knight only to have her would be lover threaten to drown her so that she must try to save herself by outwitting him. These stories may represent a warning to humans to be cautious in wishing for a fairy lover, although generally when such relationships end badly it is due to the fairy abandoning the human because of a broken prohibition, notably the aforementioned secrecy taboo.

Another famous example of a fairy lover going wrong for the human partner may be found in Keats poem *'La Belle Dame sans Merci'*. The poem tells the story of a knight who crossed paths with a fairy woman who took him *'to her elfin grotto'* and by implication became his lover. Afterwards the fairy disappeared leaving the knight to wander forever searching for her. This may be an example of the more directly harmful kind of Leannán Sí where she took some vital essence form her lover or an example of the second kind where she was merely a lover of the human knight but abandoned him for an unknown reason. As with the other anecdotal example once abandoned the knight pines away without his fairy lover. Looking at these stories and ballads we can see the challenges and difficulties this sort of Leannán Sídhe presents, as they may not always be as overtly dangerous as the first sort but they can often lead a person to the same eventual end.

Not all instances of humans with fairy lovers end badly for the human though, as some tales do make it clear that the non-human half of the pairing genuinely cares for the human partner. In accounts where a male Leannán Sidhe had a human lover he would try take care of her and if she had children with him he would make efforts to care for them as well (Campbell, 1900). Both of the following examples involve Kelpies. In one Irish tale a Kelpie loves a girl but is tricked into becoming a beast of burden on her father's farm after she finds out his true nature. After a year of such work the girl and her family consult a fairy doctor who asks the Kelpie if he would choose to be a mortal man so he in turn asks the girl if she still wants to marry him[4]; she says yes and he chooses to become mortal so the two are married (McNeill, 2001). In a less cheerful story from Scotland a Kelpie falls in love with a mortal woman and courts her. They wed and she bears him a son, but one day she realizes his true nature and flees. Heartbroken the Kelpie remains in their small home, raising their child, and waiting futilely for her to return.

Some bean feasa were also known to have Leannán Sídhe, as in the case of Eibhlin Ni Ghuinniola, about whom it was said "*a 'fairy lover', a leannán sí, was often seen with [her] as she gathered plants*". (O Crualaoich, 2003, p. 191). It was believed in such cases that it was through this connection to the Otherworld that these women gained their knowledge of magic and cures, although a Leannán Sídhe was not always involved with the wise women. Some then could maintain a relationship with a fairy lover and also remain at least for a time in our world and would benefit from the knowledge gained from their fairy associations.

Those who have a Leannán Sidhe that they do not want may find that getting rid of them is not an easy proposition. Leannán Sidhe are more difficult to drive off than other types of fairies, perhaps because the human partner initially agreed to the situation meaning that there is an implicit contract involved between the two. Breaking this is not a simple process and many examples of people who tried to flee a Leannán Sidhe show that only extreme measures are effective. Simply trying to run away does nothing, as shown by the anecdote of the man who tried moving to America to get away from the fairy lover who was draining him, only to have her follow him across the sea (Evans-Wentz, 1911). There is an Irish example of an exorcism[5] specifically aimed at removing a Leannán Sidhe from a woman, showing that in some cases they would be treated in the same way as demons and driven off, theoretically, with full rites of exorcism by a priest. In a Manx account we see a man who went with a fairy woman to a strange dance and afterwards she would appear next to his bed at night; the only way he could get her to leave was to throw an unbleached piece of linen over her head (Evans-Wentz, 1911). In that case the fairy woman couldn't be entirely driven off but could be held at bay with the cloth, which seems to have been significant because it was unbleached.

As we can see the threads of myth and folklore provide two distinct but perhaps intertwined views of the Leannán Sí. The Leannán Sí as a distinct being seduces and inspires, gives creativity but drains away life. The related beings like the Gean-cánach and Baobhan Sith similarly use their beauty and appeal to gain lovers whom they destroy in the taking, feeding on either their life force or blood. In contrast the more general fairy lovers may bless or ruin their human lover, may steal them from this world, abandon them to it, or be constant companions. One is a more overtly malevolent, seductive figure which is a distinct type of being in its own right; the other a more ambiguous term applied to different beings which in its own way embodies all that Fairy itself is - alluring, sometimes dangerous, sometimes generous.

Notes

1 To be absolute clear here because English can be annoying, 'fairy lover' meaning a lover who is a member of Fairy, not a human who loves fairies.

2 Breaking this taboo of secrecy only works in the case of Leannán Sidhe that a person wishes to keep; when one is trying to be rid of a Leannán Sidhe revealing their existence seems to have no effect. As can be seen in the section on exorcism of fairies which provides an example specifically of an exorcism of a Leannán Sidhe being rid of a fairy lover is a very difficult process indeed.

3 I'm not going to address the Roan/Selkies as Leannán Sídhe because that is an entire involved topic of its own, for example, with its own rules and obligations and gets more into abductions and fairy wives/spouses.

4 Don't ask me why he still wanted to marry her at that point, I have no idea.

5 The entire text of that exorcism can be found and is discussed in detail in the section of exorcism of fairies.

Leprechauns

Leprechauns are described in various ways across folklore. In the oldest material they look much like humans, except they are said to only be about 12 to 18 inches tall. In later folklore they are described with a similar height and as looking like older men with grey or white hair and beards.

The name Leprechaun appears under various versions and spellings as far back as 1600 in English and the 8th century in Irish. The etymology of the name is uncertain, but the leading theory is that it comes from the Old Irish lúchorpan meaning a *'very small body'* (Harper, 2017). This idea is based in the word breaking down to 'lú' meaning something small and corp, a body (a loan word from Latin) and an, a diminutive ending indicating again something small. In the electronic Dictionary of the Irish Language luchorpan is defined as 'a dwarf or water-sprite' (eDIL, 2017). There is also a very popular folk etymology that says the word comes from leith-bhrogan meaning one shoe maker, however, this probably doesn't go back further than the 19th or 18th century.

The first Irish appearance of Leprechauns - then called 'lúcurpan' - is in the Echtrae Fergusso Mac Léiti. In this story we see the protagonist interacting with the Leprechauns or more specifically they interact with him by kidnapping him while he sleeps. This story along with the related Aided Fergusso mac Leidi establishes Leprechauns as small people and also makes it clear that there are both men and women among them. This story also establishes a connection between the Leprechauns and water, as they both try to drag Fergus into the sea while he is sleeping and then, after he wakes up and captures several of them, agree to give him the power to travel under water without drowning. In the Aided Fergusso mac Leidi we see Fergus meeting the king of the Ulster Leprechauns Lubhdán and the queen Bé Bó after they journey to Emhain Macha and are captured. Although the Leprechauns cause Fergus great trouble trying to force him to free their king - stealing all the milk of the province, burning the mills, and blighting the corn - Fergus and Bé Bó would become lovers and Lubhdán would later give Fergus a poem that advised him on which trees to burn and which not to burn, as well as the associations of some of the trees.

An aspect of uncertainty with Leprechauns is whether they are their own type of fairy or are rather a general type that can include variations. In the older folklore and mythology it is plain that the Leprechauns are their own group of people, distinct in both appearance and powers from the Daoine Sí. In later folklore the word was often used as a generic term indicating all small fairies, and conflated with the other fairies who had by then been diminished. Some writers like W. B. Yeats felt that the Leprechaun, Clúracán and Fear Darrig were one single type of fairy manifested in different ways, with the Clúracán being more wild and prone to drunkenness and the Fear Darrig more malicious. Others like Croker view the differences between similar beings like the Leprechaun and Clúracán as regional variances in naming of the same being. For the purposes of this article we will address the Leprechaun as an individual being, but the reader should understand that it is not a clear cut subject and opinions vary. As Katherine Briggs says, *"The last thing to expect from folk tradition is consistency."* (Briggs, 1976, p266).

Descriptions of Leprechauns generally agree that they are small, as their name implies. A poem by William Allingham describes a Leprechaun as *"a span and a quarter in height."* or in other words 12 inches (Allingham, 1888). The Echtrae Fergusso mac Léiti describes them as about three 'fists' high, which one might estimate to be about the same size. The mythology gives us no indication they appear as anything but small people, saying that king Lubhdán's bard had fair hair while the king himself was dark haired, and that queen Bé Bó was beautiful enough that Fergus desired her despite her tiny size. Later folklore, however, tends to describe Leprechauns as exclusively male, old, grey or white bearded and sometimes wearing glasses (Briggs, 1972).

Allingham says the Leprechaun was plainly dressed in drab clothes, wearing an apron and with buckles on his shoes; he is sometimes described wearing a red hat as well (Briggs, 1972). In contrast Lady Wilde prefers to describe them as cheerfully dressed in green, however, this view cannot be traced back before her as far as I have been able to find. There is a good amount of 19th century folklore that describes Leprechauns wearing red, sometimes exclusively. One 20th century Irish source claims Leprechauns always wear red hats and live near fresh water springs (Evans-Wentz, 1911). This may represent legitimate folk belief, as red is a colour strongly associated with the Otherworld and red hats or shoes in particular are a common item for fairies to be described wearing. There has been some suggestion, however, that the descriptions of Leprechauns wearing only red is the result of one folklorist writing in the early 19th century so I would suggest that it is more likely that the red hat and drab outfit are closer to the truth.

In modern folklore the Leprechaun is a shoe-maker, always seen working on a single shoe. I have heard people say that the fairy has a malicious side and that he will try to trick a person into trying on the shoe, after which they will be unable to remove it and compelled to dance until they die. In more child friendly lore they say that the Leprechaun works to repair fairy shoes damaged during nights of dancing. The Leprechaun is believed to have great hordes of treasure as well as the ability to grant three wishes to anyone who captures him, but he is notoriously difficult to trap as he is very clever. In many stories a person may think they have gotten a Leprechaun only to take their eyes off of him for an instant and find he has disappeared. In some stories he blows the tobacco from his pipe or snuff into their faces in order to make them sneeze and have time to escape, Leprechauns being said to enjoy smoking pipes when they aren't cobbling shoes. In other stories he will divulge the location of his treasure which the person will mark with a handkerchief or rag only to return and find the entire area covered in identical markers.

Older folklore, via the mythology, showed us a complicated society which included monarchy, poets, bondwomen, and everything else we'd expect in Irish society at that time; basically the Leprechauns of 8th century Ireland had a society that mimicked or mirrored Irish society itself. The King of the Leprechauns was put under geasa [taboos] by his poet which led to the situation in which he was captured by Fergus, for example.

Yet modern folklore tells us that Leprechauns are solitary shoemakers who amass great treasure that can only be gained if they are captured and tricked into turning it over. Both views grant the Leprechaun power, but the newer view has lost the connection to water and sociability, while the older view lacked the hidden treasure and don't-look-away-or-he'll-be-gone idea.

One can see the disconnection between older folklore and newer in the views about whether a Leprechaun is solitary or social. The mythology paints a picture of social beings who live in a monarchy and were willing to fight to get their king back when he was captured by a human king. Yet renowned modern folklorist Katherine Briggs tells us that leprechauns are solitary fairies and when seen appear alone (Briggs, 1972). Yeats also supported the idea of Leprechauns as solitary fairies, as did many of the writers of his time, although this may be drawing heavily from a single Irish-American source, McNally's 'Irish Wonders', which lays out a great deal of Leprechaun lore that was simply repeated by other folklorists afterwards. The difficulty, of course, is that this written folklore has taken root and become the widespread modern lore of the last century and a half, which many people have believed is all of the Leprechauns story.

When we look at the folklore of Leprechauns we are presented with two very different pictures. The oldest mythology shows beings who are social, hierarchical, connected to water, and distinct from the Daoine Sídhe (although likely connected in some way). Modern folklore describes almost entirely different beings: solitary, male, earthy, and conflated with the Daoine Sídhe. In some cases we can surmise where a tidbit of folklore came from, for example the idea that capturing a Leprechaun would give a person three wishes is most likely a confusion of Fergus's story where he captured three Leprechauns trying to take him into the sea and agreed to spare their lives in exchange for a wish. In other cases, such as the idea of Leprechauns as fairy shoemakers, we are left guessing. Powerful society of diminutive water spirits or solitary earthly shoe-makers, both versions of the Leprechaun can be found in folklore. Which one represents the true picture of the Leprechaun? I leave that to the reader to decide.

Lios

See: Sidhe

Ljósálfar

Ljósálfar - their name means 'light elves' and they live in a world called Álfheim [elf home] or Ljósálfheim [light elf home] that according to mythology belongs to the Vanic deity Freyr. The Ljósálfar are described by Snorri as being beautiful and fair to see. Ljósálfar are said to influence the weather and like the Aesir, Dwarves, Humans, and Giants they possess runes given to them by Odin.

See: ALFAR for more on Icelandic elves

Lunantishee

A kind of fairy strongly associated with blackthorns. It is said they guard over blackthorns and bring bad luck to anyone who cuts the trees on 1st May or 1st November, or 11 May and 11 November the dates of Bealtaine and Samhain by the old calendar[1] (Evans-Wentz, 1911).

Note

1 Because of the switch from the Julian to the Gregorian calendar we sometimes see a dispute in traditional beliefs over whether it is the old or new date that an event occurs on or which holds the significance.

Lusmore

Or Lus Mór, the Irish word for Foxglove, is a well-known tale of the fairies that depicts both their idea of rewards and punishments, as well as gives a feel for general etiquette. A version can be found in Jacobs' 1894 'More Celtic Fairy Tales' as well as Yeats' 'Irish Fairy Tales' published in 1892.

In the story the eponymous Lusmore is a kind man with a deformed back. One night as he is returning home he grows tired and decides to sit down and rest for a while, only to unintentionally sit himself down near a fairy hill. As the moon starts to rise he hears the strains of beautiful, unearthly fairy music and is drawn to listen despite himself as the fairies begin singing "*Dé Luain, dé Máirt* [Monday, Tuesday]" over and over again. Lusmore listened carefully as the fairies sang, hearing a slight pause in the tune at the end of each line and when the time felt right he joined in singing and added "*agus dé* Céadaoin [and Wednesday]" at the end of the line. The fairies were so delighted by this new addition to their song that they immediately rose up and ushered the confused man into the fairy hill. He was feasted and entertained until he was exhausted and finally fell asleep. Upon waking the next morning outside the hill he found that his deformity was gone and his back was straight and healthy.

Now word of this cure got around and a woman whose son also had a deformed back came to hear of it. Nothing would do but that her son should also go to the fairy hill and be cured as well. So Jack went to the fairy hill and waited just as Lusmore had but as soon as the fairies started playing their music and singing Jack was out of patience and barely let them get through one verse before jumping in with '*Déardaoin, agus Dé hAoine* [Thursday and Friday]". The fairies were furious at this rude interruption and rose up in a whirlwind to pull Jack into the hill. They spun him around mercilessly and threw him our again with twice the bend in his back he'd had to start with.

The first portion of the story can also be found in the form of a song '*Dónall bocht cam*' or 'poor twisted Dónall', where we see the fairies' song being overheard by a man named Dónall who suffers from a bent back. Dónall, of course, provides the proper end to the song and is rewarded for it.

Lutins

A fairy found in the folklore of Brittany, Lutins form a counterpart to Corrigans. They are shape-shifters but it is said that their true form is a small wizened humanoid dressed in green. A solitary fairy the Lutin makes his home in a pond or lake and entertains himself by tricking those who travel nearby, sometimes taking the form of a black goat or horse (Evans-Wentz, 1911). Although mischievous and sometimes annoying to humans Lutins are generally not dangerous. Folklore says that the Corrigans and Lutins are often at war over the Lutins lenient attitude towards humans, who Corrigans can be very harsh towards (Evans-Wentz, 1911).

M

Mab

A character made famous in Shakespeare's works Mab was a Queen of the diminutive fairies in the 16th and 17th centuries. According to Shakespeare she is the fairies' midwife, punishes lazy maids, encourages dreams and lovers, and travels in a chariot drawn by insects. Mab appears in various literary works throughout the centuries and has become popular in recent urban fantasy.

Manannán

Manannán is a deity who is often associated with the Otherworld and in mythology rules over the Otherworldly kingdom of Mag Mell or Tír Tairngire. In some versions of the Gabail an t-Sida Manannán is also one of the Kings of the Tuatha De Danann and helps decide who will live in what fairy hill. He has strong ties with the Otherworld in general and to ruling over its inhabitants.

One of the deities that can be found in the mythology of several different Celtic nations is Manannán; called Manannán mac Lir (son of the sea) in Ireland, and Manawydan to the Welsh. His home was said to be the Isle of Man, called Manaw in Welsh and Manu in Irish; Manannán's name clearly derives from this and since this name for the island is a later development O hOgain posits that Manannán himself and his mythology are later developments as well, likely dating to no earlier than the 3rd century CE (O hOgain, 2006). The Irish initially borrowed the name from the Welsh, but then added the title "mac Lir" which was then borrowed into the Welsh as "map Llyr" (O hOgain, 2006). This demonstrates the composite nature of Manannán that has developed over time as the cultures shared mythology back and forth. To the Manx he was the first king of the Island of Man, and stories locate his grave there, as well as tell of how he would walk among the Manx fishermen as they repaired their nets (Monaghan, 2004).

Manannán appearance is described as being that of a handsome warrior (Berresford Ellis, 1987). Manannán's wife is Fand, a peerless beauty who at one point had an affair with Cu Chulainn, until Manannán used his magic to make Cu Chulainn forget about her and return to his own wife, Emer. It is said that Manannán travelled to the mortal world to father Mongán, a prince and hero, and under the name of Oirbsiu he may have fathered the Conmhaicne sept of Leinster (O hOgain, 2006). There are many stories about his various sons and daughters, who are usually treated as minor characters (O hOgain, 2006). One of his more well-known children is Áine, although some sources list her as his wife.

Manannán was originally said to live on the Isle of Man, a place which was seen as near mythical in Irish stories; later his home shifted fully into the Otherworld, to Eamhain (O hOgain, 2006). The Irish described Eamhain in rich detail as a sacred place, an island held up by four silver legs or pillars, on which grew magical apples which gave the island the full name of Eamhain Abhlach, Eamhain of the Apples (O hOgain, 2006). Other names for his domain include Mag Meall (the pleasant plain) and Tír Tairngire (the land of promise) (O hOgain, 2006). Each of these names and associations reflect the connection between Manannán's realm and the Otherworld.

To the Welsh Manannán - or more properly Manawydan - was a skilled craftsman and trickster deity (O hOgain, 2006). To the Irish, however, he was seen as the lord of the waves, to whom the ocean was like a field of solid land, as well as a master magician and God who could control the weather (O hOgain, 2006). The fish are said to be his livestock, compared to cows and sheep, and the waves themselves are called his horses; his most special horse is Enbharr, 'water foam', who could run over sea as if it were solid land (O hOgain, 2006). In the story of his meeting with king Cormac mac Art he is described as carrying a golden apple branch that rang with sweet music that could sooth people to sleep or heal the ill and wounded (O hOgain, 2006). Some sources consider him a shapeshifter, and his magical powers were numerous; he could travel faster than the wind could blow in his magical boat, he could create realistic illusions, and he had a cloak of forgetfulness that would take the memory from a person (Monaghan, 2004). It was this cloak that he used to cause Cu Chulainn to forget Fand in the story of the Only Jealousy of Emer.

Måran

Måran, singular Mår, appear at night, attacking people who are sleeping by paralyzing them and causing extreme fear and nightmares. Their name is the source of the word nightmare word: nightmare, night mare, a mår that comes at night. Mare is the Old English form of the Germanic word Mår; I will use Mår and Måran throughout to avoid any confusion with other meanings in English for the word mare. Although Måran are a distinct type of being in their own right the name for this type of fairy is usually translated as goblins, night-goblins, or incubi, establishing the way that they have been generally understood historically.

Like many other kinds of fairies what exactly Måran are is not always clear and whether or not they are fairies can be debated. Briggs in her 'Dictionary of Fairies' acknowledges their place in folklore under the names Mara and Mera but considers them demons. Further complicating matters in folklore some Måran are human witches who can purposely or accidentally spiritually travel to other humans at night and affect them, and Måran can be confused with a variety of other night time beings who act in a similar way, and sometimes with elves (Seo Helrune, 2017). This confusion may indicate that Måran can be a distinct group as well as a more general category into which other beings, including malicious human witches, may be included. Historically, however, they have often been categorized with goblins and occasionally conflated with elves, indicating that they belong among the fairy horde at least tangentially.

Just as ALFAR were originally all male beings the Måran are always seen as female. A Mår can be captured if a person being visited by her finds and blocks the exact place she entered the room; in folklore it was said that they lost their powers if they couldn't leave as they had entered (Ashliman, 2005). In several stories a man captured a Mår and then married her, as we see in versions of the involuntary FAIRY WIVES stories, and the Mår wife would become like any other human woman. But, like a SELKIE wife finding her hidden seal skin, if the Mår could find the place she'd entered and unblock it she would immediately leave even if it meant abandoning any children she'd had. Blocking the entrance is not the only way to trap a Mår: in one story the target of a Mår stays awake and sees a cat enter, nails the cat's paw to the floor, and by morning the cat has turned into a woman (Ashliman, 2005).

Mår usually attack individually effecting a person in their sleep by perching on their chest. The presence of a Mår causes paralysis and terror, and has been associated breathing difficulties, creating a feeling of pressure or weight on the chest. In folklore they are known to kill both people and animals (Ashliman, 2005). Explained today as sleep paralysis this was once known in some sources as being hag ridden or 'Old Hag' (Simpson & Roud, 2000; Seo Helrune, 2017).

Some people who are attacked by Måran also experience a sexual overtone to the experience which is partially why the word was translated as incubi and also possibly why they were associated with elves, who themselves were often associated with incubi. It should be noted, however, that elves or in this case specifically the Anglo-Saxon aelfe were usually male and the Måran were believed to be female beings, suggesting that we may indeed be looking at two different beings here with a similar method of attack in some cases. This idea is supported by

Alaric Hall in his article *'The Evidence for Maran: The Anglo-Saxon 'Nightmares'* in which he argues persuasively that Måran were in fact always seen as female and the translation of incubi was an early confusion between texts, and might more properly have been given as succubi.

Because attacks by Måran where not uncommon in the past there are many methods of dealing with them. Blocking the keyhole if the door has one, placing your shoes backwards – i.e. laces facing the bed - by the bed, and then climbing into bed backwards can protect you from attack; animals can be protected by placing a broom near them (Ashliman, 2005). Also Måran like many fairies, ghosts, and spirits can be warded off with iron which should be placed near or under the bed, and a HAGSTONE hung near the bed is also protective. A salve or powder can be made with herbs including Lupin, Betony and Garlic (Seo Helrune, 2017).

There are also a variety of charms to protect against Måran, such as this one which uses a single hair of the person's head to mime tying up the Mår while saying:

"The man of might
He rode at night
With neither sword
Nor food nor light,
He sought the mare,
He found the mare,
He bound the mare
With his own hair,
And made her swear
By mother's might,
That she would never bide a night
What he had trod, that man of might."
(Black, 1903; language modified from Shetland Scots)

There is also this one from Germany:

> *"I lay me here to sleep;*
> *No night-mare shall plague me,*
> *Until they swim all the waters*
> *That flow upon the earth,*
> *And count all the stars*
> *That appear in the firmament!"*
> (Ashliman, 2005).

Meg Mollach

One of the more famous brownie tales and one of the few to feature a female brownie. Her name is found under several variations including Meg Mollach, Meg Mullach. Meig Mallach, Maug Vuluchd, and Maggie Moulach, with the epithet 'molach' meaning hairy or shaggy.

The basic form of the story, which can be found in multiple sources and variations, tells of a BROWNIE who lurks in a mill. One night a young woman comes into the mill by herself and the Brownie begins to harass her, slowly edging closer, asking her what her name is. The woman tells him that her name is 'Me Myself'. The Brownie continues to edge closer and bother the woman until she panics and throws boiling water on him, scalding him terribly. The young woman flees and the mortally wounded brownie goes to Meg Mollach, either his mother or wife depending on the story, but when she questions him about who has harmed him all he can answer before dying is 'Me, Myself'. The young woman's cleverness protects her for a time until she is at a social event years later and tells the story to friends. When she is done speaking Meg Mollach appears and takes revenge for the death of her son, having overheard the unwitting confession.

A late 19th century author places Meg Mollach and her son, simply named 'Brownie', as spirits of Strathspey who were attached to a family named Grant, although he refers to them as ghosts (Forsyth, 1900). By that account the story anecdotally is dated back to 1700. Briggs in 'Folktales of England' recounts a version of the above story taking place in Perthshire where Meg Mollach is called Maggie Moulach and is referred to as a witch, although elsewhere she is clearly identified as a Brownie. In stories where Meg Mollach appears alone she acts as a typical Brownie taking on duties and chores around a farm (Briggs, 1976).

Mermaids

Mermaids are found across a wide swath of folklore and in a variety of cultures, including some Celtic language countries like Ireland, although it's possible they were imported into Western Europe from the Mediterranean. Simpson and Roud in the '*Dictionary of English Folklore*' suggest that this occurred during the medieval period and that while Celtic areas may have had mermaids prior to that they would have been tailless. As the folklore stands currently their characteristics are generally consistent. A mermaid appears as an attractive human woman from the waist up and a fish from the waist down, and is usually described with a mirror or comb.

Mermaids may appear in either salt or fresh water and there are several tales, like '*The Laird of Lorntie*', which feature fresh water mermaids who are otherwise indistinguishable from the ocean variety. In the sea they are seen by sailors on outcroppings of rock in the ocean, sometimes disappearing before they can be approached sometimes luring ships into shallow water where they are wrecked. They sing and their voices as much as their appearance draw men to their doom; they can also be omens of storms and bad weather (Briggs, 1976).

While modern mermaids, much like other modern fairies, are often romanticized into more gentle and helpful beings historic folklore paints a different picture. Older tales of mermaids describe them as intentionally drowning sailors and sometimes eating them (Briggs, 1976; Simpson & Roud, 2000). One Welsh tale claims that Padstow Harbour is full of sandbars because of a mermaid who was angry at being shot at by a human, so to avenge this attack she ruined the harbour (Simpson & Roud, 2000).

There is some debate as to whether mermaids are fairies or not and for a long time mermaids have been viewed as natural creatures rather than Otherworldly. The belief that Mermaids were real world beings was deeply ingrained across cultures and led to the perpetuation of sightings and of many alleged Mermaid bodies[1] being exhibited (Simpson & Roud, 2000). Like other types of fairies, however, Mermaids in Celtic lore were said to sometimes be captured as wives or to willingly take human lovers and children were produced from these unions; like the children of humans and SELKIES they would have webbed hands and feet. Like the GWRAGEDD ANNWN they were also known to pass on great knowledge to their part-human children especially of healing.

Mermaids might be intentionally captured or accidently pulled up in fishing nets. If captured they could grant wishes, but while they would keep to the exact letter of any bargain they made to gain their freedom they would also do what they could to ensure their wishes brought misfortune rather than actual blessing (Briggs, 1976). Not all stories of Mermaids are so grim and it is true that their favour could be earned through acts of selfless kindness in which case they might offer knowledge to a person or vital help.

According to some sources Mermaids will die if they are out of water for too long, losing their physical form and melting into some other substance[2] (Briggs, 1976). There is also one account of a Mermaid who was driven off by Christian prayers (Simpson & Roud, 2000). Outside of these accounts folklore offers little in the way of how to combat Mermaids or ward against them, besides avoiding them.

Notes

1 Commonly called 'gaffs' these fake Mermaids were usually the product of sewing two animals together, such as a monkey and a fish. All of them were easily exposed fakes but played into the belief that Mermaids existed as animals in this reality and lived in the ocean only needing to be caught or found.

2 The idea that certain water fairies dissolve when exposed to air for an extended period of time is also seen with some members of the Scottish Fuath and with the Asrai. The core idea seems to be that beings who live entirely in water cannot survive outside it, rather like deep sea fish which die when removed from their natural environment.

Merrows

See: Murúcha

Micoll

Micoll is another commonly invoked fairy Queen. Her name is found under many various spellings including Micol, Mical, Mycholl, Micob, and Mycob as well as Michel and Michael (Harm, Clark, & Peterson, 2015; Brock & Raiswell, 2018). Under the variant form of Meillia it is possible that Micoll might be the Milia found grouped sometimes with Sibilia, although we more often see her explicitly invoked with Titam and Burfex. Possibly a variant form of Mab, Briggs suggests that Micol is the queen of the diminutive fairies. (Briggs, 1976; Harm, Clark, & Peterson, 2015). Micoll was called on to give knowledge of "herbs, stones...trees...medicines... and the truth" as well as providing a ring of invisibility and was described as being very gentle and kind (Harm, Clark, & Peterson, 2015, page 207).

Midwife to the Fairies

Possibly the most common motif found in fairy folklore and appearing as well in anecdotal tales is the story of the human woman who is borrowed to act as a midwife to the fairies. The tale appears in different Celtic speaking countries in slight variations but follows the same general pattern. A midwife is approached by a stranger and asked to come with him to attend a birth. She goes with him and is brought to a location where she has never gone before to attend a young woman, who is often (but not always) recognized as a local girl that was thought to have died. The birth goes well enough and after the baby is born the midwife is either asked to anoint the baby's eyes with a salve and accidently rubs her own or sees the baby's being anointed and puts some of the ointment on her own as well. In some versions she immediately sees the fairy man for what he is and her surroundings are transformed from the grandeur she had previously seen to something far more humble, but in any event she is safely conveyed back to her own home. Sometime later the midwife is out, usually at a community fair, and sees the fairy man again among the human population there. She greets him and asks after the mother and child and at some point he asks her which eye she can see him with and when she tells him he promptly blinds her.

In some stories only the single eye that was touched by the fairy ointment is blinded while in other accounts both eyes lose their vision. Likewise in some versions this blinding is literal with the fairy man jabbing the woman's eye with a stick or piece of straw while in others more esoteric means are used and it is said that the eye or eyes are blown or breathed on. Rev. Kirk describes this procedure as painless and the loss of sight as immediate (Kirk & Lang, 1893).

This is one 20th century Irish example of the story told as an anecdote rather than as a folktale per se:

> *"A country nurse was requested by a strange man on horseback to go with him to exercise her profession; and she went with him to a castle she didn't know. When the baby was born, every woman in the place where the event happened put her finger in a basin of*

water and rubbed her eyes, and so the nurse put her finger in and rubbed it on one of her eyes. She went home and thought no more about it. But one day she was at the fair in Grange and saw some of the same women who were in the castle when the baby was born; though, as she noticed, she only could see them with the one eye she had wet with the water from the basin. The nurse spoke to the women, and they wanted. to know how she recognized them; and she, in reply, said it was with the one eye, and asked, "How is the baby?" "Well," said one of the fairy women; "and what eye do you see us with?" "With the left eye," answered the nurse. Then the fairy woman blew her breath against the nurse's left eye, and said, "You'll never see me again." And the nurse was always blind in the left eye after that." (Evans-Wentz, 1911, page 54)

Not all accounts of fairy midwives end with blinding, although that is the most common ending to the story. In one anecdotal account from Yorkshire that occurred in the 1920's a nurse was brought by bus and then on foot to a cave where she was asked to help midwife a pixie birth and in that story no ointment was used and the nurse lived on unharmed (Briggs, 1976).

Milk

Milk and related dairy products like butter appear often both as items suggested as offerings for the Good People and as things they prefer to steal. The idea that the fairies desire milk is an old one, and their influence over it and over cows is well documented in folklore. Many of the fairies who are given regular offerings, like the Brownie or Gruagach, were given milk.

Wimberly in 'Folklore in the English and Scottish Ballads' discusses the blessing and protective qualities of milk. He suggests, based on analysis of several ballads, that milk may have been used in purification rites as well as in rites to bless new-born babies. He also suggests that milk may have been used for washing a body in burial rites.

Mine Faeries

This type of faery can be found all over Europe as well as in countries settled by European peoples, such as the United States. Called Coblynau in Wales, Kobolds or Wichtlein in Germany, Knockers in England and Tommy-Knockers in the USA. They are found in any mine being worked by humans and can be either helpful or harmful.

Mine faeries are always seen as male and can appear in size anywhere from two to six feet tall. They are generally described as small wizened men with beards and either blue or red hats. Mine faeries usually dress to mimic the miners who are working near them so their appearance changes slightly with the times, but they are always seen carrying miniature pick axes and other mining tools. They tend to be very secretive and are easily upset if they catch anyone looking at them so it is more common to see than hear this type of faery if you work in a mine.

There are stories of helpful Knockers who would rap or "knock" on the walls of a mine shaft to indicate the locations of ore deposits, which is one possible origin of their name. In England they are known on occasion to warn miners of impending disasters such as cave-ins by creating weird noises to get the miners out of the dangerous area. In other cases, if they favoured a particular miner, they would wait until he was alone and then appear next to him, working alongside so that he could accomplish far more work than any other man alone could. Many times in such tales his jealous co-workers would eventually sneak back after him to find the source of his productivity only to be spotted by the knockers who would react violently. In one such story from the U.S. the enraged Knockers turned on their human friend believing he had betrayed their secret, and caused the entire mine to explode in flames.

In the case of the Coblynau they are viewed as more of a nuisance than anything else, being known to confuse miners with repeated knockings on the walls of the mine as well as appearing to miners. Those who were not frightened away at seeing the faeries noted that despite looking as if they were working frantically, nothing was ever accomplished. Mine faeries can also be very mischievous, playing pranks on the miners by hiding equipment and leading men astray in the tunnels.

At their worst mine faeries can be deadly. Coblynau when insulted are known to start rock slides and all forms of mine faeries are said to start fires in the mines when angered. In Germany Kobolds are considered malicious being fond of cruel jokes and tormenting miners. The Wichtlein is an omen of death which will be seen or heard knocking three times shortly before the doomed person meets their fate. There is no way to banish or remove mine faeries, if they are present they can only be treated with respect in the hopes of avoiding disaster.

Morgans

Also sometimes spelled Morrgans. A water fairy found in Wales. An obscure being in folklore said to drag away misbehaving children, they are now considered male although older stories may be rooted in the mythology of Morgan la Fey (Briggs, 1976). This confusion about the Morgans gender may be a reflection of the confusion from the spelling of various forms of the name Morgen and Morgan and the gender attached to those spellings.

Morgen La Fey

Morgen le Fay is a character first found in Arthurian stories, specifically the 12th century works of Geoffrey of Monmouth, where her name was initially spelled Morgen le Fay. It is worth noting that this spelling is significant because while both Morgan and Morgen are men's names (also worth noting) they are pronounced differently - Morgan evolved into the modern Welsh Morcant while Morgen became Morien (Jones, 1997). In the 12th century Morgen would have been pronounced, roughly, 'Mor-YEN' (Jones, 1997). The name Morgen is generally believed to mean 'sea born'.

Geoffrey was collecting local stories from Wales and publishing them in France and while he certainly didn't invent Morgen for his Viti Merlini there is no way to know for certain how much or little he shaped the character as he preserved her. Which in fairness is true for all of the Arthurian characters he wrote about. Geoffrey's Morgen was a priestess, one of nine sisters connected to Avalon. In the 15th century Morgen would be renamed Morgan by Thomas Malory and recast as King Arthur's scheming half-sister who was set against both Arthur and his wife Guinevere. Morgen is connected to healing and, perhaps, to guiding the dead or dying to Avalon or the Otherworld.

Morgens

A kind of water spirit found in Breton lore that seems very like the Welsh Morgans.

Muryans

Cornish fairies the size of ants; the name Muryans means 'ants' and is the name given to any fairy who has shrunk to this size (Bottrell, 1873). In Cornish belief fairies had their origins in humanity but had become trapped by various means in the world of Fairy and shifted into a new existence. It was believed they had once been human-sized but had shrunk over time, becoming smaller every time they changed their shape to that of a bird or animal, until they eventually were reduced to the height of ants before disappearing entirely (Bottrell, 1873).

Murúcha

An Irish sea fairy similar to traditional mermaids found elsewhere but with some notable differences as well.

In some folklore they are described very much like other mermaids with the upper torso of a human and the lower half of a fish; merrows also have webbed hands. Females are extremely beautiful but males are hideously ugly, with green tinted skin, and deep set red eyes. One difference with the Murúcha is that they can shape shift and travel on land with the aid of a red feather hat; this allows them to take the shape of a hornless cow, although if that hat is stolen from them they are trapped on land (Briggs, 1976).

As with many other kinds of fairies the Murúcha are known to occasionally take human lovers and produce children with them. Children born from the union of a Murúch and a mortal are said to look very human except that they will have some scales (Briggs, 1976).

Murúcha are sometimes associated with storms and seen as omens of bad weather, but more often in folklore they appear in helpful roles.

Music and Musicians

The fairy folk are renowned musicians and also known for their love of human musicians. They may borrow human musicians for a night and then return or they may take more permanently as it suits them. Turlough O'Carolan was said to have gained his skill as a musician after sleeping on a fairy hill and hearing fairy music, and other less famous musicians have also been known to learn from the Good People. There is a Scottish anecdote of a family known for its skill with the bagpipes who can supposedly trace the talent back to a man who as a boy was ill treated by his step-mother; a fairy man took pity on the boy's state and came to him offering him a pair of pipes and the skill to play (Evans-Wentz, 1911)

Folkloric and anecdotal accounts speak of encounters where a musician, particularly a fiddler or piper, is rewarded for playing for the fairies. Their actions towards musicians are not entirely benevolent in all cases, however, and there is one account in the Dúchas collection, volume 0274, page 193, of a fiddler who was often borrowed by the fairies and who had an eye struck out by them for refusing to eat fairy food when it was offered to him.

Their own music is heard sometimes by humans and usually described as very beautiful and enchanting. In many stories when fairies are heard singing the exact words cannot be understood although there is at least one account from Scotland where a young man heard the fairies in a hill singing a waulking song[1] (Evans-Wentz, 1911). There are also some few songs still preserved today that are said to have come originally from the fairy folk

Note

1 Waulking songs are specific chant like songs sung while working cloth, a process that is somewhat ritualized in itself. There are many traditional waulking songs, usually sung in Gaidhlig. The account given on page 98 of the 'Fairy Faith in Celtic Countries' is of the fairies singing a waulking song in Gaidhlig, which is very much in line with accounts of fairies engaging in human-like activities and speaking the local languages. In this case the song overheard was *"Ho! fir-e! fair-e, foirm! Ho! Fair-eag-an an clò!"* A rough translation of this is given as *"Ho! well done! Grand! Ho! bravo the web [of homespun]!"*

N

Names

Another taboo that we see among many of the Good People relates to names. Names have power and we find in many cases both an aversion to saying the names of certain types of the Daoine Maithe as well as an avoidance of personal names. Even nicknames have power and when we look at anecdotal evidence we find that often rather than giving a name to a fairy that a person might have regular encounters with a person or group might call them by their description.

First let's look at the wider taboo involving euphemisms. In this case the name in question is a collective one, for the entire group. There is a longstanding belief that to speak of them may draw their attention[1] and that it is always better to get positive attention than negative. Certain terms have been known to anger or annoy them, although which terms exactly aren't agreed on: at various points it was taboo to say Aos Sídhe or Daoine Sídhe or fairies, although at present fairies is the most often avoided. Euphemisms have been used since at least the 16th century to avoid the more direct terms, and these euphemisms were intended to be pleasing if they drew the fairies attention. So instead of fairies, elves, or goblins (interchangeable terms until recently) which all could raise their ire a person would say, for example, Fair Folk, Other Crowd, Mother's Blessing, or Seelie Wichts [Blessed Beings].

Beyond that we have an avoidance of personal names. Names have power, and using a being's name gives you power over them - or gives them power over you if they know and use your name. Because of this in folklore we rarely see any fairy willingly giving its name unless it's in repayment for a debt of some sort or a deeper relationship is involved. Invoking a fairy's name, or even giving one a nickname, is often enough to drive one off as we see in stories like Tom Tit Tot or Rumplestiltskin. Finding out a fairy's name or intentionally giving one a nickname is one method of banishing a being who is causing problems are endangering people. Keep in mind, however, that this method of getting rid of a troublesome fairy also angers them and that can later come back to haunt the person.

When we see discussions of fairies who were known to interact regularly with people in anecdotes or stories, often that being is known not by a name but by a descriptive term based on what they look like or where they are associated with. Yeats related an anecdote of a woman whose mother had a friend among the Good People, who they simply called 'the Wee Woman' (although she was human sized) and Brownies are usually identified by the area they occupied, such as the Brownie of Cranshaws. A Scottish clan had a Bodach attached to them which acted much like a Bean Sidhe in foretelling death and was known as the Bodach Glas, or 'Grey Man' (Briggs, 1976). In some cases we do have more well-known fairies whose names we do know, like Jenny Greenteeth or Meg Mullach[2], but these tend to be the exception rather than the rule and they seem to still involve aspects of description or places.

Generally it is best to use euphemisms when talking about the Good People, so that if you get their attention they won't be offended by how you are speaking of them. You'll rarely know a fairy being's name, and if you do by chance it's better not to use it often, but descriptive names based on physical appearance or place are acceptable. One of the quickest way to offend the Daoine Uaisle is violating the taboo they have around the use of names so it is good to keep this in mind.

Notes

1 Although not omniscient there is a pervasive belief that the fairies are often present but invisible and may therefore be near a person but unseen.

2 Molluch means top or I leave that to the reader to decide.

Nicnevin

Nicnevin appears in folklore from the 16th century onwards as a frightening figure that was used by mothers' to ensure children's good behaviour, a witch and queen of witches, and a Fairy Queen. In modern understanding she is often depicted as a queen of the Unseelie Court of Scotland.

The meaning of her name is unknown, although the official etymology is that it comes from Nic Naomhin the Gaidhlig for "daughter of the little saint"; a similar name NicClerith (daughter of the cleric) is given in the 17th century to someone said to be a close relative of Nicnevin. Other theories claim the name is NicNemhain, or daughter of Nemahin, connecting her to the Irish war goddess Nemhain. A commentator on Campbell also offers the alternate spelling of NicCreamhain, which he suggests comes from Craoibhean, 'little tree man', as the ultimate source for the name Nicnevin (Campbell, 1900).

She first appears in a 16th century poem by Alexander Montgomerie, where he describes her this way:

> *"Then a ready company came, soon after close,*
> *Nicnevin with her nymphs, in number enough*
> *With charms from Caithness and the Canonry of Ross*
> *Whose knowledge consists in casting a ball of yarn...*
> *The King of Fairy, and his Court, with the Elf Queen,*
> *with many elvish Incubi was riding that night."*[2]

This is interesting for several reasons. We are told that she appears with her nymphs - probably a general term for female fairies or maidens - in 'number enough', reinforcing a previous line that referred to her appearing with a "company". She has charms from Caithness and Ross, both counties in the extreme north of Scotland[1] giving us a geographic point for her. We are also told that her knowledge or skill consists in casting balls of yarn or thread, one might surmise possibly as a method of divination or enchantment. This is an interesting connection to the Gyre-carling, who was strongly connected to spinning, and who will be discussed in more depth later. The poem itself goes on to describe the Fairy Rade she is riding out with in dark terms mentioning that they are accompanied by many elvish Incubi (a common gloss for dangerous fairies), and it says that she is riding with an unnamed Fairy King (Briggs, 1976). This connects her directly to the Good People and counts her among their number, as their Queen.

Sir Walter Scott describes her in more depth in this passage:

> *"...a gigantic and malignant female...who rode on the storm and marshalled the rambling host of wanderers under her grim banner. This hag...was called Nicneven in that later system which blended the faith of the Celts and of the Goths on this subject. The great Scottish poet Dunbar has made a spirited description of this Hecate riding at the head of witches and good neighbours (fairies, namely), sorceresses and elves, indifferently, upon the ghostly eve of All-Hallow Mass."* (Scott, 1831).

From this we see an association between Nicnevin and storms, and we see her compared to the Goddess Hecate, as well as called a witch and described as leading a troop of witches and fairies. In the 200-odd years between the two depictions her association with witches has gone from something perhaps hinted at with her skill at magic and charms to something blatant. In the same way the description of the host she rides with has intensified and become more obviously dangerous, riding, as Scott says, 'under her grim banner'.

She is also associated in that quote with 'All-Hallow Mass', however, due to the calendar shift in 1752 which moved dates by 11 days, when it went into effect she became strongly associated with November 11th, the old-style date of Halloween/Samhain.

Because of this we see her being acknowledged on both the new and old dates of the holiday. I have seen people today calling November 11th 'Nicnevin's Night', and some people believe she rides out with her company between October 31st and November 11th[3].

Nicnevin is often identified as a witch, being called the *"Grand Mother Witch"*; her name was also used as a general name for powerful witches (Scott, 1820). In later witchcraft trials those accused were intentionally connected to the folkloric Nicnevin to solidify their guilt (Miller, 2004). There is evidence of at least three women in the witch trial records of Scotland with last names that were similar to NicNevin who were accused and killed for practicing witchcraft. The connection of NicNevin to witches is complex, with her being viewed as both a witch herself, and also the leader of all witches. By some accounts she was a human witch who was burned at the stake in 1569 northeast of Edinburgh, while others claim her as the Queen of witches (Miller, 2004). She is also explicitly called the Queen of Fairies by Sir Walter Scott writing at the beginning of the 19th century and in Montgomerie's 16th century poem.

Nicnevin and the Gyre-Carlin are closely inter-related and possibly names for the same being. As sir Walter Scott says: *"The fairy queen is identified, in popular tradition, with the Gyre-Carline, or mother witch, of the Scottish peasantry. She is sometimes termed Nicneven."* (Scott, 1802). The connection to the Gyre-Carlin is a complicated one, because she may be a separate figure who also has overlapping witch/fairy connections or she may be Nicnevin by a different name; certainly the two have extremely similar characteristics and associations. The name Gyre-Carlin breaks down to gyre, 'hobgoblin, supernatural monster' and carlin, 'a witch, a crone'. The Gyre-Carlin herself - or perhaps themselves as they may be a category of being and an individual - is described as both a witch and a supernatural woman. She is most associated with the area around Fife, where it's said that housewives who don't finish their spinning before the end of the year will have their unspun flax taken by her. The Gyre-Carlin was not limited to this one location, however, with her lore found around Scotland and the Orkneys. She was connected to the fairies for both were known to steal or bewitch babies, and she was also thought in the Orkney Islands to live in the ancient Neolithic mounds, as did the Fair Folk (Barry, 1867). The Gyre-Carlin was said to be especially active on Halloween [Samhain], New Years, and the time between Candlemas [Imbolc] and Fasteneen [Lent].

Another description of Nicnevin, which directly conflates her with the Gyre-Carlin, comes to us from a 19th century source:

> *"…a celebrated personage who is called the GyreCarline, Reckoned the mother of glamour, and near akin to Satan himself. She is believed to preside over the Hallowmass Rades and mothers frequently frighten their children by threatening to give them to McNeven, the Gyre Carline. She is described wearing a long grey mantle and carrying a wand, which...could convert water into rocks and sea into solid land."* (Cromek, 1810).

Here we see Nicnevin - called McNeven - directly connected again to the Fairy Rades or specifically those processions riding out on Halloween/Samhain. We are also given a rare physical description of her wearing a 'long, grey mantle' and are told she carries a powerful wand that can transmute earth to water and vice versa.

Nicnevin is a difficult figure to suss out. The meaning of her name is unknown and we see it in various forms thanks to the non-standard orthography of the day. Her true origins are lost to history, and she appears 400 years ago as a figure fully formed in folklore, described as leading witches and fairies through the darkness of Halloween night, her unnamed King at her side. She is repeatedly associated with witches, sometimes even said to have been a mortal witch herself, yet she is also clearly associated with the fairies and called their Queen. She rides out during liminal times of year and during storms, leading a cavalcade of 'sorceresses and elves', and she is described as 'malignant' and powerful, explaining, perhaps, the modern description of her as Queen of the Unseelie Court. The references we do have to her imply that she held a significant position in folklore, yet we have no existing myths or stories featuring her. We are left instead only with hints and later writing that seems to assume she would be known and understood by the reader. A modern understanding then, must be built on what evidence we do have and on whatever else can be gleaned from local folklore as well as individual perceptions.

Notes

1 The two regions are separated by Sutherland, but otherwise represent the northernmost area of Scotland.

2 I've translated from the Scots for ease of reading here, the original is:

> "Then a clear Companie came soon after clos,
> Nicneuen with hir Nymphis, in nomber anew,
> With charmes from Caitness and Chanrie in Rosse,
> Quhais cunning consistis in casting a clew...
> The King of pharie, and his Court, with the elph queine,
> With mony elrich Incubus was rydand that nycht."

3 This is information I have gathered by talking to various people, and should be considered anecdotal or personal correspondence. I have found nothing in actual history or folklore to support this. That said I think there is a lot of value in the modern practices that have sprung up around Nicnevin which is part of what spurred me to write about her.

Nuckelavee

The Nuckelavee is a type of water fairy found in Scotland and the Orkneys, with a particularly horrific appearance. The Nuckelavee looks like a horse with flippers instead of hooves, a man's torso rising up from its' back, elongated arms hanging down, and an oversized head lolling from side to side; the entire creature is skinless. Its blood is black, its mouth wide and gaping, and it had only a single red eye (Towrie, 2019). It makes its home in the sea and cannot bear the touch of fresh water (Briggs, 1976).

The Nuckelavee is one of the most malicious of the fairies, sometimes called a demon in folklore because of its malignant nature. The creature roamed the land near the water and would kill humans and animals it came across and destroy crops; it was also blamed for droughts and for an illness among horses called mortasheen (Briggs, 1976; Towrie, 2019). In Orcadian lore it's said that its violent tendencies are only restrained by a being called the 'Mither o' the Sea' [Mother of the Sea] and by the Nuckelavee's own avoidance of rain water and other fresh water sources, otherwise it could roam as it pleased and would do so (Towrie, 2019).

Because of its aversion to fresh water crossing a river or stream is the only way recorded in folklore to escape a Nuckelavee.

Nursing Mothers

Another popular target of fairy abductions are nursing mothers and women who have just given birth. These new mothers might be kept forever or might eventually be returned to the human world.

In one Scottish account a man was able to win back his stolen wife and child by waiting until the fairy hill opened on Samhain [31 October] and wedging the passage open with iron while he entered to bring them both out again (Evans-Wentz, 1911). In this case there is no explanation given as to why the infant was taken but the woman is explicitly said to have been nursing not only her own child but all the babies taken by the fairies. Similarly the ballad 'The Queen of Elfan's Nourice' tells the story of a woman taken by the fairies to nurse the Fairy Queen's child.

Oak, Ash, and Thorn

Referenced as a triad in the refrain of Kipling's 1906 'Tree Song' from his work 'Puck of Pook's Hill:

Of all the trees that grow so fair,
Old England to adorn,
Greater are none beneath the Sun,
Than Oak, and Ash, and Thorn.

The song itself discusses several other trees as well and mentions the practice of ritually welcoming summer but the three main trees mentioned here have come to have a reputation in modern fairylore both for protecting against fairies and as a sign of their presence.

Oberon

One of the most well-known of the Fairy Kings today, Oberon owes his modern fame to Shakespeare and his appearance in a Midsummer Night's Dream. However, Shakespeare didn't create Oberon, he initially appeared earlier in the 15th century in a French epic romance called Huon of Bordeaux (Harm, Clark, & Peterson, 2015; Briggs, 1976). Although he is a Fairy King and very powerful in both stories his description between the two accounts is very different. In the 15th century story his form is that of a 3 year old child although he is still a very powerful being, in Shakespeare he is an adult in appearance and his form is taller. In Huon of Bordeaux Oberon is described as beautiful even though he is small and deformed, and he appears wearing a glowing, jewelled gown. His physical description is not given in Shakespeare, but his power and temperament are intense and he is described as a lover of mortal women, at odds with his depiction in the French tale.

In the grimoire material Oberon appears in several sources, invoked under different guises, not always as a fairy. In one particular text where he is called into a crystal he is referred to as an angel, reflecting the perhaps changing way that Oberon was understood (Harm, Clark, & Peterson, 2015). In other grimoire material he may be called on to appear as a soldier or child, and invoked to find treasure but he also is able to give knowledge of nature, healing, and invisibility (Harm, Clark, and Peterson, 2015).

The authors of The Book of Oberon suggest that the fairy King Oberon is probably derived from the 12th century Germanic figure of Alberich who was a dwarf but whose name means 'elf ruler'. Alberich appears in the Nibelunglied and a poem called Ortnit, able to magically aid people in various ways. As Oberon he initially appears as a tiny but powerful elfin king who was unable to bear sunlight, and so shunned the day time (Purkiss, 2000). There are also several familiar spirits called on for power and luck during the Renaissance with names that seem very similar to Oberon's including Auberon and Oberycom (Purkiss, 2000; Briggs, 1976). After this Oberon can be found in various grimoire texts through the 19th century, called on as the king of fairies and also in conjunction with other spirits.

The textual material relating to Oberon can be contradictory and difficult to parse, with his physical appearance and backstory varying widely between sources. Even the name of his queen is uncertain and changes between texts. However, what remains consistent is his power and influence in whatever form he's being invoked as. For those seeking to connect to Oberon his shifting nature and many different faces should be kept in mind, as well as the consistency of his power and influence.

In Shakespeare's work Oberon's queen is Titania, but other sources name his queen as Mab or Micoll (Briggs, 1976; Harm, Clark, & Peterson, 2015).

Offerings

The practice of leaving out offerings for the fairies is a long standing one which can be found in many cultures and in various guises. The purpose of these offerings varies but most often seem to have been done to either avert potential harm caused by fairies or because it was believed something was inherently owed to them. The main thing that was offered was food, most often milk, butter, or baked goods, although sharing any food the family had is found across sources.

This example comes from the area around Sid in Broga [Newgrange] in Ireland:

> *"I knew of people...who would milk in the fields about here and spill milk on the ground for the good people; and pots of potatoes would be put out for the good people at night.'"* (Evans-Wentz, 1911, page 37).

A different Irish source from 'Fairy Faith in Celtic Countries' said that in his own area food that hadn't been touched was left out on the kitchen table at night for the fairies. The same text mentions the practice of leaving the fairies not only milk but butter, as a portion of any butter churned as was considered to belong to them.

Offerings to fairies were also used to measure goodwill, as it was considered a bad omen if food left out for Themselves wasn't taken or touched. This source from Armagh, Ireland describes a practice of leaving food out in a newly built home before it was moved into, to judge the mood of the 'place-fairies':

> *"It was very usual formerly, and the practice is not yet given up, to place a bed, some other furniture, and plenty of food in a newly-constructed dwelling the night before the time fixed for moving into it; and if the food is not consumed, and the crumbs swept up by the door in the morning, the house cannot safely be occupied. I know of two houses now that have never been occupied, because the*

> *fairies did not show their willingness and goodwill by taking food so offered to them."* (Evans-Wentz, 1911, page 75).

By this method a person or family could safely judge if the house could be lived in or if the fairies there were ill-inclined towards people.

The idea that fairies were given offerings is a very old one, and there is an implicit belief with it that these offerings are only what is due to them. If they are not given what is owed they will take it and sometimes more, such as we see in stories of fairies used to getting milk offerings who take the best cow of the herd when the milk is no longer given. As one Scottish source in 'Fairy Faith in Celtic Countries' explained it:

> *"An elder in my church knew a woman who was accustomed, in milking her cows, to offer libations to the fairies. The woman was later converted to Christ and gave up the practice, and as a result one of her cows was taken by the fairies. Then she revived the practice"* (Evans-Wentz, 1911, page 92).

MacNeill, in 'Festival of Lughnasa', mentions the Irish belief that the fairies were due a tithe of the harvest and that what was given should be the best portion. She quotes several anecdotal sources from across Ireland that all reference giving a portion of each year's harvest to the Good People, with an emphasis on the fairies taking only the best or top portion (MacNeill, 1962).

Food offerings to fairies were generally seen as having no value afterwards for humans or animals to eat as the Good People were thought to consume the vital substance of the food leaving it valueless for others. As one man from Tuam, Ireland explained it:

> *"Food, after it has been put out at night for the fairies, is not allowed to be eaten afterwards by man or beast, not even by pigs. Such food*

is said to have no real substance left in it, and to let anything eat it wouldn't be thought of. The underlying idea seems to be that the fairies extract the spiritual essence from food offered to them, leaving behind the grosser elements." (Evans-Wentz, 1911, page 44).

Ogres

A kind of monstrous giant known to eat humans. The name Ogre comes from the French for a demon or monster and first appeared in print in the late 17th century in a text called 'Contes' (Harper, 2018). Generally applied to any man-eating giant but used more in literature than in folklore (Simon & Roud, 2000).

Orcs

A word derived from the Latin word for death and the Underworld, orcus, it's thought to be a form of the word for Ogre (Harper, 2018). An obscure being in folklore Orcs were popularized by Tolkien's works in the 20th century.

Origins

There are many different theories about fairy origins, some rooted in Christian cosmology and others with a different basis. All seek to explain how the Good People fit into a wider understanding of the world as people understand it in different contexts. Ultimately there is no one simple answer for where fairies come from, likely because the fairies themselves are too diverse a groups of beings to be so easily understood.

One theory of fairy origins which is spoken of in folklore as well as in mythology is that they are the Tuatha De Danann who have gone into the fairy hills. This idea is rooted in Irish mythology, which we can see in De Gabail in t-Sida and Altram Tige Dá Meda, where the Tuatha De Danann are defeated by the Milesians and retreat into the sí, or fairy hills. There they become known as the Aos Sídhe or Daoine Sídhe, the people of the fairy hills. This idea is reinforced in stories such as the Aislinge Oenguso where the Dagda, king of the Tuatha De Danann, is referred to as the king of all the Sidhe of Ireland.

Another common view found in Ireland and Scotland is that the fairies are fallen angels of various sorts. One Irish account says that when Lucifer rebelled God opened the doors of heaven and cast the angels out, and so many were falling that finally the archangel Michael begged God to close the doors. He did so and when they closed the angels who were outside were trapped wherever they happened to be, so that those who were in the earth became demons in Hell and those who were caught in the air when the doors closed became fairies. An alternate account from Scotland is similar but has Lucifer leading the angels away rather than God casting them out and Jesus begging the gates be closed rather than Michael; in this story the angels who made it all the way to Hell were demons but those trapped in the earth or air were fairies (Evans-Wentz, 1911). This was a very common view during the medieval period, enough so that theologians of the time often debated whether fairies should properly be considered demons or not and whether they were capable of doing any good as fallen angels (Firth-Green, 2017). It is also a theme that shows up in folkloric and anecdotal accounts with stories of fairies approaching priests to ask whether there is any hope of their ultimate salvation.

There are also many accounts that claim the fairies are human dead or ancestors. This idea is found across the Celtic language speaking world.

There are also a scattering of theories that cannot be placed into any single larger category. One Irish source in the 'Fairy Faith in Celtic Countries' stated a belief that the Gentry came from outer space, perhaps echoing mythology which states the Tuatha De Danann came from the sky. A Manx source from the same text describes fairies as a type of ethereal spirit, while a Welsh source told a story where the fairies where created by the

Christian God after he passed by a woman's home and she tried to hide half her children to conceal the large size of her family from him.

The only conclusion that may be reached on the subject of fairy origins is that there is no single answer to the question, but rather multiple possible sources.

Physicality

The physicality of fairies has been a long debated point and in folklore no clear answer is provided.

In many accounts of human interactions with the Good People they seem to be as physical and solid as any living human, able to touch and interact with the tangible world. Yeats relates a story in Celtic Twilight of a woman who had a friend among the fairies who interacted physically with her, handing her a packet of herbs and once passing a meal with the family and eating food there. 'The Fairy Faith in Celtic Countries' includes many anecdotal accounts of people who were physically struck by the fairy folk and we see the same in fairy accounts recorded in the Dúchas collection.

Other accounts, however, would make the nature of fairies seem far less substantial. Rev. Kirk opined that they existed in a form:

> *"…said to be of a middle Nature betwixt Man and Angel, as were Dæmons thought to be of old; of intelligent fluidious Spirits, and light changeable Bodies, (like those called Astral,) somewhat of the Nature of a condensed Cloud, and best seen in Twilight. These Bodies be so pliable thorough the Subtilty of the Spirits that agitate them, that they can make them appear or disappear at Pleasure. Some have Bodies or Vehicles so spungious, thin, and delicate, that they are fed by only sucking into some fine spirituous Liquors, that pierce like pure Air and Oil"* (Kirk & Land, 1893, page 5).

An Irish anecdote from the early 20th century mentioned the fairy habit of suddenly disappearing and connected that to their ultimate nature:

> *"When they disappear they go like fog; they must be something like spirits, or how could they disappear in that way?"* (Evans-Wentz, 1911, page 36). When asked about the nature of fairies a Scottish source in the same text agreed, saying *"...they must be spirits from all that the old people tell about them, or else how could they appear and disappear so suddenly? The old people said they didn't know if fairies were flesh and blood, or spirits...I heard my father say that fairies used to come and speak to natural people, and then vanish while one was looking at them. Fairy women used to go into houses and talk and then vanish. The general belief was that the fairies were spirits who could make themselves seen or not seen at will"* (Evans-Wentz, 1911, page 102)

The answer may lie between the two options, or perhaps as a combination of the two, as illustrated by a story related in the works of Grimm. In the story it is said that an elf-woman entered a man's home in the form of smoke through a knothole in his door; however, once there she become as substantial as any living woman and acted as the man's wife giving him four children before leaving one day exactly as she had come (Grimm, 1888). Here we see a fairy being who can become insubstantial but can also have a physical form, physical enough to bear children to a living human, but can become insubstantial again. One Manx source in 'The Fairy Faith in Celtic Countries' agreed with this middle ground approach saying:

> *"One cannot say that they are wholly physical or wholly spiritual, but the impression left upon my mind is that they are an absolutely real order of beings not human.'"* (Evans-Wentz, 1911, pages 134 – 135)

Pixies

Appearing under variant spellings including Pixy and Pisky these fairies are found primarily in Devon and Cornwall. Like other types of fairies Pixies are known to borrow midwives, steal humans, cause mischief, mislead travellers, dance in circles, cause elf locks, and may sometimes be helpful if the mood suits them (Simpson & Roud, 2000).

Pixies may range in height from a few inches tall to five or six feet, and by some accounts may take the form of hedgehogs. Briggs describes them as red haired with pointed ears, short faces, and up-tilted noses. They are often described wearing green. A 20th century Welsh source in 'Fairy Faith in Celtic Countries' claimed to have seen pixies harassing her father's horse saying:

> "*She described them to me as like tiny men dancing on the mare's back and climbing up along the mare's mane. She thought the pixies some kind of spirits who made their appearance in early morning; and all mishaps to cows she attributed to them.*'" (Evans-Wentz, 1911, page 158).

Pixie Led

Pixie led, also called fairy led, and is a term which refers to being lost or led astray in familiar territory. Described succinctly here by a Welsh source along with its remedy:

> "*One may also hear of a person being pixy-led; the pixies may cause a traveller to lose his way at night if he crosses a field where they happen to be. To take your coat off and turn it inside out will break the pixy spell*" (Evans-Wentz, 1911, page 159).

Evans-Wentz goes on to remark on the similarity between this Welsh description and stories of being pixy led or fairy led from Ireland, Brittany, and England which all advise the same general cure.

Devonshire pixylore as reported by Keightley supports these accounts of being pixy led, describing anecdotal accounts of people led astray one familiar roads and crossing their own paths.

Plant Annwn

Literally meaning 'Children of the Otherworld' in Welsh. One term for the Welsh fairies, specifically those who owe loyalty to GWYN AP NUDD, Briggs refers to them as fairies of the Underworld and associates them with lakes in particular and with the GWRAGEDD ANNWN, CU SIDHE, and the Welsh fairy cows that live in lakes.

Pointed Ears

When we look at descriptions of fairies, under different names, from folklore we generally find their human-like appearance being emphasized. In the 'Ballad of Thomas the Rhymer' Thomas initially mistakes the Fairy Queen for the Virgin Mary; in the 'Ballad of Tam Lin' Janet has to ask Tam Lin to clarify whether he is truly a fairy or was once mortal, indicating that there's no obvious physical indicators of his nature (Acland, 2017). As Andrew Lang says:

> *"There seems little in the characteristics of these fairies of romance to distinguish them from human beings, except their supernatural knowledge and power."* (Wimberly, 1965).

Yeats, in the late 19th century relates this description of a Fairy woman given to him a woman in Ulster:

> *"She was like a woman about thirty, brown-haired and round in the face. She was like Miss Betty, your grandmother's sister, and Betty was like none of the rest, not like your grandmother, nor any of them. She was round and fresh in the face..."* (Yeats, 1902).

In all of these examples and others across folklore we see fairy people being described without pointed ears and notably with a very human-like appearance, usually the only indication of their Otherworldly nature comes through their actions, demeanour, an energy or feeling around them, or a perception people have of them as such.

So where then do we get the idea that elves and fairies have pointed ears? The answer is a bit convoluted and requires looking to the way that Christianity depicted demons, the way that Greeks described satyrs, and finally Victorian art.

The concept of elves and fairies with pointed ears in Western culture is likely rooted in Christian demonic imagery. This is because Christianity in seeking to explain the existence of elves and fairies fit them into the cosmology as a type of demon or fallen angel, which logically led to people imagining demonic characteristics onto fairies. As far back as 1320 we can find depictions of demons with pointed ears, usually along with other physical deformities, especially animalistic features (Bovey, 2006). These pointed ears and horrific appearances are in sharp contrast to the way that angelic and divine beings are depicted, emphasizing through physical depiction the hellish nature of these demonic beings. Whereas the saved souls and angels are emphatically human the demons are just as emphatically inhuman with their obvious animal features, including their ears. This is likely an intentional device to make the demons unappealing and frightening, in opposition to the relatable human-like angels. In folklore we also often see fairies described with animal features, including tails or webbed feet, as well as physical deformities like hollow backs; although fairies are as often described as beautiful as grotesque. Because Christianity chose to depict demons in the way that it did and because they explained fairies in their cosmology as a type of demon or fallen angel, and because fairylore itself described fairies as having physical features that could fit the later Christian descriptions of demons there was a certain inevitability in the artistic depictions of the two types of beings blending together.

Although it may be understandable as to why Christianity chose to show demons as horrific in artwork, pointed ears inclusive, this does beg the question of why Christianity chose to depict its demons this way when in the Bible they are described as fallen angels, and angels are certainly not horrifically animal-like in appearance. Although some angels can look disturbing based on how they are described in the Bible - cherubim for example have four wings that are covered in eyes - most are simply referred to as 'men' without any further detail, implying that while they were not human they also weren't exceptionally strange looking (KJV, 2017). In fact in stories where they show up some people may recognize them for what they are but others often do not, which we see in the story of Lot and his angelic visitors in Genesis 19; this at least implies that they can pass as human. The Bible also makes it clear that Satan and his servants – that is demons - masquerade as angels and servants of light which would seem to contradict the idea of demons having a grotesque appearance (KJV, 2017).

Looking further back though we see that there were some beings in Greek and Roman mythology that did have animalistic features and potentially pointed ears, including beings like satyrs. Satyrs were described with ears that could be either donkey like or goat like in shape, and in artwork this is easily perceived as pointed (Atsma, 2017). In the King James Version of the Bible there are references to satyrs[1], which may be a mistranslation of the Hebrew word for a type of spirit (Jackson, 2017). Even though a mistranslation is likely in that case it speaks to a cultural perception that related satyrs to demons. The word in question that is being given as satyr is sa'im which may be a corruption of the Hebrew seirim. In Old Testament demonology the seirim was a being that blended attributes of a goat and demon, based perhaps on the practice of representing a demon by a symbolic animal with similar attributes (Rodriguez, 2017). Satyrs, with their goat-like features and wild natures were an easy target to later be shifted into the bad-guys of the new religion, particularly with the goat's already existing symbolism as an animal of the wilds connected to infertility and danger. It is likely then that the classical depictions of satyrs influenced that later Christian depictions of demons.

Early depictions of elves and fairies in artwork show them in line with folklore depictions that is mostly human like in appearance although they may be either beautiful or ugly and were sometimes shown as very small. As we enter into the Victorian era we begin to see elves and fairies shown with pointed ears, probably based on popular imagery of Puck which in turn drew on demonic imagery that was drawing on the depictions of satyrs (Wright, 2009). Puck was a popular folkloric figure that had long blended fairylore and demonology, understood as a type of fairy, individual being, and also a name for the Devil (Wright, 2009). This blurring of fairylore and Christian cosmology was fertile ground for artwork and laid the foundation for a wider understanding of fairies through this lens; the artists of the Victorian era slowly refined the concept so that what began as pointed ears only on the wildest of fey beings eventually spread to pointed ears even on the delicate winged nature sprites. By the 19th century artists began depicting elves and fairies with pointed ears almost exclusively. By the 20th century we see these descriptions entering written media with both prose and poetry describing elves and fairies with pointed ears. Even Tolkien tentatively described his Hobbits with slightly pointed ears and his Elves, at one time[2] with pointed or leaf shaped ears (Dunkerson, 2017). The concept has now become ubiquitous, spreading throughout popculture and into folklore, so that it is simply taken as a given that elves and fairies have pointed ears. More recently there has been a shift particularly in anime and role playing games from the smaller leaf-shaped ears of Victorian art and Tolkien to excessively exaggerated, elongated ears that stretch above or beyond the head and are more reminiscent of donkey ears in shape.

How does this all result in a modern view of elves and fairies with pointed ears? We seem to see a pattern where satyrs were the basis for later depictions of demons and then in turn demons influenced the perception in artwork of what fairies looked like, with the idea that fairies were a kind of fallen angel. Although in folklore we don't find many descriptions of fairies' ears and particularly not of their ears being pointed, we begin in the Victorian period to see them shown this way by most artists. These pointed ears, along with some other animalistic features, become the tell-tale signs of a being's Otherworldly nature, often in art combined with wings[3]. Pointed ears became a quick way to signal to a viewer that the subject of a piece wasn't human even if they seemed so in all other ways, or in other cases to emphasize their inhuman nature.

Notes

1 For example, Isaiah 34:14: "The wild beasts of the desert shall also meet with the wild beasts of the island, and the satyr shall cry to his fellow; the screech owl also shall rest there, and find for herself a place of rest." - KJV Bible

2 The wings come from the theater and the need to signal to audiences that an actor was playing a fairy, although I suspect this too is rooted in the later connection of fairies to demons. See the entry on wings for more.

3 In fairness he did seem to later pull back from this description and it's an open ended debate as to whether his ultimate intention was for his elves to have pointed ears or not.

Possession by Fairies

I'll note as I begin that I will in this article be using the terms elf and fairy synonymously, as general terms for Otherworldly beings. This reflects the generalized use of the terms in the source material I'm referencing in writing this. For those who prefer to see the terms as applying to specific beings, understand that what follows would then apply equally to both.

That fairies or elves are capable of possessing humans is a power that they were always understood to have until recently.

Just as they can influence a person's perceptions through the use of GLAMOUR they can also directly influence a person's mind by bringing madness or even by displacing the spirit and taking over control of the person's actions. Effectively what we in modern terms would call possession, although historically we see a variety of examples of this ranging from voluntary to involuntary, temporary to longer-term. Like the more commonly understood demonic possession, however, possession by fairies was problematic enough that cures and exorcism rituals for it exist.

Demonic possession and possession by fairies seem to have been understood as different and distinct situations, but they were also seen as somewhat overlapping in nature. Looking at the Saxon evidence we see that cures for elf-possession were found alongside exorcism for demons and in the case of one example found in the marginalia of a manuscript it simply adds the word 'aelfe' into the existing Latin rite of exorcism (Jolly, 1996). The symptoms for elf-possession in the Anglo-Saxon and Saxon evidence, however, is not what we would, in modern contexts, associate with demonic possession, necessarily, and is marked by fevers, nightmares, and madness more generally. Madness in these cases was usually described as marked changes in personality, nervousness or anxiety, or significant behavioural changes. This is reflected somewhat in a later Irish anecdotal example of fairy possession from the 19th century which also involved madness. Elves are often grouped with demons and night-hags as beings which both possess and torment humans and for which there are specific prayers, charms, and herbal cures (Jolly, 1996).

There is a specific word for such possession in Old English: ylfig. Ylfig seems to have been associated with both divine possession and possession by aelfe [elves] and had both negative connotations which could require exorcism as well as some connections to prophecy (Hall, 2007). The fact that there was a particular word for this exact type of possession tells us that it was either widespread enough or understood enough in the culture to necessitate its own vocabulary and that is significant.

In Irish sources there are hints of fairy possession in the mythology, especially in some of the stories of the conceptions of heroes or kings believed to have both mortal and fairy fathers. Depending on how one reads the tales of the conceptions of Cu Chulainn and Mongan it can either be interpreted that the being in question, a member of the Tuatha De Danann who was also at the time among the aos sidhe, physically visited the woman or else possessed the body of the woman's legal spouse[1], giving the child, effectively, two fathers. There is also a clearer anecdote of fairy possession in 'The Fairy Faith in Celtic Countries' which describes a girl whose father *"held communion with evil spirits"* and whose house was built into a fairy hill, as a result of this situation the girl came to be possessed by the fairies and was eventually institutionalized (Evans-Wentz, 1911). After two years of that she was taken to nuns and then to a Fairy Doctor who eventually worked a cure for her.

During the Victorian period some writers favoured the idea that changelings[2] were the result of fairy possession rather than actual physical abduction (Silver, 1999). In these circumstances it is not the child's body that is taken into Fairy but only the soul, and the body left behind is then filled with a different spirit. One source described it as if the child was being overshadowed and displaced by the secondary spirit (Silver, 1999). The symptoms of a changeling then would also be the symptoms of fairy possession, which would be inline in many cases with what is seen in the Anglo-Saxon and European evidence: illness (fevers), nightmares, and significant behavioural or personality changes. By this logic charms to get rid of a changeling and return the human are actually a type of exorcism, seeking to drive out the foreign spirit and allow the original to return; tragically like some demonic exorcisms the possessed person/alleged changeling doesn't always survive the treatment.

Fairy possession is also found in mainland Europe. It is seen among the Romanian Calusari who dealt with a type of fairy called the Iele; the Iele possessed people as well as teaching those who followed them herbal cures (Purkiss, 2000). In Germany while outright possession is not explicitly described the Elben [Elves] are clearly connected to both madness and nightmares, two things that are closely tied to the ideas of fairy possession. Grimm, for example, relates that in German there were two closely related expressions for nightmares:

> "*dich hat geriten der mar*" [the night-mare has ridden you] and "*ein alp zoumet dich*" [an elf bridles you i.e. has a horse's bridle on you] (Grimm, 1888).

Involuntary possession by fairies seems to occur most often when a person has transgressed against the Good Folk in some way, although they may not be aware of having done so. We see an account of this in a fictional story which echoes folkloric beliefs about several boys who loudly proclaim that fairies aren't real while heading to a Midsummer bonfire, only to find themselves taken for the night by the Good People and used as horses (MacLiamoir, 1984). We see a similar story, along a longer track, in the Isle of Man in an anecdotal account of a man who would disappear every night, even if he were walking besides someone, to be taken and used by the fairies as a horse (Evans-Wentz, 1911) In the first story the boys suffer this punishment for a single night, while in the second the man is possessed by the fairies every night indefinitely. Fairy possession along more traditional lines also occurs, looking at anecdotal evidence, to children whose parents have transgressed in some way, as we saw in Evan-Wentz's story and the theory about changelings. It is also possible that such possession can be invited by an individual voluntarily, either as a result of seduction by a fairy or through a desire for prophecy.

The Calusari invited possession by the Iele through trance dancing (Purkiss, 2000).

Cures for fairy possession in the Lacunga and Leechbooks ranged from Christian rites of exorcism that included calling for the elf-spirit to be cast out to drinks made from frankincense, myrrh, and shaved agate[3] (Jolly, 1996). Exorcisms through prayers are common but so are casting out these spirits using salves, drinks, and incense. For example burning the plant aelfthone[4] sometimes along with several other herbs, such as bishopwort and lupin, is repeatedly recommended in the Leechbooks. Another, safer, option is 'smoking out' the elf or fairy using mugwort. Smoke was believed to be an effective method to drive the elf out of a person, or as Jolly says:

> "*...to purge or exorcise the internal evil*" although Jolly does also discuss the difficulty of synthesizing "*amoral creatures such as elves...into the Good-Evil paradigm of the Christian moral universe.*" (Jolly, 1996, p 136).

Indeed Christianity has struggled everywhere to fit fairies into its paradigm, often settling for an uneasy compromise that places them ambiguously between angels and demons and this may be reflected in the approach to fairy possession, which is itself ambiguous.

Fairy possession is not a subject that is widely discussed in the Western world today, yet it was once commonly understood, enough so that in the 13th century Old English had a particular term for it. Unique from demonic possession, although an overlapping concept, fairy possession was marked by fevers, madness, and nightmares all of which were thought to indicate the influence of fairies on a person's mind and by extension body. Multiple cures existed for this type of possession relying to varying degrees on the aid of an expert, either a priest or a Fairy Doctor. In context it must be understood as something that cannot be clearly labelled as either good or bad, and that can be found in various places as a voluntary practice to gain knowledge from the fairies or elves as much as it can also be viewed as a punishment from them for people who offend them.

Notes

1 For example in the Imramm Brain, Manannán says that he is taking on the shape of a man and that he will be a vigorous bedfellow to Caintigern but Fiachra will acknowledge the son as his own.

2 Personally I do not believe that any single theory explains changelings, but rather that there were likely multiple possibilities. See the entry on changelings for further details.

3 Please don't actually do this. I am in no way advocating the safety of this drink, nor do I recommend it.

4 Aelfthone is an old name for a specific kind of belladonna. I DO NOT recommend burning this. Burning this herb or consuming it could be extremely dangerous. Do not do this.

Privacy

Another taboo relating to the fairies is that they are fierce guardians of their privacy. The Good People do not like to find out they have been seen, unless they are choosing to show themselves, and they prefer people not to talk too freely about benefits they have received from the fairies.

It is a common theme in many anecdotes and stories for the fairies to protect their privacy, even violently. They are well known to react badly to being spied on in many cases and to expect humans who they favour to keep any gifts and friendship largely a secret. We see this idea played out in stories of borrowed midwives who accidently anoint their own eye with an ointment that grants true sight of fairies only to admit having the ability later and be blinded, as well as in tales of fairy lovers who abandon their human sweetheart when that human tells a single person of their existence. There are also anecdotal accounts by people who accidently saw the fairies at some casual activity and fell ill afterwards, or were noticed by the fairies at the time and attacked by them (Evans-Wentz, 1911; Duchas, 2018). In one anecdotal account a man who sees the fairies playing a game is seen by them and then beaten mercilessly (Duchas, 2018).

It is an old belief that if you have the Second Sight and see the Good People when it's clear they don't realize you can see them that you should not in any way acknowledge that you can see them; this same approach often applies to anyone who thinks they may have seen the fairies unawares. The Fairy Midwife stories illustrate the willingness of the Good People to blind those who they feel have violated their privacy in this way, and some anecdotal accounts also support this. One first-hand account from the Isle of Man discusses a man blinded for seeing the fairies:

> *"'My grandfather, William Nelson, was coming home from the herring fishing late at night, on the road near Jurby, when he saw in a pea-field, across a hedge, a great crowd of little fellows in red coats dancing and making music. And as he looked, an old woman from among them came up to him and spat in his eyes, saying: "You'll never see us again"; and I am told that he was blind afterwards till the day of his death. He was certainly blind for fourteen years before his death, for I often had to lead him around; but, of course, I am unable to say of my own knowledge that he became blind immediately after his strange experience, or if not until later in life; but as a young man he certainly had good sight, and it was believed that the fairies destroyed it.'"* (Evans-Wentz, 1911, page 131)

In some stories of those who received money from the fairies, when they spoke too openly about it or bragged they found the money stopped coming to them or even in a few stories that the wealth they had been given was reduced to leaves, gingerbread, or the like. In all but the rarest cases once offended the fairies' good favour was withdrawn and contact ceased, despite any effort by the human to regain it. As with the 'thank you' rule this is not an absolute blanket prohibition and we do see exceptions where a person is allowed to speak of them or forgiven for breaking this rule, but when they react badly they react extremely badly, as in the blinding example already given.

As with many of these taboos the exact reason for it is never spelled out explicitly but we can perhaps offer some possibilities. To begin we need to break this down into the two issues we are actually dealing with which are related but separate; their dislike of being observed against their will or without their consent, and their dislike of being spoken of by someone who has agreed not to do so. In the first case the real issue is that the Good Neighbours prefer, generally, to move unseen in the human world and when this invisibility is somehow breached by a human it upsets them. There is a clear logic to their reacting badly to being seen when they do not wish to be, since moving unseen is a main way they survive in our world and is one of the many ways they have power here. The second issue, however, is as much one of trust as concern over actual privacy as it represent someone telling a secret they have usually been asked not to tell. It is also true in a wider sense that they dislike people who brag overmuch and tend to respond to human arrogance by taking actions to punish the people; in these cases someone who receives a boon from them and then talks too much of it may find their good luck withdrawn simply because they have annoyed the Gentry with their bragging.

Why do the Good People not want everyone to know how active they are in the world or how many people are receiving their blessings? Perhaps because the Fey folk are a people with their own agency and agenda and they prefer to control who knows of them, sees them, and receives good from them.

Protection against Fairies

Folklore has always been concerned with various methods of protecting humans from fairy influence and harm, so it is no surprise that there are a wide array of methods and items to be found in the corpus of material for apotropaic purposes. These include materials, symbols, prayers, and herbs which either on their own or with proper use can effectively ward off the Good Neighbours.

Of all of these protective items by far the most often referenced is iron. This metal has protective qualities in any worked form including those that might otherwise be considered innocuous like a horseshoe or ring. Rev. Kirk asserts that there is nothing that frightens dangerous spirits more than this metal, speculating that it is because iron is found in the earth and by its location reminds these beings of their fate in Hell[1] (Kirk & Land, 1893). Even those fairies who are considered helpful or are choosing to be around humans, including some FAIRY WIVES, may be driven off by iron (Evans-Wentz, 1911). Lady Wilde suggested protecting infants from being taken as changelings by sewing a bit of iron into the hem of the child's clothes (Wilde, 1888). Another commonly recommended protection for children and babies was to hang a pair of scissors, opened into the shape of a cross, above the cradle (Briggs, 1976). A horseshoe can be hung up over the door way, points up, which not only acts to ward off fairies but is also said to draw good luck. An iron knife or cross is also an excellent protection, either carried or hung up above the door or bed (Briggs, 1976). In Welsh belief a knife, particularly of iron, was so effective a protection that should friendly fairies visit a home all knives were hidden from sight lest they be offended and if a traveling person was attacked by the fairies he had only to pull his blade for them to disappear (Sikes, 1880). Another method found in Germanic and Norse traditions is to hammer an iron nail into a post near the doorway or alternately part of the door frame. Additionally, it is said to be as effective to draw a circle using an iron nail or knife around what you want to protect (Gundarsson, 2007).

Related to the use of iron is the specific use of cold iron. Many people are familiar with the term 'cold iron' and associate it today with pure or simply worked forged iron - what is technically called 'pig iron' or 'crude iron'. Historically the term cold iron was a poetic term for any iron weapon and is synonymous today with the term 'cold steel'. So when you see a reference to cold iron it is talking about an iron weapon, usually a sword or knife. For example Welsh fairies are said to flee at the sight of cold iron or any blow from it, and in Scotland a cold iron was laid near new mothers to protect them from fairy interference (Jackson, 1883). Wirt Sikes in his book 'British Goblins' relates a story of a man pursued by fairies through the mountains who escapes after pulling an iron knife at which the fairies disappear.

Fairies can and will enter into homes at night if certain conditions are not met, often relating to the proper care of the home. Many of these may seem antiquated now but should, nonetheless, be considered here. In Scotland it was said that if wash water was left standing, the fire wasn't properly raked, or the spinning wheel not properly set the fairies could get in past any other existing protections (Campbell, 1900). The same belief relating to wash water is found in Ireland, where the presence of dirty water in a home was also thought to allow the fairies access, although people were encouraged in some areas to leave fresh water out for them as an invitation for them to enter (Wilde, 1888).

Labouring women might be protected by iron, a piece of bread, or the Bible, any of which would be kept near them as they gave birth (Kirk & Lang, 1893). The woman and baby could be given special milk from a cow that had been fed an herb called pearl-wort, or else leather could be burned near them (Evans-Wentz, 1911). Iron tongs might be kept near the cradle or a pair of iron scissors might be opened up to form the shape of a cross and placed nearby. The period between birth and baptism was seen as especially dangerous for both infant and mother who must be carefully guarded lest the fairies steal one or the other away. Christian prayers are often used as a form of protection against many things, fairies included. In one Manx account a woman lying in bed holding her infant heard the sounds of fairies all around her and felt her baby being pulled from her arms so she cried out to the Christian God causing the fairies to flee (Evans-Wentz, 1911).

One anecdotal source mentions the colour red having protective qualities and while we do find specific charms, such as rowan and red thread, which have apotropaic qualities the folklore more widely doesn't emphasize the colour red on its own generally being protective. Red is one of the more common colours that fairies are known to wear, the Welsh Tylwyth Teg for example wearing red coats and Leprechauns wearing red hats in some folklore.

During the winter, and especially around New Year's when the fairies could be more active, holly was used for decoration and for its ability to ward off the Good People (Campbell, 1900). It was believed in Scotland that rowan was the best protector against the fairies, with rowan branches collected on the eve of Beltane and hung up around the home, or tied with red thread and hung over the door (McNeill, 1959). Burning Mugwort would drive off the aelfe according to the Leechbooks.

Salt is used as a protection against fairies. Multiple sources attest to the fairies aversion to salt in their food, including Campbell and Evans-Wentz, and the protective quality salt ensures that human food is not interfered with.

Fairies are also averse to human waste and urine in particular. Urine was thought to drive out the Álfar and Huldufolk if released on ground belonging to them. By some accounts when Bridget Cleary's family was trying to cure her of the changeling they thought had taken over they may have doused her in urine.

Bells are also known in folklore to drive off fairies of all types, particularly church bells. There are several accounts of fairies who left an area after a church bell was raised. Some fairies like the Nuckelavee cannot bear fresh water, while others, like Trows, are weakened or immobilized by sunlight.

Note

1 Kirk's exact wording is somewhat convoluted here but the above is my interpretation of this passage on pages 13 and 14 of the Secret Commonwealth:

"…all uncouth, unknown Wights are terrified by nothing earthly so much as by cold Iron. They deliver the Reason to be that Hell lying betwixt the chill Tempests, and the Fire Brands of scalding Metals, and Iron of the North, (hence the Loadstone causes a tendency to that Point,) by an Antipathy thereto, these odious far-scenting Creatures shrug and fright at all that comes thence relating to so abhorred a Place, whence their Torment is either begun, or feared to come hereafter".

Púca, The

The Púca - also called by a wide array of variant names including Phooka, Pooka, Pwca [Welsh], Bucca [Cornish] and Puck [English] is a type of being found in folklore across hundreds of years. Some even connect Shakespeare's character Puck to the folkloric Púca, although Shakespeare naturally took a lot of literary liberties. Puca was used in early Middle English as a name for the Devil (Williams, 1991). The old Irish púca is given as 'a goblin, sprite' and similarly the modern Irish is given as hobgoblin (eDIL, 2018; O Donaill, 1977). These translations give a clue to the Púca's nature, which may be described as mischievous but can in folklore be either helpful or harmful. In some sources the Púca was seen as purely evil and dangerous, while others described it as potentially helpful and willing to do work around the home if treated well

(MacKillop, 1998).

The Púca is known to take on many forms, most often appearing as a dark horse, but also as an eagle, bat, bull, goat, a human man, or a more typical goblin-like small fairy; in the 1950 movie 'Harvey' there is a Púca which is said to take the form of giant rabbit (Briggs, 1976; Yeats, 1888; MacKillop, 1998). In the form of a horse the Púca will lure riders onto its back and then take them on a wild ride only to dump them in a ditch. This is a reasonably harmless trick though given that the kelpies and Each Uisge when pulling the same trick end it by drowning and eating their riders. The Púca has also been known to work on farms and in mills, both in human form and in horse form (Briggs, 1976). This, perhaps, best encapsulates the Púca's personality, using the horse form to both trick and cause minor harm as well as to work and help. In other stories the Púca will sometimes trick a person, even cruelly, and reward them later. In one case a Púca gave a piper a ride, forcing him to play as they went, only to have the piper find the next day that the gold he thought he'd been paid had turned to leaves and his pipes would play nothing but the noises of geese; but when he tried to tell the priest later and demonstrate he found that his playing had become the best of any piper in the area (Yeats, 1888). And perhaps that is the best summary of the Púca after all.

The Púca is a mysterious being, if indeed there is only one of him as some claim, or a complicated type if there are more than one. Generally all of the above named beings - the Púca, Pwca, Bucca and Puck - are considered together to be the same, however, while it may be that they are different cultural iterations of one being it might also be that they are simply similar enough to be classed together. The Welsh Bucca is said to be a single being who was once a God, while the English Puck is thought by some to perhaps be a type of pixie (Evans-Wentz, 1911). In contrast some older Irish folklore would clearly indicate the Púca was not solitary but a group of beings. It was said by one person interviewed in Ireland at the turn of the 20th century that the 'Pookas' were men who went invisibly to racecourses mounted on 'good horses' (Evans-Wentz, 1911). In Welsh and British folklore the Pwca and Puck were both said to mislead travellers and the British Puck stole clothes (Briggs, 1976; Purkiss, 2000).

The Púca also had a special association with autumn and with the turning of the year form summer to winter. In some areas it was said that any berries which remained on the bushes after Michaelmas [September 29] belonged to the Púca, who would spoil them for human consumption (Briggs, 1976). In other areas it is said that it is after Samhain [October 31] that all the remaining berries belong to the Púca, and that he will urinate or spit on them to claim them. In either case it is clear that he was entitled to a portion of the wild harvest, the food that grew without being cultivated. The Púca was also associated more generally with roaming on and around Samhain and it was said that Samhain was sacred to him (Yeats, 1888).

Although generally helpful the Púca can play pranks which may be malicious and if it's necessary to convince one to leave a home or area folklore would suggest the same method used (albeit less intentionally) that rids a home of a Brownie - the gift of clothes (Briggs, 1976; Yeats, 1888). In particular the gift of fine quality clothes as the Púca seems to have high standards. If, however, you feel you have a Púca around that you enjoy you might try offering it the traditional cream or the less common offering of fish, as some say they enjoy that (Evans-Wentz, 1911).

Puck

A figure from English folklore often equated or compared to the Irish Púca.

See: Púca

Pwca

See: Púca

Q

Queen of Air and Darkness

A title which has gained greatly in popularity and is often applied to Mab today, it was first seen in print in a 1922 poem by A.E. Housman. Titled simply 'III' it is found in his 'Last Poems' and features an unknown narrator killing an enigmatic being called the Queen of Air and Darkness who foretells the narrator's death following her own.

Her strong enchantments failing,
Her towers of fear in wreck,
Her limbecks dried of poisons
And the knife at her neck,

The Queen of air and darkness
Begins to shrill and cry,
"O young man, O my slayer,
To-morrow you shall die."

0 Queen of air and darkness,
I think 'tis truth you say,
And I shall die to-morrow;
But you will die to-day.

The name would be used as the title of a 1939 TH White novel and in 1972 for the title of a Poul Anderson novella. It has also been used explicitly for the title of fictional fairy Queens in the works of LK Hamilton and Jim Butcher. Additionally the Queen of Air and Darkness is the name of a goddess in the 'Dungeons and Dragons' role playing game. In modern fiction the name is given to several characters in novels, often attributed to the Queen of the UNSEELIE COURT.

Queen of Elfland

A common general title for the Queen of the Otherworld in Scotland, particularly the Lowlands, which we find from about the 16th century onward is the Queen of Elfland. Variants on this include Queen of Elfin, Queen of Fairy, Queen of Elfame, Queen of Elfhame, and Queen of the Seelie[1] Court. She is never given a first name in either ballad material or anecdotal accounts.

When she appears in folklore she is often alone although in a few accounts she does have a nameless king by her side and she is also known to ride out in procession with the FAIRY RADE. Her horse is white, probably a sign of her rank, and she is described as both very beautiful and well dressed in either green or less often white. In both anecdotes and ballad material she has been compared to Mary, as Queen of Heaven, perhaps in an attempt to convey the Otherworldly nature that her form radiates.

The Queen of Elfland is an unpredictable figure who may show unmotivated compassion or may steal a coveted person into Fairy for her own reasons. Her benevolent nature can be illustrated by her actions in the Ballad of Alison Gross where she finds a man who has been enchanted into the shape of a worm and returns him to his true form, apparently for no other reason than pity (Acland, 2001). In contrast in several versions of the 'Ballad of Tam Lin' when the young boy who would later be called Tam fell from his horse the Queen caught him up and took him into Fairy with her, stealing him away from the mortal world. Likewise in the Queen of Elfin's Nourice she has taken a human woman, separating her from her new-born, so that the woman can nurse the Queen's own baby, and no amount of weeping by the woman will sway the Queen to release her until the royal baby is old enough to be weaned.

In stories and ballads the Queen has an obvious interest in human men, particularly attractive ones as well as musicians. She will sometimes take these men permanently, sometimes bind them to her service for 7 years, and sometimes as we see with a few of the Scottish witches and cunningfolk leave them in mortal earth but maintain a connection to them. Going with the Queen of Elfland may or may not be voluntary. In the 'Ballad of Thomas the Rhymer' we see the Queen appearing to Thomas and compelling him to go with her into Fairy, keeping him in her service for 7 years, but paying him when he is finally returned. In some versions of the story the Queen eventually came back for Thomas, sending white deer to lead him back to Fairy where he still remains. In the Ballad of Tam Lin the eponymous character tells his mortal lover that he had come to be among the members of Fairy when he fell from his horse and was caught by the Queen of Fairies who took him *"in yon green hill to dwell"* (Acland, 1997). In a similar ballad, 'The Faerie Oak of Corriewater', the Queen of Fairies has taken a young man into her service as a cupbearer, paying him with a kiss; his sister tries and fails to rescue him. A Scottish witch, Andro Man, said in his trial he had repeated sexual encounters with the Queen of Elfland, which he called 'Elphin' (Henderson & Cowan, 2007).

The idea that she slept with Andro Man is interesting as we see a similar concept in the ballad material. In some versions of 'Tam Lin' the Queen seems to have a sense of affection for Tam Lin, although it's unclear whether it's romantic or maternal. In the earliest versions of Thomas the Rhymer, under the name Thomas of Erceldoune, the Queen and Thomas become lovers before she brings him with her into Fairy. And in the ballad of 'The Faerie Oak of Corriewater the Queen' is paying her new human cupbearer with 'a kiss' although the ballad implies that perhaps a bit more than a simple kiss is involved. It is possible looking at the evidence that the Queen uses sex and intimacy to bind men to her service.

The Queen's interest in humans extends beyond just men and we also find folklore about her interactions with women. These stories lack the sexual overtones of the previous examples but do include the wider themes of kidnapping and service. In 'The Queen of Elfin's Nourice' a nursing mother is abducted and put into the Queen's service, with the promise that the woman will be freed if she nurses the Queen's child until the child reaches a certain age (Child, 1882). The Queen also appears in the Scottish witch trial documents, with several Scottish witches saying they had sworn their loyalty to the Queen of Fairies, rather than the expected Christian Devil. Isobel Gowdie, one of the most well-known Scottish witches, described the Queen of Fairy well dressed in white and claimed she had been taken into the fairy hill and given as much meat as she could eat (Henderson & Cowan, 2007). Meat was a luxury food and it may be that Isobel being fed as much of it as she could want was form of payment for her services. Accused witch Bessie Dunlop claimed that the Queen of Elfland came to her when Bessie was in labour with her child, and part of the reason that Alison Pearson accused and went to trial was for allegedly spending time with the '*Quene of Elfame*' (Henderson & Cowan, 2007). Many of the trial accounts of Scottish witches detail stories of witches who were brought by a fairy or fairies into the Otherworld to meet with the Queen, or sometimes the Queen and King; these witches told various stories of things they had done or seen while there. These visits and the relationship with the Queen could involve being given knowledge of healing herbs and skills and in some cases potentially of cursing and elfshot. Several of these witches said it was this Queen who directed them in their witchcraft and assigned them a fairy as a familiar spirit (Wilby, 2005).

Ultimately the Queen of Elfland is an enigmatic figure, possibly several different Fairy Queens whose various folklore have been collected together because she remains nameless. What can definitely be said about her is that she seems to have more than a passing interest in humans and is willing to directly seek out those who may be of use to her. Whether or not that is good for the human in question varies greatly in each account.

Note

1 Seelie also has multiple variant spellings. See entry on seelie for more on this.

Queen of Elfans Nourice

A ballad describing a mother who has been taken by the Fairy queen to nurse the Queen's child. The woman is pining for her own new-born who she has been separated from, but the Queen will not return her until her job is done. The piece offers fascinating insight into both sides of the stolen NURSING MOTHER motif.

I heard a cow low, a bonnie cow low,
And a cow low down in yonder glen;
Long, long will my young son weep
For his mother to bid him come in.
I heard a cow low, a bonnie cow low,
And a cow low down in yonder fold;
Long, long will my young son weep
For his mother take him from the cold.

Waken, Queen of Elfland,
And hear your nurse moan.'
'O moan you for your meat,
Or moan you for your money,
Or moan you for the other bounties
That ladies are want to give?'
'I moan not for my meat,
Nor moan I for my money,
Nor moan I for the other bounties
That ladies are want to give.

But I moan for my young son
I left at four nights old.
'I moan not for my meat,

Nor yet for my money,
But I mourn for Christian land,
It's there I gladly would be.'
'O nurse my child, nurse,' she says,
'Till he stands at your knee,
And you'll win home to Christian land,
Where glad it's you would be.
'O keep my child, nurse,
Till he goes by the hand,
And you'll win home to your young son
You left at four nights old.'

'O nurse lay your head
Upon my knee:
See you not that narrow road
Up by yon tree?

That's the road the righteous goes,
And that's the road to heaven.
'And see not you that broad road,
Down by yonder sunny hill?
That's the road the wicked go,
And that's the road to hell.'
(Modified from Child, 1898)

Ráth

See: Sidhe

Redcaps

A dangerous kind of Goblin, Redcaps are known to haunt the ruined locations of murders, and although there have been a few stories of less malevolent Redcaps the majority have a vicious nature. They get their names from the red hat they always wear which they dye in fresh human blood. In general appearance they look like stooped, wrinkled older men, with large teeth, fingers ending in talons, wearing iron boots and usually carrying a weapon like a pike (Briggs, 1976). Redcaps, as indicated by their choice of footwear, are one kind of fairy which is not affected by iron. In folklore they are impervious to most human weapons but can be driven off using Christian prayers or at the sight of a cross (Briggs, 1976).

There is one folkloric account of a man who bound a Redcap to be his fairy familiar and the goblin acted to protect him from harm by weapons (Briggs, 1976)

Religion of the Fairies

There is not one single cohesive religion to be found among the fairy folk but we do find hints of different beliefs and practices in the folklore relating to them.

Grace Hutchins in the tale of SELENA MOOR tells her former love that the fairies are star-worshippers and one source in Ireland refers to the Gentry as having come *"from the planets"* (Bottrell, 1873; Evans-Wentz, 1911, page 53).

There were claims that the fairies did celebrate some kind of festivals although what exact kind is uncertain. One source from Ireland stated:

> *"Persons in a short trance-state of two or three days' duration are said to be away with the fairies enjoying a festival. The festival may be very material in its nature, or it may be purely spiritual."* (Evans- Wentz, 1911).

In contrast to these examples there are also accounts of fairies who act as Christians or are very concerned with Christian theology, particularly with their own potential salvation. One story recorded in the Dúchas folklore collection, volume 0276, page 192, talks of a man who was invited into a fairy hill to witness the baptism of a fairy baby. There are also widespread accounts of fairies who inquired of people, including priests, about whether they would or could achieve salvation with other Christians; when the answer inevitably was no the fairies' reaction was usually violent.

Perhaps on a related note some of the middle-eastern Jinn are said to be Muslim while others are not, indicating a possibly wider pattern where some Otherworldly beings follow human religions and others do not. This may tie into the idea that some fairies were once living humans while others were never human at all.

While the Irish fairies seem to have an appreciation of religion and ritual, at least one Welsh source claims the Tylwyth Teg are averse to such. This account in 'Fairy Faith in Celtic Countries' describes a human man who wants to wed a fairy woman but the couple must do so with some degree of secrecy because, as the story goes, *"they had to go about it quietly and half secretly, for the fair-folk dislike ceremony and noise."* (Evans-Wentz, 1911, page 162).

Retreat of the Fairies

There have been multiple accounts over the last 600 years of the retreat of the fairies from the human world, often attributed to the advance of the Christian faith. Chaucer, in the Wife of Bath's Tale circa the 14th century, stated that:

"In the days of King Arthur, Britain was full of fairies.
The elf queen danced in meadows with her companions.
This is what I read, anyway.
Now, no one sees elves any more, because of the prayers of friars.
These friars search all over the land, blessing every building and house, with the result that there are no more fairies."
(Canterbury Tales, lines 863 – 866)

Whereas Chaucer blamed the Christian church generally and Catholics more specifically for the fairies' retreat, the 16th century bishop and poet Richard Corbet blamed Protestants. In his poem 'Farewell, Rewards, and Fairies' he claimed the fairies were themselves Catholic:

"By which we note the Fairies
Were of the old Profession.
Their songs were 'Ave Mary's'
Their dances were Procession.
But now, alas, they all are dead;
Or gone beyond the seas;
Or farther for Religion fled"

A 19th century Scottish tale would again claim the final retreat of the fairies from earth, as two children saw a parade of small fairies riding south and one was brave enough to ask them where they were going to which one fairy replied *"The People of Peace shall never more be seen in Scotland"* (Briggs, 1976, page 96). Of course, this permanent retreat proved rather less than permanent as sightings of fairy beings continued afterwards and continue to this day.

There are also stories of fairies retreating not from the mortal world in its entirety but from specific areas. There is a place in Perthshire, Scotland named after the fairies once thought to live there but it's believed they fled when the train began passing through, because of the train's whistle (Evans-Wentz, 1911).

Fairies were also said to have been driven out of several areas by the sound of church bells which they seemingly can't abide. Katherine Briggs records two separate accounts of fairies that moved from their home areas complaining of the relentless noise of the bells, one from Inkberrow and the other from Exmoor (Briggs, 1976).

Despite these claims anecdotal accounts of fairies persists into the modern era, and despite claims that the Fairy Faith itself has ceased the beliefs and practices also continue among the living Celtic language cultures and diaspora.

Rescue from the Fairies

If a living human was taken by the fairies there are several means mentioned in folklore for how they might be rescued. The fairies were generally reluctant to give up a person they had taken, so none of these methods are guaranteed to work and many may initially result in increased fairy violence before capitulation.

A person might be taken entirely, might be taken with a changeling left in their place, or the person's physical body might remain behind but their spirit would be taken. Yeats in The Celtic Twilight related a story of a young girl bodily taken by the fairies who was returned after the local people at the direction of the garda [police officer] burned the field of ragwort she had last been seen in; the girl told of her abduction by the fairies after she was brought back. In contrast several anecdotal accounts in The Fairy Faith in Celtic Countries talk about people who seemed to have died and then were revived with the belief that they were taken, in spirit, by the fairies and their body left behind. One eye witness account, found on page 72 of that text, describes three children who stumbled across a group of fairies dancing; a fairy woman ran at the children and struck one with a reed; the children ran home but upon arriving home the girl who had been struck collapsed apparently dead only to be revived later by the prayers and actions of the local priest.

In an anecdotal account from the 'Fairy Faith in Celtic Countries' a woman taken by the fairies could have been rescued if her husband had gone to a specific place at night when she and the Fairy host would be passing by and grabbed her when he saw her, and similarly folklore says that rev. Kirk was taken by the Good People and could have been saved if a relative had thrown an iron knife over his head when he appeared at his son's baptism after his apparent death. In both cases the people failed to act and the taken humans were not rescued. In contrast in the Ballad of Tam Lin we see a story of a woman who is told to pull her fairy lover from his horse when the Fairy Rade passes by and hold him through a variety of frightening transformations in order to win him back to humanity and as her spouse, which she successfully does.

If someone encountered the SLUA SIDHE and believed the fairy host had a captive with them they could toss some dirt from the road, a glove, or an iron knife at the host while saying 'this is yours, that is mine' and they would be compelled to free whoever they had taken. Campbell also suggests that a left shoe or hat may be thrown for the same effect. One 20th century anecdote tells of a method of recovering someone who was among the fairies by praying and whistling three times, with the person returning on the third whistle (Evans-Wentz, 1911). The exact prayer used is not given.

Prayer sometimes plays a part in rescue of people from Fairy as we see in the above example, although generally combined with other actions. In such accounts the person praying is usually someone with authority, rather than a lay person. However, there is at least one account from the ballad of Alice Brand where a man who has been transformed into a fairy is returned to his former human state when a woman makes the sign of the cross over his forehead three times. This does represent an unusual method compared to the wider bulk of folklore, however, and may hinge on the person in question having been a Christian when he was human.

See also CHANGELINGS for methods specific to rescuing people believed to have been taken and replaced with a changeling.

Rón

See: SELKIES

Robert Kirk

One of the most well-known authors on the subject of Scottish fairies Kirk was a protestant minister in 17th century Scotland who initially achieved renown for translating the Bible into Gaidhlig. Serving in Aberfoyle, an area replete with fairylore, Kirk would later begin writing down the local beliefs and stories in a series of notebooks. Before this project could be finished, however, he became ill and although a relative helped him by recording his words as Kirk dictated them, the minister would die before he was finished.

Kirk's death is surrounded with mystery even today. He collapsed while walking near a fairy KNOWE, something that he habitually did, and that later led to speculation that he had actually been taken by the fairies possibly for his attempts to write about them. After his death folklore would spring up around Kirk, claiming that he had been taken to serve the Fairy Queen herself, possibly as a chaplain to the fairies, and a story began circulating that he had appeared to a relative declaring himself a captive in Fairy who could be freed if iron was thrown over his head when he was seen at his posthumous son's christening (Smith, 1921; Walsh; 2002). This was not done and Kirk remained in fairy, according to common belief.

Kirk's book on Scottish fairies would later be published by Sir Walter Scott in 1815, although that version had multiple errors; his work would later be republished with the assistance of folklorist Andrew Lang under the title of 'The Secret

Commonwealth of Elves, Fauns, and Fairies'. Kirk's notebooks can be found today in the Edinburgh University Library and National Library of Scotland. An excellent analysis of Kirk's life, work, and writing on the 'Secret Commonwealth' was written by Kevan Manwaring titled 'The Remarkable Notebooks of Robert Kirk' and can be accessed online.

Robin Goodfellow

An English fairy made famous by Shakespeare Robin Goodfellow is generally viewed as an individual being more so than a type of fairy although he falls into the general category of a HOBGOBLIN. He is a trickster spirit, sometimes malicious and sometimes kind, who could take a variety of forms including that of a horse (Simpson & Roud, 2000). His name may be understood as a generic one: Robin was a nickname for the devil but also associated with hobgoblins[1] and Goodfellow may be either a reference to his sometimes beneficial nature or a euphemism encouraging that sort of response from him (Wright, 2009; Simpson & Roud, 2000).

Because he is a shapeshifter Robin Goodfellow was sometimes confused with or equated to the English PUCK, and in later folklore there is crossover between the two. Shakespeare emphasizes this in his play 'A Midsummer Night's Dream' where Robin Goodfellow is explicitly identified by the name of Puck. There are early 16th century references to Robin Goodfellow misleading travellers, which connects him as well to the WILL'O'THE WISP, and other more helpful tales which seem to connect him to BROWNIES. All of these beings are considered types of Hobgoblins.

In folklore Robin is said to be the child of the English fairy king OBERON and a mortal woman; he was not born with fairy powers but gained them later and was taken fully into Fairy as an adult (Simpson & Roud, 2000). It's said that robin's mother, who was human, raised him until he was six but that he was such a mischievous child that she finally threatened to whip him, at which the boy ran away; falling asleep later dreamt of fairies and woke up to find a scroll next to him that explained his nature and granted him several powers including shape shifting (Keightley, 1850).

Robin Goodfellow was a popular spirit across England during the 16th and 17th century. In 1636 he appeared in a small book titled 'Robin Goodfellow; his mad pranks and merry jests' which detailed Robin's birth and life as well as some of his adventures (British Library, 2018). The text is rare today but valuable in that it gives us a fuller picture of Robin's character than his appearance in Shakespeare's more popular work which preceded it by about 30 years. It describes Robin as a spirit who acts in both rural and domestic settings, who tricks people but often in order to help teach them moral lessons, leads travellers astray, and includes a woodcut of him as a satyr-like figure with goat legs and horns, carrying a broom, surrounded by dancing figures (British Library, 2018). This imagery and activity is in line with both his Shakespearean antics as well as his wider conflations with Puck and other types of fairies.

According to Keightley Robin would do some chores around a farm or home in exchange for milk and bread, but was offended by any offer of clothing.

Note

1 As discussed in the section on hobgoblins the 'hob' portion of the name is a shortened version of Robin.

S

Salt

Salt is another substance often mentioned for having apotropaic qualities against fairies.

At least one 20th century Irish source mentions that the Daoine Maithe don't eat food with salt in it (Evans-Wentz, 1911). Food being carried out of a house at night was sprinkled with salt to protect the substance of it from being taken and the luck of the family from being taken with it (Campbell, 1900).

Second Sight

Second Sight or Spirit Sight is an ability to see spirits and fairies which a person may be born with or which can be acquired through various means. Those who are born with the Sight are might be known for their ability to perceive spirits and to have some knowledge of events occurring elsewhere, which may be the result of a kind of clairsentience or be information passed to them by fairies.

People born with the Sight were often known to be FRIENDS OF THE FAIRIES and to be taken by them either permanently or for periods of time. Such people also seemed at least partially exempt from the usual rules applied to fairy privacy and are able to see fairies and interact with them without the usual consequences that come with accidental sightings, at least from the fairies directly. Both Wilby in her book 'Cunningfolk and Familiar Spirits' and rev. Kirk in 'The Secret Commonwealth' mention that people connected to the fairies and who can see them would be startled, even terrified on occasion, when seeing them unexpectedly.

Some people were said to have gained the sight because of or after an illness, as we are told here:

> *"Mike Farrell, too, could tell all about the gentry, as he lay sick a long time....Mike surely saw the gentry; and he was with them during his illness for twelve months."* (Evans-Wentz, 1911, page 55).

In one Welsh anecdote from the Fairy Faith in Celtic Countries a baby is given the Second Sight when their eyes are anointed by a special fairy oil, given the baby's father by a fairy woman[1]. From this it may be gathered that the Sight can be in inherent ability a person has or can be something that is gained at some point throughout life.

It is also possible according to stories to gain the Sight temporarily with the aid of an outside factor. Possessing a four leaf clover is supposed to dispel all enchantments, including fairy glamour, and allow a person to see the Fair Folk even when they don't want to be seen (Yeats, 1888). In both Scottish and Welsh anecdotal accounts and the writings of rev. Kirk we are told that a person may temporarily gain the Second Sight if a person stands on the foot of someone who has it, or conversely if the Second Sighted person stand on the other person's foot; this physical connection seems to impart the ability – at least in the moment – from one to the other (Kirk & Lang, 1893; Evans-Wentz, 1911).

Those who gain the Sight in other ways can have it taken from them if the Good People become aware the person possesses it, as the fairies guard their privacy and do not like being seen unintentionally. Rev. Kirk mentions this fairy habit of blinding those who can see them making it clear that they take both the natural sight as well as Second Sight but he emphasizes that this is done painlessly and instantly (Kirk & Land, 1893). The tales of FAIRY MIDWIVES feature this blinding prominently, usually ending with the midwife in the story losing an eye, or both eyes, when her ability to see the Other Crowd is found out.

Note

1 This account is oddly parallel to the MIDWIFE to the FAIRY tales but slightly reversed, in that the father goes out for a midwife but returns with a fairy woman who gives him the oil and instructions to place it on the baby's eyes. The man does so but accidently gets a bit on his own eye, and later sees the fairy woman at a market and is asked which eye he sees her from, after which she promptly blinds that eye (Evans-Wentz, 1911, page 140).

Seeing Fairies

For those who lack the natural possession or gifted possession of the SECOND SIGHT it is possible to see fairies under certain circumstances. The fairies can choose to reveal themselves to anyone at any time, and this may be selective so that even within a group only one person may see the Good People. We can see this in the 'Echtra Condla' where Connla can see the fairy woman but his father cannot, in an incident in the Tain Bo Cúailgne where a fairy man comes to see Cu Chulainn and passes unseen through the forces of Connacht although Cu Chulainn and his charioteer Laeg can see him, and in an account of the AMADÁN NA BRUIDHNE related by Yeats where a woman alone among a group could see the Fairy Fool as he approached them. There are also a few accounts of fairies being seen in the company of humans apparently unawares, like O Crualaoich's anecdotal account of a bean feasa who was seen in the company of a fairy, possibly her LEANNÁN SIDHE.

There are also certain times when it is more likely for a human to see the fairies and these include on the Quarter days, especially Bealtaine and Samhain, as well as at liminal times like twilight and midnight. It is at midnight that Janet sees the FAIRY RADE passing by in the Ballad of Tam Lin, for example. Campbell mentions twilight, heavy mists, and heavy rain as other periods when a human might be more likely to see fairies as well as when they have been mentioned in conversation or insulted (Campbell, 1900). We see this later shown in Mac Liammóir's

'Oíche na Féile Eoin' story in Oícheanta Sí wherein a group of boys is mocking the fairies and denying belief in their existence only to have a fairy appear in the guise of strange boy who accompanied them to the community bonfires and eventually led them off into the darkness to be taken by the fairies and ridden across the countryside for them.

Seelie

A Scots word with a variety of spellings, particularly sely, and meanings including "lucky, happy, blessed"; the adjective is applied euphemistically to fairies in Scotland. McNeill uses this term in relation to the Scottish fairies, calling them both 'Seelie court' and 'gude wichts' (McNeill, 1956, page111). Court in this sense meaning a group or company, and wichts meaning beings. Seelie fairies are those who are benevolently inclined towards humans and likely to help around homes and farms (McNeill, 1956). It should be remembered though that they are as able and likely to cause harm as any fairy. The use of the term Seelie in relation to fairies dates back to at least the 15th century in Scots and can be found in a book from 1801; in the 'Legend of the Bishop of St Androis' it says:

"Ane Carling of the Quene of Phareis
that ewill win gair to elphyne careis;
Through all Braid Albane scho hes bene
On horsbak on Hallow ewin;
and ay in seiking certayne nyghtis
As scho sayis, with sur sillie wychtis"
[one woman of the Queen of Fairies
that ill gotten goods to Elphin carries
through all broad Scotland she has been
on horseback on Halloween
and always in seeking certain nights
as she says, with our Seelie wights]

Seelie Court

One of the two main Courts of Fairy found in Lowland Scottish folklore, the Seelie court was likely originally a euphemism for all fairies and only later came to be seen as a distinct grouping of kindly inclined fairies.

As a group of fairies the Seelie court appears in Scottish folklore, especially in the Lowlands, as a general term for all fairies and as a specific for a group of more kindly inclined beings. The term seelie here is related directly and strongly to their temperament with Jamieson calling it the *"pleasant or happy court, or court of the pleasant and happy people"* (Jamieson, 1808). It is important to remember in context that in Scots 'court' can mean either a royal court as well as a group or company of people, and we see the term used both ways when applied to Seelie. There are clear references to a Queen of the Seelie Court, such as we see in the ballad of Alison Gross where the Queen stumbles across a mortal man cursed into the shape of a worm when she and her 'Seely Court' were riding nearby.

The Seelie Court is usually considered to be more benevolently inclined towards humans and won't cause harm without a reason and warning (Briggs, 1976). This should not be interpreted to mean they are harmless, however, as they did retaliate against those who wronged them and were as mercurial and sometimes cruel as any other group of fairies. They were also as likely as any other fairies to engage in activities like stealing the substance from crops or taking people. An early 19th century poem, the 'Ballad of Lady Mary O'Craignethan', ties the Seelie Court to the kidnapping of a human woman by a man of fairy (Sands, Brymer, Murray, & Cochran, 1819).

Exactly what kinds of fairies may be included in the ranks of the Seelie court may be debatable, although those beings who are usually helpful to humans would be logical. The term is also used in a euphemistic sense to reference all fairies.

Selena Moor

Selena Moor is a folktale from Cornwall which exhibits several common motifs from fairylore including the HUMANS BECOMING FAIRIES, CHANGELINGS, and ESCAPE FROM FAIRIES, as well as some unusual aspects.

The story is related in a late 19th century book of Cornish folktales and begins by describing an area of land in Cornwall, since tamed, which was once an expanse of wild moorland and swamp. One year around the autumn equinox a certain man, a middle aged bachelor named Mr Noy, was heading home from the public house when he went missing and was gone for three full days. The entire population of the area searched for him but no sign was found until on the third day some men heard the sound of Mr Noy's dogs and horse and tracked him into the edge of the swamp where he was found sleeping in a ruined building. When they woke him he was confused and thought it was the day he had disappeared and moreover that he was a great distance from his home although he was within a mile of it. Eventually he related to his neighbours that he had tried to shortcut through the moor after leaving the pub the night he was last seen and in doing so had found himself inexplicably travelling in a strange and unfamiliar place full of trees and quite unlike anything in his local area. Wandering for a long time he had finally heard music playing and thought to follow that to seek help. He saw lights through the trees and heard people and thought it must be some farm folk out celebrating Harvest Home[1], but his dogs and horse refused to go further so before proceeding he tied the horse to a tree and left the dogs there with it (Bottrell, 1873).

When he reached the clearing Mr Noy saw a group of what he described as *"undersized mortals"* with tables and cups set out that were all made for the size of the people. Among them he saw one person his own size, a young woman who was playing music for the gathered group to dance to and who at times would break off to go into the nearby house and bring out more drink to refill the cups with. The music was so enchanting that Noy stepped forward to join in but seeing him the young woman caught his eye and gestured instead for him to follow her back into the orchard, handing off her instrument to an old man near her. Once in the trees Noy recognized her as Grace Hutchins his own sweetheart who had died several years previously and been buried in the local churchyard. Grace explained that she had stopped him because if he had joined the dance then he, like her, would be trapped among the fairy people and when he moved to embrace her she stepped away, saying "*embrace me not, nor touch flower nor fruit; for eating a tempting plum in this enchanted orchard was my undoing.*" (Bottrell, 1873, p 98). She goes on to tell him that while everyone thought she had died on the moor it was a CHANGELING that had been buried in her place and she, as far as she knew, lived on trapped among the fairy people. She went on to tell him how she had gotten lost on the moor one day trying to follow after him and found herself after some wandering in a strange place full of roses and high walls with fruit hanging ripe and full all around. As she told him:

> "*The music, too, seemed very near at times, but she could see nobody. Feeling weary and athirst, she plucked a plum, that looked like gold in the clear star-light; her lips no sooner closed on the fruit than it dissolved to bitter water which made her sick and faint. She then fell on the ground in a fit, and remained insensible, she couldn't say how long, ere she awoke to find herself surrounded by hundreds of small people, who made great rejoicing to get her amongst them, as they very much wanted a tidy girl who knew how to bake and brew, one that would keep their habitation decent, nurse the changed-children, that weren't so strongly made as they used to be, for want of more beef and good malt liquor, so they said.*" (Bottrell, 1873, page 99).

She had lived like that in the ensuing years and had come to believe that these fairy people had once been mortal like herself but were now only shadows slowly dissolving. She told him they had neither hearts nor feeling and that everything in their life, including all the tempting food, was merely illusion, and she also said that these fairies were not Christians but instead worshipped the stars. She did say, however, that the small people were very kind to her and that she was adjusting to her new life, later even telling Noy that while he should leave while he could that night if he wanted to join her among the fairies later he could choose to. She said that some among them took the form of goats in order to steal a goat that was in milk from a flock to feed the changeling children and when Noy questioned her she told him that the fairy people had both human children they had taken and some rare children born to them, saying,

> *"…they are fond of babies, and make great rejoicing when one happens to be born amongst them; and then every little man, however old, is proud to be thought the father. For you must remember they are not of our religion," said she, in answer to his surprised look, "but star-worshippers. They don't always live together like Christians and turtle-doves; considering their long existence such constancy would be tiresome for them, anyhow the small tribe seem to think so."* (Bottrell, 1873, page 100).

Grace told Mr Noy that she was in the habit of coming to watch over him in the form of a bird and that her love for him was eternal. Then she was called back among the fairy folk to serve another round of drinks and Noy thinking quickly pulled a glove from his pocket and turning it inside out cast it down, at which point he felt a blow on his forehead and fell asleep. His neighbours were sceptical, as much of what he had said was repeating well-known local fairylore, but the experience changed Noy greatly and he died within a year after falling into a depression pining for Grace.

William Bottrell in recording this tale notes that it is strikingly similar to another local folktale featuring a famer named Richard Vingoe who also wandered and was lost until he found himself in a strange place with fairy people feasting and men playing a game of hurling; he would have joined the game except a young woman pulled him away and he realized she was his lost fiancé. She led him a ways apart and kept him from the fairies while explaining what they were and how she had come to be there. She led him safely back to familiar territory and left him there where he decided to lay down and rest for a bit only to wake a week later. Like Noy he was deeply changed by the experience, his behaviour changed afterwards, and he died unhappy.

The stories were alike enough that Bottrell guessed they were different versions of one tale, although we may perhaps also see instead a similar theme playing out. In both stories it is clear that a human may be taken by the fairies by engaging in their activities and that once taken the human is transformed by the fairies into one of their own number. This person is assumed to be dead by the rest of their community although as Grace says she did not think that she had died but been replaced by a changeling. It is also a common element of both stories that the person who escapes their brush with the fairies is, nonetheless, drastically effected by it and pines for what they experienced, even briefly, among the Undying People.

Note

1 Harvest Home or Gulthise as Bottrell calls it is a folk celebration that occurs around the autumn equinox when the harvest is taken in.

Selkies

Selkies are a fascinating ocean fairy who can take the form of either a human or a seal. Called Rón or Roane in Irish, and Selkies, Silkies, or Selchies in Scotland, Shetland or the Orkneys. The name 'Selkie' is derived from the Scottish word 'selch' itself drawn from the Old

English seoh, all meaning seal (Heddle, 2016). The Irish word rón also means seal. Their folklore is fairly consistent across any area although there are some slight variations; for example Orkney Selkies are known to have some ability at prophecy and Rón are gentler and more forgiving than their Scottish counterparts. Selkies are also one of the kinds of fairy who are very intertwined with humans making Selkie lore slightly more prominent particularly in coastal areas.

Selkies in their seal form are indistinguishable physically from ordinary seals except for their eyes which are unusual and expressive. In human form they are noted to have dark hair and eyes, and folklore differs on whether they appear to be exceptionally attractive or ordinary. The key to the Selkies ability to transform was its seal skin which was both a part of the fairy and also separable from it, making it both a source of power and a weakness. In some Scottish folklore it's claimed that the human form is the Selkie's true one, and the seal form is only assumed with magic (Briggs, 1976). Without the seal skin the Selkie could not transform into its seal shape and in its seal form, according to some folklore, if the skin was damaged or forcibly removed the Selkie would die[1]. In the folklore of the Orkneys the Selkies shape shifting is somewhat limited, with some tales claiming they can only come ashore in human form on Midsummer and others that they must wait 7 or 9 days in the sea before returning to land again (Towrie, 2019).

Orkney folklore offers a few explanations for the origins of Selkies. From a more Christian perspective it is said that they may be the angels who fell into the sea when God was expelling the rebellious angels from heaven, while other stories say they are the souls of drowned humans or those who have committed a great wrong and been condemned into the form of a seal as punishment (Towrie, 2019).

Selkie stories generally feature either the FAIRY WIFE theme, with the Selkie wife compelled to her mortal husband's side, or else a variation of the LEANNAN SIDHE motif with the human and Selkie coming together in a more voluntary manner. The latter type of story is somewhat less common and tends to involve male selkies and female humans. Some scholars interpret Selkie stories in a way that views the male Selkies as more noble and the females as more emotionally driven, but that is an oversimplification (Silver, 1999). Briggs repeats a tale exemplifying this concept of a young woman dissatisfied with her husband who conjured a Selkie lover for herself and had many children with him over many years. Male Selkies have reputations for being both amorous and rather fickle (Briggs, 1976). As the previous example shows, however, they are able to maintain longer relationships when they choose to, although more often, as noted by the Orcadian folklorist Dennison, they would simply come ashore seeking an unsatisfied woman open to their attentions and then return to the sea (Towrie, 2018). Unlike some other male fairies who had human lovers male Selkies did not seek to take their human lovers into the waves with them very often; what stories we do have along that vein involve the human being turned into a Selkie or drowning. In the Fairy wife type stories the Selkie is forced into the relationship when her seal skin is stolen by an amorous human man who finds it. Bound on land without the transformative magic of her seal skin the Selkie goes with him as his wife, keeping his home and bearing him children, until the day she finally finds out where her seal skin has been hidden. In many version of these stories it is one of her own children that eventually finds the cleverly hidden skin and reveals its location to her. Once she has her skin back she returns immediately to the water, abandoning her unwanted spouse as well as her children. In many cases it does seem the children at least were loved by the Selkie and there are stories of Selkies who would after returning to the sea ensure that their children always had plenty of fish and excellent fishing.

Much folklore describes the union between humans and

selkies and the children produced. The children of selkies and humans are said in folklore to be born with webbed hands or feet, a trait that carries down a family line. One famous example of this comes from the Orkneys where a woman named Ursilla was said to have taken a Selkie lover and had many children by him, all of whom were born with webbed hands and feet; these webs were cut with iron shears and turned into a hard growth upon the hands and feet (Towrie, 2018). This trait was passed down through the descendants of Ursilla so that while the story passed into folklore the evidence of the birth defect associated with it was noted by folklorist Walter Dennison in an 1893 article her wrote detailing Ursilla's story[2]. When the mother is the Selkie she may abandon her half-human children when she has a chance to return to the sea; when the father is the Selkie he may take his child with him or leave them with their mother. In one account from the Orkneys a woman and Selkie have a child and after a year the Selkie returns to take the boy with him into the sea but lets the human mother know where she might be able to go at the shore to see her son (Heddle, 2016). Several families including the MacColdrums and MacRoons claim descent from Selkie women.

There have been several popular movies featuring these fairies in the last several decades including 'The Secret of Roan Inish' which was based off an earlier novel and 'Song of the Sea'.

Notes

1 Briggs relates an example of this idea from Shetland where a fisherman catches and skins a seal, tossing the body back into the water; a mermaid sacrifices herself to retrieve the Seal-man's skin saving his life (Briggs, 1976).

2 The full account by Dennison, which relates Ursilla's story including her marriage, seeking out of a Selkie lover, and Dennison's own meeting with one of her descendants, can be found on the Orkneyjar website here http://www.orkneyjar.com/folklore/selkiefolk/ursilla.htm

Selling the Soul

Most of us are familiar with the idea of classical witches selling their souls to the Devil, but there is another concept we see as well in folkloric sources: a person selling their soul to the fairies. The implication in the wider narrative is that the soul is being pledged to the Queen of Fairy but it is rarely spelled out as such. This is usually done as a combination of a required renunciation of the person's previous faith and either a pledge of loyalty to the Good People or else a more formal agreement to give over one's soul to them, with the implicit understanding that ultimately one's loyalty then is owed to the Fairy Queen or King. We see this in examples from the Scottish witch trials where an agent of the Fairy Queen approaches a person and offers them things they would want, often good luck and success, in exchange for the person giving up Christianity and swearing loyalty to the fairies instead.

The idea of a person selling their soul is seemingly ubiquitous in Christian accusations against early modern witches. It hinges on the belief that the soul could be offered by a person to non-Christian powers in exchange for worldly benefits to the person, with the understanding that this would cost the person their potential salvation within Christianity. Although most well known in relation to diabolism, this concept is seen as well in witchcraft trials relating to those who dealt with or worked with the fairies. Emma Wilby argues in her book 'Cunning folk and Familiar Spirits' that while we might be tempted to see the idea of selling the soul to fairies as a later Christian distortion of tradition it does reflect genuine beliefs surrounding those who dealt with fairies and the much older ideas in the culture that to deal closely with fairies was understood to represent accepting a fate bound to them (Wilby, 2005). These older fairy beliefs were likely vestiges of pagan practice, held over by the initial approach of the Church to fairies as beings that fell into an ambiguous area, but shortly before the witch hunts began in Scotland there was a shift in the ecclesiastical view to seeing fairies as more clearly demonic and including them, sometimes interchangeably, with the Devil and demons (Henderson & Cowan, 2007). This was a significant shift in perspective in Scotland, although we do not see a similar shift in Ireland where fairies remained in that grey area between good and evil, clearly outside of the main accepted belief system but persisting as powerful beings with connections to the dead and the pagan Gods.

At this point I think we need to look at exactly what we mean with the phrase 'sell your soul' and unpack the concept, particularly separating it from the embedded negative connotations. The expression is, of course, one that comes to us from a Christian context and implies trading one's soul, implicitly to a negative entity, in exchange for worldly benefits. However, this idea hinges on the wider belief that one's soul has already been given to the Christian God and that selling your soul elsewhere is bad because it means giving up the benefits that would otherwise come from that God. But I think there's a valid argument that commitment to any God or religion is just as much of a 'sale' of the soul, in that one is committing oneself to that specific deity in exchange for specific benefits, and with an understanding that there are specific requirements one will have to live by. What makes selling your soul to the Devil, or the fairies, or pagan Gods, negative is more about perspective coming from one religion to another than anything else. Ultimately what we are discussing here is not that different from a person dedicating themselves into any religion, or to any deity, except that whereas the promises of Christianity hinge on the afterlife entirely the promises of the fairies involve both the mortal life and the afterlife.

Next I think we need to look at what we mean by 'soul'. This may sound simple but it's actually a bit more complicated because there isn't any clear agreement on what a soul actually is, or even if it is one holistic thing. For some cultures the soul is comprised of multiple parts which can be separated, while others see the soul as one unit, the animating force that inhabits the body. Generally in the older material when we see the soul discussed what is meant is the consciousness of a person that contains their personality; the words soul and spirit are used interchangeably. However, even in the fairylore material we see the idea that a person can be away with the fairies that a part of their spirit can be in Fairy while the rest of them remains here, hinting at the possibility that even this conscious soul can be divided or at least focused in two places simultaneously (Wilby, 2005, Evans-Wentz 1911). It is possible then that in any case where we see a person committing their soul to something or someone they are only pledging a part or aspect of the soul, possibly that which is the unique personality, and that other parts may go elsewhere. I am not going to dictate to anyone how to view what a soul is, I will only say here that what we see discussed in the texts and folklore is something separable from the body which retains the essence of the person's character in life. When you pledge your soul and the time comes for that to be collected your body is left behind and it is this part of yourself that's taken[1].

There is a formulaic approach to selling one's soul to the fairies which involves first renouncing your old religion or God and then overtly promising one's self to the new. This is not done spontaneously by an individual but usually at the specific request of the fairies or at the urging of a specific fairy, often the person's existing fairy familiar. Emma Wilby discusses this at length in chapter 6 of her book 'Cunning Folk and Familiar Spirits'[2] mentioning examples from the Scottish witch trials where we see the renunciation and promising pattern. This is not a bargain that only favours the fairies, however, and we always see the person offered something valuable in return. Cunning woman Joan Tyrry claimed she learned her healing skill from the fairies; Jean Weir was given a small piece of wood by an envoy of the Fairy Queen which allowed her to spin unusually quickly and inexplicably fine quality yarn; Bessie Dunlop was offered gear and goods (Wilby, 2005). It is worth noting that the narrative of selling the soul to the Devil is largely absent from English witchcraft trials (Gregory, 2013) and that such confessions and connections specifically to Fairy were unique to areas with strongly ingrained existing fairy beliefs and were notably absent in other places.

Renunciation - In these examples we find the fairies, usually through the intermediary of a fairy familiar sent to the person, asking for an explicit renunciation of the person's 'Christendom' and baptism, although there were also examples where they required the person to keep making a show of going to Church or even encouraged them to be sure they were adequately devout. There are also cases where the renunciation was implicit rather than explicit, such as we see with Alison Peirson, who was never asked to verbally renounce Christianity but was instead asked to agree to be faithful to a green-clad fairy that appears to her, in exchange for his good favour; her responding yes to his request was perceived as an implicit renunciation of her other religion (Wilby, 2005). In the cases of implicit renunciation a person agreeing to be faithful to or to act as an agent of the fairies - in effect skipping to step two - was viewed as carrying with it the inherent rejection of the person's previous pledges to any other faith.

Promising - After the person's previous religion or God was renounced they were required to pledge their loyalty to the fairies, usually in the form of a fairy familiar or envoy. Bessie Dunlop promised that she would be 'loyal and true to [her familiar Thom] in any thing she could do', and Alison Peirson swore to be faithful (Wilby, 2005). In one singular account Joan Willimot was asked to promise her soul to a fairy woman, which she did (Wilby, 2005). Those who made these oaths would later be taken to Fairy and presented to the Fairy Queen, or Queen and King, or at the least would be regularly urged to go to Fairy if they refused to leave this world. It is possible that this travel to Fairy marked the final sealing of this agreement, something that may be supported by Wilby's assertion that to travel to Fairy was to give one's soul, implicitly, to the fey folk for the time one was there. Those who had sworn loyalty to a fairy or to the fairies more generally would have fallen into the ultimate hierarchy of Fairy itself and owed their loyalty to the monarchs of the group they were dealing with.

In some cases the person might be formally presented to the Queen of Fairy, while in others, such as Isobel Gowdie, the Queen might give the person a gift from her own hand, or as in the case of Andro Man might have sex with the person (Wilby, 2005). All of these actions can be viewed as fully committing oneself - one's soul - to Fairy generally and to its monarch specifically. This renouncing and promising was sometimes noted to follow a specific ritual format where the person would place their hand on the sole of one foot, and place the other hand on the crown of their head (Wilby, 2005). This can be seen as a pledging of the person's entire self - of everything between one hand and the other - to the powers they are speaking to. This also shows an important difference from the similar soul selling ritual in diabolism which usually involved the person giving blood to the Devil, or later signing their name in blood.

It is clear that the common belief of the time was that those who dealt with fairies and went with them into Fairy, particularly if negotiation was involved, understood that their soul could end up in Fairy when they died (Wilby, 2005). This is not a surprising idea given how complicated the relationship is between the fairies and the dead; it was a well ingrained belief that sometimes a person who died had actually been taken into Fairy and we see a wide range of anecdotes supporting this. Reverend Robert Kirk was believed to have been taken by the fairies, possibly for writing too much about them (Briggs, 1976). Evans-Wentz in the 1911 text 'A Fairy Faith in Celtic Countries' includes several stories of people thought to have died in various manners who were then seen or believed to have become part of the company of Fairy. The idea then of consciously committing oneself to that fate wouldn't have seemed outlandish, especially for those who were dealing with fairies and were already aware that it was a possibility simply because of their existing interactions with the Otherworld. We don't see this explicit giving of the self or soul to the fairies in the Irish material but arguably we do see the implicit giving occurring, particularly with the witches and bean feasa who were said to have Leannán Sídhe.

The final question that should perhaps be asked here, is why the Fair Folk would want to enter into these bargains. They offer practical advantages to the human in the human world in exchange for that person's sworn loyalty and for a commitment of the person to the fairies. These particular bargains are specific to the class of people later termed witches and cunning folk, so it is likely that there were specific reasons why these people were seen as desirable to the fairies, however, in a wider sense, the pattern of fairies taking people is well established. Looking at these stories gives an idea of why the Good People might want to take human beings, and ultimately the answer always comes down to pragmatic uses of one sort or another. In the more common stories the people taken were brides, young men, nursing mothers, babies, musicians, and people who were considered especially beautiful or well mannered. In some cases, such as the musicians, the person might only be taken temporarily to entertain the fairies with their skill. Some Irish witches and Fairy Doctors were said to have been taken by the fairies for a period of seven years before being returned to the human world with great knowledge and magical skill, while others were often known to be away with the fairies. In most other cases, however, the taking was permanent and the person's fate might be less pleasant, with various forms of servitude and use as breeding stock being common and sacrifice, such as in the Lowland fairies teind to Hell, not being unheard of.

Ultimately when we consider the evidence for people dedicating themselves to the fairies through transactions which involved an explicit or implicit renunciation of the previous faith and pledging of loyalty to the Good People, we see what amounts to the conversion to a new religion. Although couched in negative terms because these narratives come to us from a religion that saw these fairies as evil spirits and was being repudiated by these witches and cunning folk, the actual pattern followed and promises involved are little different than those of any person converting from one religion to another. The only major difference, and the most significant, is that the world of Elphame is no land of eternal bliss and rest for the soul but another life entirely, and the fate of the soul once there should be seriously considered.

Notes

1 Generally anyway. In the vast majority of examples the physical body is left behind and the spirit goes to Fairy and is transmuted there, however, there are some anecdotal examples where the body is also taken. For brevity I am only focusing here on the soul and situations where the soul is being taken; for a more thorough discussion of wider examples see changeling lore.

2 Wilby also discusses later 19th and 20th century Scottish examples were a practitioner might make an agreement with fairies for a specific amount of time; in these cases the deal is not a permanent pledging of the self but a temporary partnership. In these later examples the terms were agreed in a contract with the Good People offering specific services or knowledge in exchange for payments, and with the terms lasting for a prescribed period of time (Wilby, 2005).

Serving Fairy

We sometimes see people referencing or discussing the idea of a person being in service to Fairy or going into Fairy for a set amount of time and then coming back to mortal earth, at least for a while. Often in folklore when this occurs it is for a very precise amount of time and what we most often see is 7 years. This pattern repeats in both folklore and ballads.

It's said that the bean feasa and fairy doctors in some instances would be 'taken' for 7 years and then come back to serve the human population. Or, as Yeats puts it:

> *"The most celebrated fairy doctors are sometimes people the fairies loved and carried away, and kept with them for seven years"* (Yeats, 1888).

Although the text does also clarify that not all fairy doctors are taken in this manner, it is interesting to note that 7 years is specified so exactly for those who are. We also see this number showing up in some of the ballad material as the number of years that a person will be taken to serve in Fairy before being returned to earth.

Thomas the Rhymer was gone seven years and then returned, at least temporarily. In the ballad after meeting the Queen of Elfland by chance she says to him:

> *"Now, ye maun go wi me," she said,*
> *"True Thomas, ye maun go wi me,*
> *And ye maun serve me seven years,*
> *Thro weal or woe, as may chance to be."*

Thomas is then taken into Fairy and serves the Queen for the required 7 years before being returned to earth with a pair of shoes and new coat - both green[1] - and the gift of prophecy and true speech. By some folklore accounts she later sent a white hind and stag to guide him back to the Otherworld.

In the ballad of 'The Faerie Oak of Corriewater' the Fairy Queen says that the young man she's taken to be her cupbearer will serve her for 7 years.

"I have won me a youth," the Elf Queen said,
"The fairest that earth may see;
This night I have won young Elph Irving
My cupbearer to be.
His service lasts but for seven sweet years,
And his wage is a kiss of me."

In this instance the person being taken is filling a specific role, although it is also implied that he will also be the Queen's the lover. Unlike True Thomas Elph Irving's payment for his 7 years of service is simply a kiss from the Queen, indicating that what exactly one does in the Otherworld or the reason one is taken has an important impact on how one may be treated and the compensation one receives.

Although it's never explicitly stated in the ballad of Tam Lin, and there is much debate about how long Tam Lin has been in Fairy and how old he was when he was taken, it may possibly be argued that he had served the Queen for less than 7 years. When he convinces his pregnant lover, Janet, to free him he tells her that the fairies pay a tithe to Hell every 7 years, that the tithe is due November 1st (within a few days), and that he is afraid that he will be given in payment because he is *'so fair and full of flesh'*. While not conclusive the implication is that he may not have been there for the previous tithe, hence his concern that Janet free him before the next one. It is, of course, also worth noting that here again we do see the number 7 showing up as significant.

As with anything relating to Themselves there are other options seen, including being taken permanently or, as sometimes happened with nursing mothers, being taken until the fairy baby was weaned. However, 7 years of service seems to be a common contract, and is a number we see repeated in ballads and folklore.

Note

1 Green is a colour strongly associated with the Good People.

Seven

Seven is a number that often appears in fairylore in various ways. Yeats, for example, mentions that some Fairy Doctors who learned their skills from the Good People were taken by the fairies for a period of seven years (Yeats, 1888). In some selkie folklore it is said that a selkie can only come on land once every seven years (Heddle, 2016). In Thomas of Erceldoune, the predecessor of the Ballad of Thomas the Rhymer, when Thomas first meets the Fairy Queen she is accompanied by seven hounds and he and the Queen have sex seven times before the Queen takes Thomas into Fairy. He is then taken for what he believes is three days although seven years pass in the human world; in the later Ballad the agreement is for seven years of service to the Queen.

One of the most prominent applies to time and shows up in the ballad material where we find references to seven years of service to fairy and the fairies tithing to Hell every seven years[1]. The choice of the number seven here may relate to its significance more generally in fairylore but may also be a reflection of legal precedent at of the time. English law contemporary to the ballads gave seven years as the maximum length of time a person could be indentured as a servant and the time that had to pass for a person to be declared dead; it was also the usual length of apprenticeship before a person could claim to have mastered a craft (Acland, 1997). This may indicate that the deeper meaning of the number seven was a legal and cultural one, and would have been understood to imply to the audience that a person having spent seven years with the fairies and been returned had fully served the time they owed and mastered what could be taught to them by the Good People.

There is also a reference in Carmichael to seven in relation to the elements:

> *"...the 'seachda siona,' seven elements, would probably be fire, air, earth, water, snow, ice, and wind - perhaps lightning."* (Carmichael, 1900, page 349).

Note

1 Although it should be noted in alternate version of the teind or tithe to Hell stories the tithe may be due every year rather than once every seven years. Lyle's article in vol. 70 of Folklore 'The Teind to Hell in Tam Lin' discusses this in detail.

Seven Sisters

The Seven Sisters are a grouping of seven named fairies found within the grimoire material. These are: Lilia, Restilia, Foca (Fata), Fola (Falla), Afryca (Afria/Africa), Julia (Julya), Venulia (Venalla). In the 11th century these sisters initially appear listed as seven fevers in charm texts (Brock & Raiswell, 2018). In later grimoire material the seven sisters are said to be under the rule of Micob and each has a specific sigil associated with her; it is suggested that they can be called on for knowledge of herbs, medicine, and in a ritual to gain a ring of invisibility (Harm, Clark, & Peterson, 2015). Little else is directly known about the sisters, however, the number seven is generally considered significant to fairies and in fairylore.

See: Micoll for more

Shapeshifting

Shapeshifting is something we see in various fairylore and may be part of the nature of a fairy, a learned skill, or in some cases forced upon another being.

There are many examples of fairies within folklore who

have the ability to take an assortment of forms and often there is no certainty as to which, if any, form is their true one. The Banshee in some stories can appear as a bird as well as a woman and similarly besides appearing as a beautiful woman and the Baobhan Sìthe is known to take the form of a wolf or crow. Púca can appear as human-looking or as a variety of animals including goats, ponies, bulls, eagles, and rabbits. Kelpies may take the form of humans or horses and selkies are well known for having both human and seal forms.

There are also those among the Fair Folk who do not belong to a type of fairy known for shapeshifting but who, nonetheless, change shapes in stories and anecdotes, perhaps through magical skill. Hares and hedgehogs had a reputation for potentially being fairies or witches shape changed with magic (Briggs, 1976). In one anecdotal account from the Isle of Man a man reported encountering a group of small black pigs which were a group of fairies shape changed and which disappeared as soon as he called out to them (Evans-Wentz, 1911). These magical shape changes might be used to work mischief, to travel unseen, or to work further magic by getting close to a person or object.

Besides these two kinds of shapeshifting there are also many tales of forced shapeshifting ranging from mythology to folklore. Briggs describes this as a common theme found within mythology, and indeed it is quite common particularly among Irish myths were we see even the Gods are not exempt from these forced changes (Briggs, 1976). In the 'Wooing of Etain' the sorceress Fuamnach changes her rival Etain into a fly, and in the 'Fate of the Children of Lir' the aforementioned children are cursed into the shape of swans. In the Fenian myths we see Fionn's wife Sadb cursed into the shape of a deer after she refuses the attention of a mysterious druid, and Fionn's sister is forced into the shape of a dog by a rival causing his nephews to be born as hounds. In some cases these forced shape changes can be cured while in others they are permanent.

Sidhe

Sidhe, also spelled sí, sidh or sith, pronounced shee, is an Irish word meaning either fairy mound or used as an adjective to indicate something has a fairy quality to it. We see it used in older material to indicate a person of the sí or in compound words like bean sidhe, fairy woman. In modern usage it has also become something of a slang term for the fairies themselves, shortened from Aos Sidhe or Daoine Sidhe which both mean 'people of the fairy hills'.

Many of the sidhe in Ireland are the locations of older archaeological sites, often burial mounds. Some people speculate that this is the source of the connection between the fairies and the dead, although that subject is rather more complicated than that. Other names for a fairy hill besides sidhe include ráth and lios, both terms for old Iron Age hill forts that have also taken on associations with the fairy hills and fairies more generally.

Sibilia

Sibilia is mentioned as being both the 'empress' and 'princess' of all fairies to whom all others are servants (Harm, Clark, & Peterson, 2015). She appears in two grimoire rituals that I know of, one in an ancillary capacity merely referenced as having dominion over other fairies while in the other she is invoked into a candle flame to reveal the truth and answer questions put to her. Brock and Raiswell mention that she may be invoked along with Milia and Achilia reflecting a pattern sometimes seen of using alliterative names.

Silence

A fairy prohibition that effects those who benefit from their blessings and aid in particular and which may be tied to their guarding of their privacy. In multiple anecdotal accounts we find fairy blessings withdrawn or stopped if a human speaks too freely, or at all, about having received them.

There is a Scottish story of a woman with a Leannán Sidhe who loses him and her sanity after telling her sister about him (Briggs, 1976). In a slightly more benign case from Devonshire went as follows:

> *"A young woman of our town, who declared she had received the reward of sixpence for a like service, told the circumstance to her gossips; but no sixpence ever came again, and it was generally believed that the Pixies had taken offence by her chattering, as they do not like to have their deeds, good or evil, talked over by mortal tongues."* (Keightley, 1850, page 299).

Size of Fairies

The size of fairies is an often debated subject, yet folklore paints a clear, if varied, image of them. While modern depictions tend to favour small, childlike imagery looking at the wider scope of material we find everything from miniscule ant sized beings to gigantic fairies twice as tall (or more) than humans. The most common depictions fall into two main categories: those that are around 2 feet tall and those that are the height of an average human being.

What we find in many of the stories and ballads is that fairies look very much like human beings except that they have an aura of Otherworldliness to them or in some other intangible way project their fairy qualities. As Andrew Lang puts it:

> *"There seems little in the characteristics of these fairies of romance to distinguish them from human beings, except their supernatural knowledge and power. They are not often represented as diminutive in stature, and seem to be subject to such human passions as love, jealousy, envy, and revenge...The People of Peace (Daoine Shie [sic]) of Ireland and Scotland are usually of ordinary stature, indeed not to be recognized as varying from mankind except by their proceedings..."* (Andrew Lang, 1910).

Slua Sí

Among the ranks of the malicious fairies one of the more dangerous may be the Slua Sidhe[1] [Irish] or Slua Sithe [Scottish], the Fairy Host. Unlike most other types of fairies where there can usually be found at least one or two cases of benevolent behaviour towards an exceptional human the Slua Sidhe delight in tormenting humans. They are considered some of the most daunting of the Scottish fairies (Briggs, 1976).

The Slua travel in the air going in clear weather with the sound of a flock of birds and often the whirlwind is attributed to them so that it is called the séideán sidhe, fairy blast, or sitheadh gaoithe, thrust of wind, or sometimes by the similar sounding sidhe gaoithe, fairy wind (O hOgain, 1995; MacKillop, 1998; Evans-Wentz, 1911). When travelling this way the Host passes unseen by most humans, although some people claimed to see them in the clouds (Carmichael, 1900).

The Fairy Host can appear at any time but certain times present greater dangers. Any time after dark was a risk but especially midnight; as one Scottish source explained it:

> *"...the hosts travel in the air above places inhabited by people. The hosts used to go after the fall of night, and more particularly about midnight."* (Evans-Wentz, 1911, page 108).

Most stories of people encountering the Slua begin with the person being out alone at night, so that anyone who needed to be out at night was advised to be careful. People who had to travel alone at night needed to be cautious to avoid the host.

The Slua Sidhe delights in snatching humans up and compelling them to join in the Host's activities, including harassing other humans (O Súilleabháin, 1967). These activities might include kidnapping humans which the fairies want for brides as well as humans they take for no other purpose than just to torment them. A person who was out alone at night or who was somewhere they weren't supposed to be might be taken up by the Slua and once taken would have little choice but to go along with them until the fairies released them. A person taken this way might be referred to as *"in the fairies"* (O Súilleabháin, 1967). When a person was taken they might be carried to another county, province, or even across to another country, then left to slowly find their own way home. This is something we see in a variety of stories but can be typified perhaps in Hyde's *'Guleesh Na Guss Dhu'* which describes the adventures of a young man who finds himself among the Host and travelling to Italy and France with them. Although the story of Guleesh ends well enough for him, no one who is taken by the Slua is ever truly safe as they are always mercurial and dangerous to humans.

Other folklore of the Slua Sidhe relates to those who are out and see the Host passing with a human captive. There are several methods to force the Slua to release people they may be carrying along but one of the most well-known, repeated for example by McNeill in 'The Silver Bough', is to toss a handful of dirt from the road, a left shoe, or an iron knife into the air while yelling *"This is yours, that is mine!"*. Common wisdom says that the person being carried would then be freed. Such a person who had been taken by the Slua and returned from them could be sought out for advice on fairies and were considered knowledgeable on the subject in the same way that people who were friends of the fairies would be (O Súilleabháin, 1967).

In Scotland some people believe that the Slua Sidhe, who are also called the fairy host of the air, are spirits of those humans who died with unforgiven sins or filled with sin (McNeill, 1956; Briggs, 1976; Carmichael, 1900). Evans Wentz related stories of the Slua as both the mortal dead and as fallen angels, showing that the belief was not entirely clear-cut (Evans Wentz, 1911). In Irish folktales related by authors like Yeats and Hyde, however, the fairy host are distinct from the human dead and act like fairies in other tales, engaging in behaviour such as stealing human brides to force them to wed members of their own group. The Slua may include fairy horses, hounds, and a variety of fairy beings, as well as the human dead. There is no simple division to be found here and it is likely that the Slua represent both fairies who were never human and some who may once have lived as humans but are now counted among the Host.

The fairy host, like other fairies, is usually invisible to humans but can be sensed in the appearance of a sudden wind and the sound of voices, armor clinking, or people shouting (O Súilleabháin, 1967). Hyde describes it in the story "Guleesh Na Guss Dhu" this way:

> *"...he heard a great noise coming like the sound of many people running together, and talking, and laughing, and making sport, and the sound went by him like a whirl of wind..."* (Hyde, 1890, p 76).

According to some Irish folklore the Slua appears as a dust devil which moves over roads and hedges as the Good Neighbours travel (JCHAS, 2010). When the whirlwind appeared people would react by saying *"Good luck to them, the ladies and gentlemen"* or by averting their eyes, turning their backs, and praying (O hOgain, 1995; JCHAS, 2010, p. 319). The use of a phrase wishing luck to potentially harmful spirits and calling them 'ladies and gentlemen' reflects the common practice of appeasing the more dangerous fairies both by speaking of them in polite, positive terms and also of wishing them well, giving a blessing in hopes they respond in kind. This was done to avert any harm caused by the close proximity of the Host and to hopefully avoid drawing their attention in a negative way. The sí gaoithe [fairy wind] which indicated the Slua was present, could bring illness or cause injury as it passed by, contributing to its fearsome reputation (MacKillop, 1998).

Note

1 The Slua is sometimes seen as related to the idea seen on the continent of the Wild Hunt as spirits who travel the air and can take people.

Solitary Fairies

A term used to describe those fairies who prefer to lead a solitary existence, differentiated from the TROOPING FAIRIES who would rather stay in groups. Like many such categorizing terms these are fluid and may change based on circumstance and story.

Spinning

Spinning has many associations with magic and fairies in folklore and folktales. A variety of famous tales involve spinning, usually following a pattern where a fairy appears to a mortal who has been given an impossible task involving spinning and offers to complete it for a price. This price varies from the human themselves (if they are female) to a firstborn child and can be avoided if the human can find out the fairy's name. We also see a version of this in the modern Westernized tale of Sleeping Beauty[1] where the curse on the eponymous princess involves a spinning wheel.

In at least one anecdotal account a woman who wished for help to get her spinning done received fairy aid, but the fairies ended up being as much of a problem as an assist, as the story illustrates:

> *"...his father knew a woman in the neighbourhood who was in a hurry to have her stock of wool spun and made into cloth, and one night this woman secretly wished to have some women to help her. So the following morning there appeared at her house six or seven fairy women in long green robes, all alike chanting, "A wool-card, and a spinning-wheel." And when they were supplied with the instruments they were so very desirous to get, they all set to work, and by midday of that morning the cloth was going*

> *through the process of the hand-loom. But they were not satisfied with finishing the work the woman bad set before them, but asked for new employment. The woman had no more spinning or weaving to be done, and began to wonder how she was to get the women out of the house. So she went into her neighbour's house and informed him of her position in regard to the fairy women. The old man asked what they were saying. "They are earnestly petitioning for some work to do, and I have no more to give them," the woman replied. "Go you in," he said to her, "and tell them to spin the sand, and if then they do not move from your house, go out again and yell in at the door that Dun Borve is in fire!" The first plan had no effect, but immediately on hearing the cry, "Dun Borve is in fire!" the fairy women disappeared invisibly. And as they went, the woman heard the melancholy wail, "Dun Borve is in fire! Dun Borve is in fire! And what will become of our hammers and anvil?"--for there was a smithy in the fairy-dwelling.'"* (Evans-Wentz, 1911, page 110).

In Shetland it was believed that the first six days of Yule were when the fairies were most active and that spinning wheels and wool had to be stored during this period or eth Good People would get into them and ruin them (Tobar an Dualchais, 2018).

Note

1 The modern version of Sleeping Beauty is very different from the older 16th and 17th century versions recorded by Basile and Perrault. The oldest version I am aware of – 'Sun, Moon, and Talia' – does not involve fairies although it does include clear themes and plot found in later versions of 'Sleeping Beauty'.

Spriggans

In Cornish lore Spriggans may be equated to elves and are explained as pagan ancestors and stolen humans who are too good for Hell and too bad for Heaven, thus trapped on mortal earth (Bottrell, 1873). Bottrell says that the word Spriggan means sprite.

Stolen Bride

Besides the Midwife to the Fairies the Stolen Bride may be the next most well-known of fairy story themes. In the typical version of this tale we see a bride carried off on or around her wedding night, taken to be the bride instead of a fairy man. In some versions of the story the woman can later be rescued while in many accounts she is lost to the world of Fairy and may appear later as the labouring mother in the Fairy Midwife accounts. Often there is also crossover with changeling stories, and the human woman is thought to have died and is mourned by her family but may be seen later particularly by the man she was to marry.

Yeats made famous this Irish account:

> *"A young man going at nightfall to the house of his just married bride, met in the way a jolly company, and with them his bride. They were faeries, and had stolen her as a wife for the chief of their band. To him they seemed only a company of merry mortals. His bride, when she saw her old love, bade him welcome, but was most fearful lest he should eat the faery food, and so be glamoured out of the earth into that bloodless dim nation, wherefore she set him down to play cards with three of the cavalcade; and he played on, realizing nothing until he saw the chief of the band carrying his bride away in his arms. Immediately he started up, and knew that they were faeries; for slowly all that jolly company melted into shadow and night. He hurried to the house of his beloved. As he drew near came to him the cry of the keeners. She had died some time before he came."* (Yeats, 1888, pages 123 – 124).

In a Manx account the man had a chance to rescue his stolen bride, but was thwarted by the second woman he had married:

> *"A Ballaleece woman was captured by the fairies; and, soon afterwards, her husband took a new wife, thinking the first one gone for ever. But not long after the marriage, one night the first wife*

appeared to her former husband and said to him, and the second wife overheard her: "You'll sweep the barn clean, and mind there is not one straw left on the floor. Then stand by the door, and at a certain hour a company of people on horseback will ride in, and you lay hold of that bridle of the horse I am on, and don't let it go." He followed the directions carefully, but was unable to hold the horse: the second wife had put some straw on the barn floor under a bushel.'" (Evans-Wentz, 1911, page 130).

Svartálfar

Svartálfar means 'black elves' and in Icelandic mythology they possess their own world, Svartálfheim [black elf home]. The Duergar or dwarves also live in Svartálfheim creating a longstanding confusion about whether Svartálfar are truly elves in their own right or are actually another name for dwarves. Both are associated with mountains and mountainous regions, but seem to have a distinct and separate focus in activities and interactions with people. Grimm believes that the Svartálfar were good natured beings and argues that they received worship from people into the 19th century.

See ÁLFAR for more

T

Taboos

Dealing with the Good People is complex and comes with a series of taboos, or things that either must be done or must not be done. Some taboos include those relating to saying THANK YOU, FOOD, PRIVACY, and SILENCE which are addressed in depth in individual sections.

Other taboos include not interfering with sites known to be associated with the fairies or with fairy activities. The cost of breaking any prohibition of the fairies is usually high and may include madness, illness, or death. An anecdotal account from Kilmessan talks of a man who was found dead and was believed to have been taken by the fairies as a punishment for interfering with one of their processions of FAIRY RADES (Evans-Wentz, 1911). Folklore surrounding rev. Robert Kirk claims he was taken by the fairies for his attempts to write about them.

Tam Lin[1]

One of the most significant Scottish ballads, from a fairylore perspective, is undoubtedly Tam Lin, which can be found under variant names and versions dating back to 1549. As eminent folklorist Katherine Briggs puts it "*It is perhaps the most important of all supernatural ballads because of the many fairy beliefs incorporated in it.*" (Briggs, 1976, p 449). An indication of the importance of the ballad may be its popularity over the centuries and its prolific nature. Indeed there are nearly 50 versions of the ballad that I am aware of, and probably more that I am not aware of, each with variations which can be minor or major in nature. However, the wider theme of the ballad remains consistent: a young woman goes to a well in a wood that is rumoured to be guarded by a fairy who takes a toll from all trespassers, she becomes pregnant by him, and returns to free him from the fairies on Halloween night.

1. O I forbid you, maidens all,
That wear gold on your hair,
To come or go by Carterhaugh,
For young Tam Lin is there.
2. There's none that go by Carterhaugh
But they leave him a treasure,
Either their rings, or green mantles,
Or else their maidenhead.
3. Janet has tucked up her green skirt
A little above her knee,
And she has braided her yellow hair
A little above her eyebrow,
And she's away to Carterhaugh
As fast as she can go
4. When she came to Carterhaugh
Tam Lin was at the well,
And there she found his steed standing,
But away was himself.
5. She had not pulled a double rose,
A rose but only two,
Till up then started young Tam Lin,
Says, Lady, you'll pull no more.
6. Why pull you the rose, Janet,
And why break you the stem?
Or why come you to Carterhaugh
Without my command?
7. "Carterhaugh, it is my own,
My daddy gave it to me,
I'll come and go by Carterhaugh,
And ask no leave of you."
8. Janet has tucked up her green skirt
A little above her knee,
And she has braided her yellow hair
A little above her eyebrow,

And she is to her father's house,
As fast as she can go.
9. Four and twenty ladies fair
Were playing at the ball,
And out then came the fair Janet,
The flower among them all.
10, Four and twenty ladies fair
Were playing at the chess,
And out then came the fair Janet,
As green as any glass.
11. Out then spoke an old grey knight,
Laying over the castle wall,
And says, Alas, fair Janet, for you,
But we'll be blamed all.
12. "Hold your tongue, you old faced knight,
Some ill death may you die!
Father my child on whom I will,
I'll father none on you."
13. Out then spoke her father dear,
And he spoke meek and mild,
"And ever alas, sweet Janet," he says,
"I think you go with child."
14. "If that I go with child, father,
Myself must bear the blame,
There's not a lord about your hall,
Shall get the child's name.
15. "If my love were an earthly knight,
As he's an elfin grey,
I would not give my own true-love
For any lord that you have.
16. "The steed that my true love rides on
Is lighter than the wind,
With silver he is shod before,
With burning gold behind."

17. Janet has tucked up her green skirt
A little above her knee,
And she has braided her yellow hair
A little above her eyebrow,
And she's away to Carterhaugh
As fast as she can go.
18. When she came to Carterhaugh,
Tam Lin was at the well,
And there she found his steed standing,
But away was himself.
19. She had not pulled a double rose,
A rose but only two,
Till up then started young Tam Lin,
Says, Lady, you'll pull no more.
20. "Why pull you the rose, Janet,
Among the groves so green,
And all to kill the bonny babe
That we got us between?"
21. "O tell me, tell me, Tam Lin," she says,
"For his sake that died on tree [i.e. Christ's sake],
If ever you were in holy chapel,
Or christendom did see?"
22. "Roxbrugh he was my grandfather,
Took me with him to stay
And once it fell upon a day
That woe did me betide.
23. "And once it fell upon a day
A cold day and windy,
When we were from the hunting come,
That from my horse I fell,
The Queen of Fairies she caught me,
In yonder green hill to dwell.
24. "And pleasant is the fairy land,
But, an eerie tale to tell,

Yes at the end of seven years,
We pay a tiend to hell,
I am so fair and full of flesh,
I'm afraid it will be myself.
25. "But the night is Halloween, lady,
The morn is Hallowday,
Then win me, win me, if you will,
For well I know you may.
26. "Just at the dark and midnight hour
The fairy folk will ride,
And they that would their true-love win,
At Miles Cross they must bide."
27. "But how shall I know you, Tam Lin,
Or how my true-love know,
Among so many uncouth knights,
The like I never saw?"
28. "O first let pass the black, lady,
And soon let pass the brown,
But quickly run to the milk-white steed,
Pull you his rider down.
29."For I'll ride on the milk-white steed,
And yes nearest the town,
Because I was an earthly knight
They give me that renown.
30. "My right hand will be gloved, lady,
My left hand will be bare,
Tilted up shall my hat be,
And combed down shall my hair,
And that's the tokens I give you,
No doubt I will be there.
31."They'll turn me in your arms, lady,
Into a lizard and snake,
But hold me fast, and fear me not,
I am your child's father.

32. "They'll turn me to a bear so grim,
And then a lion bold,
But hold me fast, and fear me not,
And you shall love your child.
33. "Again they'll turn me in your arms
To a red hot rod of iron,
But hold me fast, and fear me not,
I'll do you no harm.
34. "And last they'll turn me in your arms
Into the burning coal,
Then throw me into well water,
O throw me in with speed.
35. "And then I'll be your own true-love,
I'll turn a naked knight,
Then cover me with your green mantle,
And hide me out o sight."
36. Gloomy, gloomy was the night,
And eerie was the way,
As fair Janet in her green mantle
To Miles Cross she did go.
37. At the dark and midnight hour
She heard the bridles sing,
She was as glad at that
As any earthly thing.
38. First she let the black pass by,
And soon she let the brown,
But quickly she ran to the milk-white steed,
And pulled the rider down.
39. So well she minded what he did say,
And young Tam Lin did win,
Soon covered him with her green mantle,
As happy as a bird in spring
40. Out then spoke the Queen of Fairies,
Out of a bush of broom,

"Them that has gotten young Tam Lin
Has gotten a stately-groom."
41. Out then spoke the Queen of Fairies,
And an angry woman was she,
"Shame betide her ill-fared face,
And an ill death may she die,
For she's taken away the handsomest knight
In all my company.
42. "But had I known, Tam Lin," said she,
"What now this night I see,
I would have taken out your two grey eyes,
And put in two eyes of a tree."
Language modified from traditional Scots ballad

This is the most common version of the Ballad of Tam Lin. Let's take a closer look at the material.

The name Tam Lin, which elsewhere sometimes appears in variants as Tam-a-Line, Tam o the Lin and Tamlane is not a proper name but what we might understand as a nickname or name with epithet. Tam is a version of Tom. Lin, or Linn, has several meanings in Scots but the most likely here is a waterfall or pool of water; a Lane is a slow moving stream. Tam Lin may be read as Tom of the Pool or Tom of the Waterfall and Tamlane similarly as Tom of the stream, which, of course, makes perfect sense for a fairy who guards a well in the Carterhaugh woods. In some alternate versions the fairy knight is named as True Thomas, conflating this story with that other ballad of a Fairy Queen abducting a man, possibly due to both characters having similar names, Tam, Tom, and Thomas.

Tam Lin initially appears as a mysterious figure who controls the woods of Carterhaugh. He expects a toll from trespassers of something valuable which is listed here as either jewellery, green cloaks, or the virginity of maidens. The mention of green is interesting, as green is particularly a fairy colour and was seen as an unlucky colour for women to wear for this reason. The mention of it here may be the first hint of fairy involvement. Janet - given different names in some other versions - has heard the warning about Tam Lin and decided to go to Carterhaugh, in alternate versions such as we see in 39C going *"By the only light of the moon"*. It should be noted here that Janet has been told that Tam Lin expects sex from maidens and is intentionally going there, which at least implies that she accepts this as a possibility. She has also dressed in a green skirt, which as was just mentioned is a fairy colour normally not worn by women. I have always personally seen this as indicating that Janet knew exactly what she was doing and intended to go find herself a fairy lover.

Janet arrives in the Carterhaugh wood at the well that Tam Lin guards and finds Tam Lin's horse, but not Tam Lin himself. The verse states that Tam Lin is at the well, however, implying that although she may not see him he is nearby. It is possible that this is an allusion to fairy glamour or enchantment. Finding the fairy horse but not the guardian she was looking for she picks two roses, taking from the place that Tam Lin guards. This naturally, immediately, summons Tam Lin to her side. You have to admire Janet's directness here, as we see her intentionally invoking Tam Lin with her actions. I might suggest that this is not generally the wisest course of action, as usually disturbing or violating a place guarded by fairies results in retribution; in this case we see instead a conversation.

The interaction between the two as related in the ballad doesn't include any sex, although we will find out later that occurred but was not directly mentioned; in various alternate versions the sex is more obviously stated and is usually clearly consensual but not always so. For example:

"He's taken her by the milk-white hand
Among the leaves so green

And what they did I cannot say
The leaves they were between" (39I)

and

"He took her by the milk-white hand
And gently laid her down,
Just in below some shady trees
Where the green leaves hung down." (39J)

In some later versions of the ballad the sexual encounter between Janet (by any name) and Tam Lin is clearly non-consensual. This requires an entire essay of its own to unpack and I highly recommend reading Acland's article *'Is Tam Lin a Rape Story?'*

What we do have in 39A, however, is Tam Lin challenging Janet over her trespassing on the place he guards and her pulling of the roses. Janet's response is to tell him that she is the one who owns Carterhaugh and so doesn't need his permission. Janet's willingness to challenge Tam Lin and refusal to back down may be a key factor in Tam Lin choosing her to save him from Fairy.

As far as we can tell from the ballad Janet has no further contact with Tam Lin after returning home to her father's hall. It soon becomes obvious to those around her that she is pregnant and one of her father's knights accuses her of as much, worrying that she will get them in trouble. Here we see an illustration of why I like Janet so much in this version of the ballad. She has been publicly accused of a significant social transgression - sex out of wedlock and pregnancy from it - and her response is to yell back and tell the knight, effectively, to shut up and curse him with an ill death, that whoever she has a child with it won't be him. Now that it's been brought out in public her father also asks if she is pregnant, although we may note he speaks to her 'meek and mild'. She doesn't outright admit that she is, but says that if she is she will take the blame for it because no man in her father's hall is responsible.

Janet then does admit that her lover is one of the Other Crowd, and despite having as far as we are aware only one tryst with Tam Lin she declares that he is her true love and that she will not give him up for any mortal lord. She then describes his horse, an interesting bit of lore from our perspective, as lighter than the wind and having silver horse shoes in front and gold in back. The horse shoes are interesting, although tangential, but give us an idea of what fairy horses may be shod with since iron is obviously not an option. Why the two different kinds of metal? It's hard to say but it could represent the animal's ability to travel between the two worlds.

Janet immediately goes back to Carterhaugh after this and once again finding the horse at the well and not Tam Lin, pulls two roses to invoke him. He appears and tells her to stop but also asks her why she wants to abort the child she is carrying. Although in other versions of the ballad Janet is advised to take such an action or is pulling not roses but abortifacient herbs in this version there has been no mention of such implying that Tam Lin has some supernatural knowledge of her intentions. Janet questions him about whether he is truly one of the Gentry or is a mortal man and he tells her how he was claimed by the Fairy Queen after falling from his horse. It is quite likely that this is an analogy for dying, and reinforces the blurred lines between the fairies and the dead that is often seen throughout folklore.

At this point in another version, 39I, we see the following passage which isn't present in 39A but is pertinent for our discussion here:

31. The Queen of Fairies kept me
In yonder green hill to dwell,
And I'm a fairy, lyth [joint] and limb,
Fair lady, view me well.
32."But we that live in Fairy-land

No sickness know nor pain;
I quit my body when I will,
And take to it again.
33.'I quit my body when I please,
Or unto it repair;
We can inhabit at our ease
In either earth or air.
34.'Our shapes and size we can convert
To either large or small;
An old nut-shell's the same to us
As is the lofty hall.
35.We sleep in rose-buds soft and sweet
We revel in the stream;
We wander lightly on the wind
Or glide on a sunbeam.
36.'And all our wants are well supplied
From every rich man's store,
Who thankless sins the gifts he gets,
And vainly grasps for more.'

I'm including this here, as it appears in Child's notes, because I feel that it offers some essential information about the nature of fairies. In this version Tamlane has just told Janet that he knew her as a child and that he was born a human son to the Earl of Murray before being taken by the Queen of Fairies. Yet he also explicitly tells her that he is *'a fairy, lyth [joint] and limb'*. This confirms that the fairies may take a person and by some means transform that person into one of their own kind. He then goes on to describe to her what it is like to be a fairy, including the facts that they do not get sick or know pain, can leave their bodies or re-enter them, change their sizes, and exist as either physical beings or ethereal ones (*'we can inhabit at our ease in either earth or air'*). He finally references something mentioned by both rev. Kirk in the 17th century and Campbell in the 19th writing on fairies, that fairies will take the substance or produce of food if a person speaks ill of their own crops or stores and that it is one this that they live.

He also expresses his concern over being given to Hell as part of the teind paid on All Hallows (See TITHE TO HELL for more on this) and tells her that she can rescue him if she is brave enough. What follows is a very specific method of rescuing a person during a fairy procession, although it is possible that this only works because Janet is very brave and because she is carrying Tam Lin's child. In other examples of this method being used the person doing it shared a blood relationship with the person they were trying to save, and I suspect that being related by blood in some manner is an essential factor, which may be why Tam Lin hadn't mentioned it earlier, although the timing of Halloween may also have played a part. In a similar story, THE FAERIE OAK OF CORRIEWATER, a woman tries and fails to save her brother in a similar situation, indicating that this method is certainly not fool proof and that Janet was indeed risking her life to save Tam Lin.

Janet is advised to go to Miles Cross on Halloween and wait for the fairy procession to ride past at midnight, perhaps meaning that the timing of midnight on Halloween is essential, or perhaps merely referencing that this was the usual point that the fairy rade rode out. In some versions it is specifically mentioned that he is riding with the Seelie Court:

> *"The night, the night is Halloween,*
> *Our seely court maun ride,*
> *Thro England and thro Ireland both,*
> *And a' the warld wide."*
> - "A fragment of Young Tamlane," Hinloch MSS, V, 391(Child, 1898)

I feel it important to add that in an alternate version, 39D, the protagonist carries holy water and uses it to make a 'compass' or circle around herself before the fairies emerge from the mound. This can be seen as a protective gesture on her part and also perhaps explain why the fairies do not perceive her presence until she breaks the circle to grab Tam Lin down from his horse.

It is mentioned that because of his renown Tam Lin will be riding on a white horse; the idea of white horses carrying people of significance in Fairy is something we see repeated often in different places but it is worth noting here. The Queen of Fairies herself is said to ride on a white horse in many stories, and white animals are often messengers of the Otherworld. In the few versions where he is not riding a white horse he is riding next to the Queen herself, mounted on a 'blood-red steed', with red also having significant - and far grimmer - Otherworldly meaning. Janet is alerted to the approach of the fairy rade by the sound of bridle bells, as the ballad says 'she heard the bridles sing' referencing the belief that fairies attached silver bells to their horses bridles and manes when they rode in processions.

Once she has pulled him from his horse we see the fairies turning Tam Lin into a variety of fearsome things, finally ending by turning him into a coal which Janet must throw into a well. From the water Tam Lin emerges as a naked man and Janet covers him with her green cloak, claiming him with this act. It is likely that there is great significance in his final forms being heated iron and a burning coal and that he must, in a fiery form, be thrust into well water. Tam Lin did himself guard a well and wells were often sacred and viewed as both powerful and healing.

Having withstood these trials and won Tam Lin the fairies cannot take him back again, although it's unclear whether he has regained his mortality or not. For her efforts Janet wins a bridegroom and a father for her child, but she is also cursed by the Fairy Queen, who wishes of her 'an ill death may she die'. Arguably Tam Lin is the truest winner here, having avoided being tithed to Hell, being returned to mortal earth, and getting a well-off wife and child into the bargain. The Queen's parting words imply that if she had foreseen these events the she could have prevented it by either literally blinding Tam Lin or, perhaps, by altering his sight less literally so that he wasn't moved by Janet's beauty, depending on how we choose to interpret her giving him the eyes of a tree. It is implied in some, and out righted stated in others, that the Fairy Queen loved Tam Lin herself, although it is ambiguous as to whether this was romantic love or more maternal, she having taken him in many versions when he was only a boy:

> *"Out and spak the queen o fairies,*
> *Out o a shot o wheat,*
> *She that has gotten young Tamlane*
> *Has gotten my heart's delight."*
> -'Tamlane,' "Scotch Ballads, Materials for Border Minstrelsy," No 96 a

It is easy to see from all of this why the 'Ballad of Tam Lin' is so valuable in studying fairylore. Janet, arguably, goes out seeking a fairy lover and finds one. She does this by dressing in green and going to a well in a wood that is known to have a fairy guardian who takes a toll from trespassers, including having sex with them. She possibly goes at night, by the light of the moon, perhaps a full moon? She invokes him by picking forbidden flowers, the property of the fairies. The two talk and it is later implied (stated in other versions) they have a tryst which results in a pregnancy, putting Janet in a difficult position with her family, so she goes back to Carterhaugh and invokes Tam Lin a second time. He then gives her a means to rescue him, something that may only work because the timing is right and Janet is stubborn, fearless, and carrying his child. We learn about how to invoke fairies, and what payments they may expect. We learn as well how a mortal might become one of the Good People, what that might mean, and how he might be rescued. We see that a fairy lover can be gained, and even won away from the fairies, if one is brave.

Note

1 A version of this article also appears in my previous book 'Travelling the Fairy Path'.

Thank You

It is a TABOO among the fairy folk for us to say thank you to them.

Anecdotally I have met a variety of people across demographics who share this prohibition, not only with strictly Celtic fairies but also with less clearly culturally defined one. I also found a reference in Katherine Briggs Dictionary of Fairies to this taboo. This is something that we can see directly with some specific fairies like brownies and pixies who will become enraged if thanked verbally.

Why is this a taboo? It is hard to say as folklore offers no clear explanation, but we can offer a few suggestions. One school of thought is that saying thank you implies that the Daoine Uaisle are in some way lesser than you and serving you, which offends them - and is why they react with anger. Another thought is that saying 'thank you' is seen as acknowledging a debt owed, and it is never a good idea to owe an unspecified debt to any of the Good People. It is also possible that saying thank you, or overtly acknowledging what They have done for you, is problematic because they prefer not to have that sort of attention or focus on themselves.

What then is one to do if one feels the Other Crowd have done something helpful or kind? Briggs suggests that, *"no fault can be found with a bow or curtsy"* (Briggs, 1976, p196). I have found that a gift returned for a gift works well, as does a general expression of gratitude for the event or item itself (not the giver). Saying things like 'I am so glad that this worked out this way' or 'I am so happy that this is here' for example.

Thomas the Rhymer

Another of the most important ballad pieces relating to fairylore is Thomas the Rhymer, based on the earlier prose piece 'The Romance and Prophecies of Thomas of Erceldoune'. In its prose form the story goes back to the 15th century with the ballad dating slightly later (Henderson & Cowan, 2001). If he were a real person, and some speculation exists that he may have been, he likely lived during the late 13th century (Murray, 1885). In all versions it tells the story of a man named Thomas who meets the Queen of Fairy, travels with her to her realm, serves her there in some capacity, and then is returned to the human world with a parting gift from the Queen. Below I'll include a modernized version of the ballad.

1.True Thomas lay on Huntlie Bank,
A wonder he spied with his eye
And there he saw a lady bright,
Come riding down by Eildon Tree.
2. Her shirt was of the grass-green silk,
Her mantle of the velvet fine
At each tuft of her horse's mane
Hang fifty silver bells and nine.
3. True Thomas, he pulled off his cap,
And bowed low down to his knee
"All hail, you mighty Queen of Heaven!
For your peer on earth I never did see."
4. "O no, O no, Thomas," she said,
"That name does not belong to me;
I am but the queen of fair Elfland,
That am hither come to visit you."
5. "Harp and sing, Thomas," she said,
"Harp and sing along with me,
And if you dare to kiss my lips,
Sure of your body I will be."
6. "Fare me well, fare me woe,

That fate shall never daunt me;"
Soon he has kissed her rosy lips,
All underneath the Eildon Tree.
7. "Now, you must go with me," she said,
"True Thomas, you must go with me,
And you must serve me seven years,
Through good or bad, as may chance to be."
8. She mounted on her milk-white steed,
She's taken True Thomas up behind,
And yes whenever her bridle rung,
The steed flew swifter than the wind.
9. O they rode on, and farther on--
The steed went swifter than the wind--
Until they reached a desert wide,
And living land was left behind.
10. "Light down, light down, now, True Thomas,
And lean your head upon my knee;
Abide and rest a little space,
And I will show you wonders three."
11. "O see you not that narrow road,
So thick beset with thorns and briers?
That is the path of righteousness,
Though after it but few enquires.
12. "And see not you that broad broad road,
That lies across that lily meadow?
That is the path to wickedness,
Though some call it the road to heaven.
13. "And see not you that bonny road,
That winds about the ferny hillside?
That is the road to fair Elfland,
Where you and I this night must go.
14. "But, Thomas, you must hold your tongue,
Whatever you may hear or see,
For, if you speak word in Elflyn land,

You'll never get back to your own country."
15. O they rode on, and farther on,
And they waded through rivers above the knee,
And they saw neither sun nor moon,
But they heard the roaring of the sea.
16. It was dark dark night, and there was no star light,
And they waded through red blood to the knee;
For all the blood that's shed on earth
Runs through the springs of that country.
17. Soon they came on to a garden green,
And she pulled an apple from the tree:
"Take this for your wages, True Thomas,
It will give the tongue that can never lie."
18. "My tongue is mine own," True Thomas said;
"A good gift you would give to me!
I neither able to buy nor sell,
At fair or tryst where I may be.
19. "I'd be able neither to speak to prince or peer,
Nor ask of grace from fair lady:"
"Now hold your peace," the lady said,
"For as I say, so must it be."
20. He has gotten a coat of the even cloth,
And a pair of shoes of velvet green,
And till seven years were gone and past
True Thomas on earth was never seen."
(Child, 1898, language modified to modern English)

In the prose version and some ballad versions Thomas meets the Queen when she is out hunting with her seven hounds, while in most versions of the ballad she is simply out riding. In most versions she is riding a white horse caparisoned with bells, although in an alternate version her horse is grey and she is carrying nine silver bells (Child, 1898). The bells are likely important, something we see in other stories as well, possibly a means to travel between worlds.

When he sees her Thomas calls her a wonder and mistakes her for the Queen of Heaven, although she is quick to correct him. She is wearing a fine green dress and identifies herself as the Queen of Elfland, except in one version where she refers to herself simply as a lady from a strange land. In the prose version Thomas propositions her, and despite her claims that sleeping with him will destroy her beauty, the two have sex seven times in a row (Henderson & Cowan, 2001). The Queen's warning comes to pass as she becomes disturbing to look at but Thomas chooses to remain with her anyway. In the ballad she asks Thomas to play and sing for her then in some versions takes him into her service while in others she offers him in a kiss saying that if he agrees she will be *'sure of his body'*.

The two then travel together into the world of Fairy. At one point Thomas either begins to complain of hunger or asks for food, depending on the version, indicating fruit growing nearby. The Queen denies him this fruit, often an apple, claiming it is dangerous for him and in some versions offers him bread and wine instead while in others she instructs him to lay his head down on her knee. She then offers to show him three wonders, using the same word in the text, farlies, which Thomas used to describe the Queen when he first saw her. She points to three paths[1] leading to Heaven, Hell, and Fairy respectively. Each path is characterized by the effort it takes to get to that destination, with the path to Heaven thorny and difficult, the path to Hell broad and easy, and the path to Fairy winding and beautiful.

Thomas is warned that he must remain silent while he is in Fairy, an unusual prohibition in fairylore. The reason for this is not given in the ballad version, however, in the prose version, the Queen has regained her beauty at this point and tells Thomas that she is married and her husband will be furious if he find out she and Thomas are lovers so for his own safety he must only speak to her (Henderson & Cowan, 2001). In the prose version

Thomas remains in Fairy for three days before the Devil shows up to collect his tithe[2] and the Queen sends Thomas home lest he be chosen. In the ballad versions the two travel for a longer period of time, with the Queen finally offering Thomas an apple as payment for his service to her, saying it will give him the gift of true speech. He tries to refuse, knowing this gift is as much a curse as a blessing, but she insists. In older versions, however, Thomas is given a choice by the Queen between a gift of prophecy or a gift of skill with the harp and he chooses prophecy as the greater skill (Henderson & Cowan, 2001). In all versions Thomas is missing from earth for seven years before being returned.

Folklore claims that Thomas lived on earth for a rime after that but was eventually taken into Fairy again. The belief is that the Queen sent a doe and stag as a sign to him that she was coming to bring him back to her world (Henderson & Cowan, 2001). By this account he is there still.

Notes

1 In the prose version she shows him four roads.

2 See Tithe to Hell for more on this.

Titam

Titam is also called Titem, Tytarit, Titan, Tytan, Tytar, and even Setan or Chicam (Brock & Raiswell, 2018; Harm, Clark, & Peterson, 2015). The Book of Oberon suggests that Titam may be connected to or a variant name for Shakespeare's fairy Queen Titania although Briggs argues that Titania is a variant of Diana instead. Because of the obscure nature of the material and the non-standard spelling between sources it is difficult to favor either theory, although it may be that both have some truth in them. Titam is often invoked with Micoll and Burfex in the grimoire material.

Time

Time moves very differently in the world of Fairy than in the mortal world and those who experience fairies sometimes suffer time related consequences even if no obvious fairy ill will is involved. A person who joins in dancing in a fairy ring may find when they leave that while they think only a single night has passed it has actually been years. In one Scottish account a groom disappeared the night of his wedding and emerged on what he thought was the next morning only to find that decades had passed and of all the people at the wedding only one still lived, and she an old woman (Evans-Wentz, 1911). In a Welsh example a boy was taken by the Tylwyth Teg and left their company after what he thought was a fortnight, only to find when he returned home that two years had passed (Evans-Wentz, 1911).

Tithe to Hell

In Scottish folklore there's a belief which says that the Good Folk must pay a teind (tithe) to Hell; this idea appears first in writing in two poems and seems from there to enter the wider lore particularly in the modern period. The teind is an interesting folkloric belief because it is not found in Ireland, nor was it a belief throughout Scotland until a much later period, originally being seen only along the southern border. In his extensive writing on the Scottish Fey in the 17th century, for example, rev. Robert Kirk makes no mention of such a teind, and it appears in only one contemporary witchcraft trial in Edinburgh, yet today it is often discussed as if it were factual for all the Good Folk.

It is worth noting as we begin, however, that this may not simply be a Scottish belief but a particularly regional Scottish belief, appearing originally in the areas around the river Tweed. The oldest textual evidence for the Teind comes from the 15th century 'Romance and Prophecy of Thomas of Erceldoune', later known as 'Thomas the Rhymer' and is tied by place and personal names into the area around Dryburgh Abbey and Melrose along the Tweed (Murray, 1918). The second oldest literary source for the teind is the poem 'The Ballad of Tam Lin' dating to the 16th century set at Carterhaugh in Selkirk, also near the Tweed, along one of its tributaries (Murray, 1922). The two locations are about 8 miles apart. In contrast Rev Kirk was living and writing in Aberfoyle, about 80 miles to the north. This geographic difference may be significant, and part of the explanation for why the teind seems to have been so strongly present in one specific area and almost unknown elsewhere.

The teind itself is the idea that the Good People must pay a tribute to Hell on a regular basis, generally said to be every seven years (Briggs, 1976). The exact agreement and terms vary by source with the single witchcraft confession claiming it was a yearly tithe and the two poems clearly stating it is paid every seven years. It is also called both a teind in some variations and a kane in others; teind in Scots means tithe, a payment of a tenth part, while kane is a Scots word for a payment by a renter to his landlord (Lyle, 1970). The difference between a teind and a kane is, of course, hugely significant, as the first clearly implies the loss of a tenth of the population every seven years, if we assume seven years was the standard, and the second does not. Indeed the text of Tam Lin often implies that he expects to be the only one given to Hell as he says *'I fear 'twill be myself'* (Lyle, 1970). It would seem that there is more logic to the idea of a single offering rather than of a tenth of the entire population being given every year or every seven years, but the evidence exists to support either interpretation and no certain interpretation can be given.

In the trial of Alison Pearson the accused witch confessed to learning her craft from the fairies and said that *"every year the tithe of them [the fairies] were taken away to Hell"* (Scott, 1830). The Fairy queen in 'Thomas of Erceldoune' references the Devil fetching his fee from the fairies and suggests that Thomas will be chosen because he is so strong and pleasant:

"To Morne, of helle the foulle fende,

Amange this folke will feche his fee;
And thou arte mekill mane and hende,
I trowe wele he wode chese thee." (Murray, 1918).
[Tomorrow morning, of Hell the foul fiend,
Among this folk will fetch his fee;
And you are very strong and skilful
I believe well he would choose you]

Similarly Tam Lin, while pleading with his lover to save him from his fate says that:

"But aye at every seven years,
They pay the teind to Hell;
And I am sae fat and fair of flesh
I fear 'twill be mysell.' (Child, 1802)

This seems to suggest that the tithe was a regularly anticipated event and that those chosen for the teind are picked for physical health and personality. It is the best who are chosen and given, and so in both poems the ones who would be the teind and those who care for them try to avoid this fate.

The core concept behind this payment seems to be the idea that the Good Neighbours are the vassals or subjects of Hell and its ruler and so owe it and him rent on a set basis. This rent is paid, we might say, in the currency of Hell - souls. The earliest versions of 'The Romance and Prophecy of Thomas of Erceldoune' imply the risk to Thomas from the tithe isn't only from his strength and skill but also apparently in their desire to preserve their own and offer humans instead. The same theme is found in Tam Lin where it is not the fairies who fear going for the tithe but the human-born Tam Lin. Lyle's article *'The Teind to Hell in Tam Lin'* argues that the belief in the teind grew out of a need to explain the belief in changelings (Lyle, 1970). From this perspective people in seeking to understand why fairies stole human beings came to fit them and their motives into a Christian worldview; fairies were fallen angels who lived as tenants to the Devil, trapped as it were outside of both Heaven and Hell they needed to pay rent to their landlord and did so by stealing humans to spare having to give up their own folk. A key aspect to this argument is the fact that in both poems the teind is due to be paid the next morning and the men in the story can be saved that night if they escape Fairyland before the payment (Lyle, 1970). In Tam Lin this occurs explicitly on Samhain, a time in Scotland when the bi-annual rents came due, reinforcing the idea that the tithe or kane was a rent payment (Lyle, 1970).

Ultimately we can conclude that the teind is a fascinating and unique belief found in the southern area of Scotland as early as the 16th century. It reflects the idea that the fairies paid rent to Hell in the form of lives, preferably stolen human ones, probably once every seven years. A person could avoid being this teind if they could be rescued from Fairy on the eve of the payment, otherwise if they were fair enough and well-mannered enough the Devil might choose them as payment. The belief itself might be a way to explain why the fairies took humans to begin with and left changelings, or it could perhaps be an echo of an older pagan practice or offering sacrifices to the spirits themselves for the humans to pay rent, as it were, to live in the territory of the gods or Fey. Ultimately we will never know with certainty.

Transformation to a Fairy

There are references to fairies having children of their own as well as having children with humans, but we also see another means of fairy reproduction and that is through the transformation of humans into fairies. In the ballad of Tam Lin the eponymous character was born human but describes himself as a fairy after having been taken by the Queen of fairies and made into one of their number. In an anecdotal account from Ireland a young boy was taken by the Good People and kept for three days during which they attempted to strip him of all things earthly, but failing to find a blackberry thorn under one of his nails were unable to turn him into a fairy and were forced to return him (Narvaez, 1991).

In the tale of SELENA MOOR we are told of Grace Hutchins who was human but taken by the Cornish fairies to become one of their number. In both that tale and anecdotes from Ireland in the Fairy Faith in Celtic Countries different sources suggest that people who were prone to TRAVELLING TO FAIRY in trances as living humans are more likely to be taken this way. Grace Hutchins tells her former lover:

> *"People believed, and so it seemed, that I was found on the moor dead; it was also supposed that I must have dropped there in a trance, as I was subject to it. What was buried for me, however, was only a changeling, or sham body, never mine I should think"* (Bottrell, 1983, page 98).

There has long been debate about the connection between fairies and the human dead and it is generally agreed that some portion of the Fair Folk were once living humans with a variety of anecdotal sources suggesting that it was possible to recognize the recently deceased among the fairies. There are many accounts of belief in Sligo that people who drowned were particularly likely to be seen later among the fairies (Evans-Wentz, 1911). Not all human dead became fairies, however, with a variety of other afterlife options and only those specifically chosen by the Fair Folk join them after leaving the human world.

According to one person from Sligo, Ireland when the fairies take a person they take both the physical body as well as the spirit and transform the person's body into one like their own (Evans-Wentz, 1911). This is in line with the quote given above from the Cornish story of Selena Moor, where Grace Hutchins claims she was physically taken and a changeling left to be buried in her place. A Scottish source agrees, stating that when fairies took living humans *"they took body and soul together."* (Evans-Wentz, 1911, page 102).

Not all those who are taken are removed entirely from the human world and there are stories of those who have at least intermittent contact with their former human family. In one account from Grange, Ireland, a woman taken by the fairies was known to return at night to comb out the hair of her three children and appeared once to a neighbour to ensure her children were taken care of by revealing where she had hidden money she had earned when she was still human (Evans-Wentz, 1911). And, of course, in Tam Lin we see Tam Lin taking a human lover.

The actual process of transformation is uncertain but may involve at least in part having the captive person eat fairy food. One person from Sligo in 1909 described it thus:

> *"Once they take you and you taste food in their palace you cannot come back. You are changed to one of them, and live with them forever."* (Evans-Wentz, 1911).

This may partially explain the deep prohibition against eating fairy food, and the idea that to eat fairy food binds a person irrevocably to Fairy.

Travelling to Fairy

Travelling to Fairy or with the fairies is a complex subject in folklore and we find it in both stories and anecdotal material. In some cases there is a clear and complex process needed in order to gain access to the world of Fairy while in others it is presented as a common, even nightly, occurrence for some people.

Ritualized travel is found particularly in folklore and ballads and would seem to follow a specific, if somewhat varied process.

Anecdotal accounts of travelling to fairy are less formal and, in many cases, seem to be less voluntary on the human's part. We see travel to Fairy here divided roughly into two types: those who physically travel to a different world or place, and those who travel to Fairy in dreams or trances. Isobel Gowdie said she was physically brought to the Fairy queen who fed her meat, and one accused Scottish cunningman asserted he had been brought inside a fairy hill (Wilby, 2005). Irish mná feasa [wise women] were sometimes said to fall into trances in which it was thought they were away with the fairies and afterwards they would say they had been far away and talk of things that would soon happen (O Crualaoich, 2003).

There are many anecdotal accounts from Ireland of people who travelled to Fairy in dreams or trances and returned. These experiences could last anywhere from a few hours, to a full night, to several days or even years (Evans-Wentz, 1911). People who travelled this way may remember the details vividly afterwards or may not, although there was some supposition that claims of memory loss were faked to protect the person from the possible ire of the fairies for revealing too much after the fact (Evans-Wentz, 1911).

It was sometimes believed that those who were ill, especially for extended periods of time, were being taken by the fairies. Such people might eventually recover and later be known for continuing to spend time among the Good People (Evans-Wentz, 1911).

Trows

A term found in the Shetland and Orkney Islands of Scotland, likely imported to there from Norse areas during occupation periods. Possibly a variant of the word trolls. Trow is considered roughly synonymous to other Scottish terms for fairies including sighean (Gibson, 1837).

In some folklore Trows are described as very human in appearance, although they may appear old, shrivelled, or physically deformed. In other stories, however, they are described as clearly inhuman, unattractive, and twisted, even in sometimes appearing as a mix of human and horse. They are often described in unflattering terms as having oversized feet, large noses, flat faces, and short limbs. They can range in height from three to six feet depending on the story. They are often said to dress in grey, although sometimes they appear in green, red, white, or black (Briggs, 1976, Bruford, 1991).

It was claimed that the witches in these areas dealt with the trows, much as we see the witches in other areas dealing with fairies, and as in other areas the trows were known for shooting magical arrows that caused illness and death and for swapping changelings for beings they wanted (Hibbert, 1891). In Shetland the Trows prefer night time and fear the sun which traps them on earth until it sets (Briggs, 1976). Like some other kinds of fairies Trows will make themselves welcome in human homes at night while the inhabitants are sleeping, coming in to sit by the fireside; they are known to dislike people who lock their doors for this reason (Briggs, 1976). Trows live in mounds that are often called knowes and like other fairies they will steal humans, most often brides, and enjoy music and causing mischief.

Trooping Fairies

One method of dividing fairies into groupings was by their social habits and form this we get the Trooping fairies for those fairies of a gregarious nature. The term is also used sometimes as a sort of generic for all fairies, something like the euphemistic terms would be, but it should best be understood in its proper context.

Tuatha De Danann

One of the groups of beings who invaded Ireland often described as the old gods of that land. The Tuatha De Danann ruled over the land until being driven into the SIDHE by the Milesians. The Tuatha De Danann are closely tied to the fairies in Ireland and many of their members became Kings and Queens of Fairy in later folklore.

See Daoine Sidhe

Tylwyth Teg

One of the main groupings of fairies in Wales is the Tylwyth Teg [Fair Family[1]] and this term may be a name for Welsh fairies more generally. Another euphemistic name for them is Bendith Y Mamau [Mother's Blessing] which Briggs' suggests might have been used by people particularly to avert being taken into Fairy by them (Briggs, 1976). They were generally considered benevolent and kind beings and many sources described them as 'good' although like any fairies they could cause mischief or harm if motivated to. This 20th century Welsh source summarizes the general opinion of the Tylwyth Teg at the time:

> "'*In most of the tales I heard repeated when I was a boy, I am quite certain the implication was that the Tylwyth Teg were a kind of spirit race having human characteristics, who could at will suddenly appear and suddenly disappear. They were generally supposed to live underground, and to come forth on moonlight nights, dressed in gaudy colours (chiefly in red), to dance in circles in grassy fields… I think the Tylwyth Teg were generally looked upon as kind and good-natured, though revengeful if not well treated.*" (Evans-Wentz, 1911, page 142).

It should be noted though that while this reputation for goodness and benevolence generally held throughout anecdotal accounts the opinion wasn't universal and there were sources who felt that the Tylwyth Teg were dangerous or antithetical to humans. At least one 20th century Welsh source defined them as evil spirits and indicated that children had a particular fear of them (Evans-Wentz, 1911).

They are described in anecdotal accounts as appearing both as small, no taller than a seven-year-old child, and as the height of an average human adult and are usually blond (Evans-Wentz, 1911; Briggs, 1976). Like other fairies they were able to pass invisibly or to disappear when they chose to (Evans-Wentz, 1911). They appear across a wide selection of Welsh folklore described variously as young and beautiful or old and wizened, as the size of children or the height of an average adult human, wearing red or wearing white, making it difficult to make many definitive statements about the Tylwyth Teg. This may support the idea that rather than a specific grouping Tylwyth Teg is actually a more generic term.

The Tylwyth Teg live in the earth, in lakes, and on islands in the ocean (Briggs, 1976). Specific regions in Wales tended to assign one location as home to the Tylwyth Teg more than others so that in North-western Wales stories are more likely to say they live underground while in Southern Wales they live in lakes and in South-western Wales they are found living on islands in the sea. The folklore of each region is then based on or in this view.

Tradition holds that they enjoy dancing and are usually seen at night and that they are more usually inclined towards kindness. Despite this general benevolence they were known to take human children as other fairies did and replace them with CHANGELINGS and to lead travellers astray to amuse themselves (Evans-Wentz, 1911).

The Tylwyth Teg were particularly renowned for their singing and dancing, activities which they seemed to enjoy passing their time with. Wherever they danced fairy rings marked by rings of mushrooms would appear. If a human was drawn into their dance they would pass what they thought was a single night, only to find when they left that a year had passed (Evans-Wentz, 1911). They might also keep the person forever.

The Welsh Tylwyth Teg were particularly connected to children, both by taking changelings as other fairies do and also for rewarding or punishing children based on behaviour. One Welsh source believed that the Tylwyth Teg would take bad children and turn them into evil spirits (Evans-Wentz, 1911). The folklore suggests that they lure children in to their dances and may keep those children for a time or forever. Unlike other fairies, however, they do sometimes release children who wish to return home, as one anecdotal account related, where a child who was taken wished to return to his mother and was allowed to do so (Evans-Wentz, 1911).

Like other groupings of fairies the Tylwyth Teg are said to have a King and Queen. Who exactly their King is may vary depending on whether we are interpreting them as a generic term for all Welsh fairies, in which case we would look to Gwyn ap Nudd and Arawn. A source in Fairy Faith in Celtic Countries named a different King and his Queen saying:

> *"The king of the Tylwyth Teg was called Gwydion ab Don, Gwyd referring to a temperament in man's nature*[2]*. His residence was among the stars, and called Caer Gwydion. His queen was Gwenhidw. I have heard my mother call the small fleece-like clouds which appear in fine weather the Sheep of Gwenhidw.'"* (Evans-Wentz, 1911, page 151).

Notes

1 I am giving the meaning of Tylwyth Teg here as Fair family because that is the most common translation you will find. The actual reading is more nuanced and in fairness I think it should be mentioned here that Tylwyth has meanings including family, tribe, household, and ancestry; Teg can be understood as fair, beautiful, or fine. I encourage readers to avoid overly narrow interpretations of the English.

2 It's worth noting here that Gwydion means 'tree born' and Gwydion ab Don is a personage from the Mabinogion, like Arawn, although Gwydion is never as far as I'm aware directly associated with the Otherworld or Fair Family. Rather Gwydion is a sorcerer and the uncle of the God, Llew Llaw Gyffes. As

to Gwenhidw, she is an obscure figure; Dumezil mentions the name in his book 'Gods of the Ancient Northmen' where he notes an appearance of the character and some variations of the name as well as suggestion a possible breakdown of the name's parts into 'white' and 'charm' or 'witchcraft'.

U

Uraisg

A solitary Scottish fairy who would sometimes gather together into groups. Briggs considers them a type of Brownie because they can be helpful around homes and farms while Carmichael describes them as monstrous and dangerous to those who come across them. Dwelly calls them both a Brownie and a 'water-god'. The name is sometimes spelled Ùraisg (plural Ùraisgean), Uraisg, and is Anglicized to Urisk.

Sources generally agree that the Uraisg is a half-man, half-goat although they differ on whether he appears to be ugly or attractive. Carmichael says he is:

> *"…a monster, half-human, half-goat, with abnormally long hair, long teeth, and long claws"* (Carmichael, 1900, page 373). In contrast Dwelly describes him as *"a jolly personable being, with a broad blue bonnet, flowing yellow hair and a long walking-staff."* (Dwelly, 1902).

Uraisg may help around human habitations in which case they prefer to be given or to take milk, although they may frighten humans who see them. When in the wilds they tend to be found around small bodies of water, perhaps the reason for Dwelly referring to them as 'water-gods', and when they gather in groups that is also known to happen around lakes and waterfalls.

Unseelie

A Scots word now more commonly seen spelled Unseelie but originally more often spelled unsely and with a variety of other forms. In essence the word represents the opposite of its counterpart seelie, just as the fairies it describes are the opposite of the Seelie fairies. Generally it can be defined as a person who is unhappy, unfortunate, or unlucky and in the context of the fairies the implication isn't that they are these things but that they bring these things with them. The word is a form of the Scots word unsell, a noun for a wicked or troublesome person, and related to the Old English word unsele meaning unlucky; all of these meanings should be taken into account when trying to understand Unseelie fairies.

McNeill calls the Unseelie *"wicked wights"* and says that they are perpetually ready to harm humans which is why special precautions were taken against them. Their power is greatest on the quarter days and this is when the most care must be taken to ward against them and avoid encounters with them (McNeill, 1956). They are not limited to these times, however, and can be dangerous at any time if a person is unfortunate enough to run across them.

Unseelie Court

The Unseelie Court are the gathered grouping of those beings who are more baneful to humans. The word court in this context can refer to both a group or company as well as royal court, so it is both all malevolently inclined fairies in general as well as the specific ones connected to the monarchy of the Unseelie. In modern belief[1] Nicnevin is considered the Queen of the Unseelie Court, although older folklore doesn't speak to that specifically.

Just as the SEELIE COURT are those most inclined to help humans without a reason the Unseelie Court are those who are most inclined to harm without reason. They need no motivation to act malevolently and often seem to delight in tormenting people for their own amusement. There are other reasons a person may find themselves at risk from the Unseelie Court besides offering them entertainment and the main secondary reason is as a food source; many of the Unseelie Court beings are known to eat humans.

Which beings fall into the auspices of the Unseelie Court are a matter of opinion as folklore isn't conclusive and some beings can be fluid in their relations to humans. Kelpies, for example, are generally dangerous to humans, but may sometimes be helpful and even caring towards them. Others, however, are solidly against human safety and interests, such as the Redcaps. The Slua Sidhe is also often strongly connected to the Unseelie Court (Briggs, 1976).

Note

1 See the entry on Nicnevin for more on her connection to the Unseelie.

V

Vampires

Vampires as they appear in folklore are not usually considered a type of fairy, however, there are some traditional fairies that have vampiric qualities or are sometimes classified as vampires including the LEANNÁN SIDHE and BAOBHAN SITHE. This is a bit of a grey area and opinions will vary as to whether these are actually true vampires in the classical sense or simply beings who may be described with the adjective because they feed on a human's life force or blood.

W

The Wee Wee Man

A Scottish ballad wherein a traveller encounters a small fairy man, no taller than the length of a finger, near a well. Despite his tiny size the little man shows the traveller great feats of strength and also of magic.

It was down by Carterhaugh, father
Between the water and the wall
There I met with a wee wee man
And he was the least that ever I saw.
His length was scarce a finger's length
And thick and nimble was his knee
Between his eyes a flea could go
Between his shoulders inches three.
His beard was long and white as a swan
His robe was neither green nor grey
He clapped his hands, down came the mist
And he sank and he sainted clean away.
He's lifted up a stone, six feet in height
And flung it farther than I could see
And though I'd been a-trying bold
I'd never had lifted it to my knee.
"Wee wee man, you are so strong,
Tell me where your dwelling be" -
"It's down beneath yon bonny green bower
Though you must come with me and see."
We roved on and we sped on
Until we came to a bonny green hall
The room was made of the beaten gold
And pure as crystal was the glass.
There were pipers playing on every spare

And ladies dancing in glistering green
He clapped his hands, down came the mist
And the man in the hall no more was seen.
(Child, 1882; language modernized)

The Wild Hunt

The Wild Hunt is a collection of spirits - some say ghosts, or fairies - that travel through the air in storms led by a Huntsman. Who the Huntsman is varies as widely as the geographic areas the hunt is found in and the names it is known by. There have been entire books written about the Wild Hunt - and I highly recommend Claude Lecouteux's "Phantom Armies of the Night: the Wild Hunt and the Ghostly Processions of the Undead" - so this section will by necessity be very limited in its scope but I'd like to offer an overview. I have encountered the Hunt myself a time or two and it is likely that another follower of a Fairy-based witchcraft will also meet them or see them at some point and its best to go into that with an understanding of who and what they may be.

So, to begin, the Hunt is found in Germany, France, Denmark, Normandy, Sweden, Norway, England, Scotland, Ireland, Wales, and the United States (Jones, 2003). The Hunt is interesting though in that although found across a wide geographic area and among different cultures it always takes on a unique local character, often with a specific local spirit or God taking on the role of Huntsman. In the Germanic areas the Hunt is often led by Odin (Wodan), Frau Hulde, or both together, the Welsh Hunt is led by Gwynn ap Nudd, and the English by Herne, while in France it is led by Harlequin, and in other areas a variety of fictional or historic figures including sir Frances Drake (Jones, 2003). The hunt in Germany is also sometimes led by Frau Perchta or the White Lady, Frau Gauden, who led groups of dead children or witches through the sky and were seen as good omens of abundant crops in the coming year (Berk, & Spytma, 2002) Some modern sources try to relate the Hunt led by

Harlequin to the Norse goddess Hel, but it more likely that the name derives from the 12th century term "*Herlethingus*", a word used to describe wandering spectral troops during the time of Henry the 2nd (Berk, & Spytma, 2002). In Orkney the Hunt is led by Odin but may also be the Trows riding out on pale horses to steal cows (Towrie, 2013). In Scotland the Hunt is the Unseelie Court, perhaps relating to the Irish idea of the Slua Sí, the fairy host who travel through the air attacking the unwary. Often when the Huntsman - or woman - is not a God or Otherworldly spirit it is said to be a person who so loved hunting in life that they rejected any other afterlife but to continue hunting and were rewarded or cursed to perpetually hunt for all eternity (Grimm, 1883).

The Wild Hunt is known by many names. In Orkney it is called the Raging Host (Towrie, 2013). Associated with Odin the Hunt was called Odin's Hunt/Odensjakt, Odin's Army, Wilde Jagd, the Wild Ride, Asgardeia, Oskerei, Horrific Ride, Thunderous Ride, and also the Ride of the Dead, and the Family of Harlequin (in France) (Towrie, 2013; Berk, & Spytma, 2002). Other names include the Furious Host or Wild Host and in America, the Ghost Riders. Each named Hunt has its own unique characteristics and backstory but all have the same general character and wider purpose.

The Wild Hunt travels in the air, and appears as a group of dark riders, led by a Huntsmen who may be headless, with a pack of fearsome hounds, and accompanied by a horde of spirits who sometimes appear as the newly dead or battle dead (Jones, 2003). When the Hunt is led by Gwynn ap Nudd the hounds are white with red ears, and are called the Cwn Annwn or Gabriel Hounds (Berk, & Spytma, 2002). The Hunt always includes horses and hounds, both usually black, but sometimes white or grey, and always fierce; in some accounts the animals breath fire and they are often missing limbs or with extra limbs and may display the same gruesome wounds as the battle dead accompanying the Hunt (Berk, & Spytma, 2002). The presence of the Hunt is signalled by the unearthly sound of hooves, hunting horns, and baying hounds appearing usually in the night sky and sometimes in storms (Towrie, 2013).

Mary Jones relays a historic account of the Hunt from 1127 CE:

> *"...it was seen and heard by many men: many hunters riding. The hunters were black, and great and loathy, and their hounds all black, and wide-eyed and loathy, and they rode on black horses and black he-goats. This was seen in the very deer park in the town of Peterborough, and in all the woods from the same town to Stamford; and the monks heard the horn blowing that they blew that night. Truthful men who kept watch at night said that it seemed to them that there might be about twenty or thirty horn blowers. This was seen and heard...all through Lenten tide until Easter."* (Jones, 2003).

This description gives the time the Hunt appears as during "Lent" which might be assumed to be roughly March and April. In Switzerland the Hunt was said to appear during summer nights, and those who do not quickly get out of the way of the passing Hunt will be trampled by it (Grimm, 1883). More often in folklore the Hunt was said to ride in late fall and winter, particularly during the 12 nights of Yule. Grimm tells us that in Germany it was believed the Hunt rode during the time from Christmas to 12th Night or whenever the storm winds blew (Grimm, 1883). Yule was seen as a time of high supernatural influence when the Dead were more present (Towrie, 2013). In my own experience with the Ghost Riders of America they appear around Samhain and ride until the first week of January, but in times of great unrest or disturbance they may appear as well.

In many cases the Hunt is connected to Fairy in some way, but it is equally strongly connected to the spirits of the Dead.

Towrie conjectures that the Orkney trows, themselves connected to the Wild Hunt, may have originally been considered spirits of the dead (Towrie, 2013). The dead are often seen in the retinue of the Hunt and that includes both those who may be recognized as recently dead as well as the ancient battle dead, some displaying hideous wounds. Some folklore also says that the wild Hunt rides out seeking the dead, chasing certain types of ghosts or spirits.

The Hunt appeared for different reasons depending on where it was - in some cases hunting a mythic animal or creature, in others pursuing lost souls or even seeking to punish wrong-doers (Towrie, 2013). As a Fairy Rade[1] the Hunt is usually hunting human beings, either with the purpose of kidnapping them or tormenting them; in some cases the person might go mad (Berk, & Spytma, 2002). In some cases the Hunt might offer to take a living person to ride with them, but the risk of doing so was great; the person might never return or might become a permanent part of the Host[2]. Seeing the Hunt could be an ill-omen and the Hunt itself could kill or drive a person mad, but conversely in some areas it was believed meeting the Hunt bravely and politely could earn a person great reward. There are several folk tales, like the story of "Wod, the Wild Huntsman" where the main character meets the Hunt and comes away with gifts of meat and gold as a reward for his cleverness. Showing proper respect would also earn a person a reward, but conversely rudeness would result in the person being thrown a severed human limb, if he was lucky, or his own dead child, if he wasn't; in some cases the Hunt would turn on the person mocking them and tear the person to pieces (Berk, & Spytma, 2002; Grimm, 1883).

Protection from the Wild Hunt is best achieved through avoiding them by not traveling at night, especially during Yule or other dangerous times. Shelter can also be sought at the first sound of hunting horn or hounds in the air. However, should those fail or not be possible and should you meet the Hunt, and do not feel like taking your chances with them, there is this charm from 14th century Germany:

"Woden's host and all his men
Who are bearing wheels and willow twigs
Broken on the wheel and hanged.
You must go away from here."
(Gundarsson, trans. Höfler; Berk, & Spytma, 2002).

Notes

1 The Fairy Rade or Fairy Ride is a concept seen in many cultures of a procession of higher ranking fairies who ride out together, often at specific times of year like Samhain and Midsummer. Crossing paths with a Fairy Rade is dangerous, although we can see examples in stories such as the tale of Tam Lin where a mortal is recovered from the fairies after being won back during a Rade. The Fairy Rade sometimes is similar to or confused with the Wild Hunt.

2 Some modern spirit workers and traditional witches do choose to ride with the Wild Hunt. I won't say I've never done it, but I also won't encourage other people to try it. There is always a danger with the Hunt that you won't come back.

Will o' the Wisp

The Will o' the Wisp is an interesting thing to study, possibly a ghost or a fairy from one view and a swamp phenomena by another, one that may be explained by scientific means but whose folklore persists. There is debate even today about whether the Will o' the Wisp is supernatural or a natural occurrence and explanations for it include both optical illusions as well as spontaneous ignition of swamp gasses. There is also a rich array of folklore around it which offers many explanations of it from that viewpoints as well as stories of dealing with it

In recent times it has become less common for people to see Will o' the Wisps, and many accept the scientific explanation although science itself has never been able to reproduce or measure them successfully. When the phenomena appears it can be as small as a candle flame or as large as a torch, pale or bright, and the light will reflect off of nearby objects (Sanford, 1919). Colours can vary and may include green or white and the phenomena has been seen passing through windows and doors and inside buildings although it is most commonly seen over or near water, particularly swamps. Explanations for what causes it include bioluminescent plants and animals, gases given off in the process of decay, and bubbles of plasma, although no single theory can or has been proven (Drudge, 2016).

In folklore the Will o' the Wisp has many different names which are indicative of the folklore attached to it. The common name of Ignis Fatuus is Latin for 'fool fire'. It is also known variously as Bill-with-the-wisp, Hobbledy's Lantern, Jack-a-lantern, Jenny-with-the-lantern, Jenny-burnt-tail, Peg-a-lantern, Joan-in-the-wad, Kit-in-the-stick or Kitty-candlestick, Kitty-with-the-wisp, the Lanternman, Pinket, Friar Rush, Gyl Burnt-Taylf, Hinky punk, and Hobby Lantern (Briggs, 1976). It's possible that like so many other types of fairies we are not looking at one specific being but rather a range of beings who all fall under the umbrella term of 'Will o' the Wisp' because of how they appear and what they do. In that case any being who shows up in the dark of night bearing a light to mislead travellers could be called a Will o' the Wisp even if we also know it as another distinct being such as the Pwca.

The nature of the Will'o'the Wisp can be either mischievous or malicious depending and they have been known to both lead travellers harmlessly astray and also to lead them to their deaths. They do this by appearing as lights in front of lost travellers; as the traveller follows the light the light moves and leads them astray. In the case of the mischievous spirits this may mean into a ditch or in circles but for the dangerous ones it could mean off a cliff or into a bog where they drown. They are also known to attack people directly in some folklore, physically chasing them, driving them mad with a touch, or causing a burning sensation on the bottoms of the feet (Ashliman, 2016).

The Will o' the Wisp is often explained as a human spirit of some sort that has been cursed to wander by night bearing a light. The purpose of this light also varies and depends often on why the spirit is cursed to wander. In some areas of Scotland it was said to be the spirit of a girl who had died and spent her afterlife searching the area near the shoreline for a plant used in dyeing cloth; and that she did so because she'd been too greedy in hoarding the dye when she was alive (Ashliman, 2016). In other stories, for example, it was someone who illegally moved boundary markers or cheated neighbours and is set to wander with a light to show where the true boundary is. In the Netherlands and parts of Germany there is a belief that Will o' the Wisps are spirits of unbaptized children who will approach people and try to lead them to water hoping to be baptized (Ashliman, 2016). They can be dealt with by either offering them baptism or throwing graveyard dirt at them.

By other accounts though the Will o' the Wisp is a fairy. In Wales both the Ellydon and Pwca take on the role of the Will o' the Wisp, leading travellers astray. Stokes describes one such incident with the Pwca here:

> *"[A] peasant who is returning home from his work, or from a fair, when he sees a light traveling before him. Looking closer he perceives that it is carried by a dusky little figure, holding a lantern or candle at arm's length over its head. He follows it for several miles, and suddenly finds himself on the brink of a frightful precipice. From far down below, there rises to his ears the sound of a foaming torrent. At the same moment the little goblin with the lantern springs across the chasm, alighting on the opposite side;*

> *raises the light again high over its head, utters a loud and malicious laugh, blows out its candle, and disappears up the opposite hill, leaving the awestruck peasant to get home as best he can."* (Stokes, 1880).

In parts of Germany they are viewed as a type of gnome who can help lost travellers if petitioned to do so and paid for their help, but who will also lead astray those who annoy them (usually by seeking them out); protections against them include walking with one foot in a wheelrut (Ashliman, 2016). In another German story they are described as having wings and flying, and one appeared to attack a girl while she walked because she was singing a song which mocked the spirit (Ashliman, 2016).

There is a distinct crossover as well between the two beliefs, that the Will o' the Wisp is human spirit and that it is a fairy, which we see in many versions of the Jack o Lantern story. In that classic tale, generally viewed by folklorists to fall into the auspices of Will o' the Wisp lore, a person makes a deal with the devil but outwits him by some means and eventually finds himself turned away from both heaven and hell alike. Left to wander in the cold darkness between worlds after a time he finds a light or is given one, which he uses to light his way. In a version of the story related by Stokes in 1880 the reader is explicitly told that the man, having been turned away from both afterlives, was turned into a fairy (Stokes, 1880). This is reinforced by Danish lore which states that a Jack o Lantern is the soul of 'an unrighteous man' and that one should never call on him or point him out if you see him but that turning your cap inside out will protect against him, which is true to fairylore (Ashliman, 2016). This may reflect wider beliefs that fairies themselves are those who belong to neither heaven nor hell, something we see in both narratives about the fairies origins as fallen angels and also some beliefs that relate dead humans as fairies.

The Will o' the Wisp is an intriguing and unusual fairy - or spirit - one of the few that science has sought to explain and also one of the more well documented as a phenomena. I have never seen one myself, but my husband has once in the swamp behind our home. Are they natural phenomena? Ghosts? Fairies? I think perhaps the answer is all of the above.

Wings

The oldest depictions and descriptions of fairies do not include them having wings and when they are described as flying it usually through some esoteric process. Folklore and anecdotal accounts of fairies prior to the 18th century do not feature winged fairies. Fairies would fly by enchanting and object, often an herb like Ragwort, into the form of a horse which could travel through the air (Briggs, 1976). The Slua Sidhe and the Wild Hunt were able to travel through the air on their own power but are never described in older accounts with wings of any sort.

In the late 18th century and then into the 19th century actors depicting fairies in plays begin to be seen in art and early photographs wearing stylized wings, possibly to signify their Otherworldly nature to the audience. During the Victorian period we begin to see fairies in artwork shown with wings, along with the wider shift into the Victorian aesthetic of fairies as young, softer looking beings, often children or adolescent in appearance. The wings in these cases are usually insect wings like those of dragonflies or butterflies in line with the wider diminishing of fairies into insect like and insect sized beings strongly associated with flowers and nature.

Anecdotal accounts of winged fairies are not found until the 20th century and are extremely rare until into the 21st. Anecdotal accounts found in Evans-Wentz 'Fairy Faith in Celtic Countries' from 1911 and in the 1991 work edited by Narvaez 'The Good People' notably lack winged fairies or references to winged fairies, as do the folklore gathered by Yeats, Wilde, Campbell, Carmichael, Sikes, and other early folklorists. Despite this the 2018 'Fairy Census' conducted by Simon Young includes a multitude of anecdotal encounters with winged fairies very much in line with the Victorian and later Hollywood and fiction influenced ideas of fairies.

Witches

Witches and fairies have a long and complicated relationship with each other. Both Irish and Scottish witches were said in some sources to learn and gain their powers both for healing and harming from the Good People (Hall, 2005; Yeats 1888).

Many Scottish witches made did not gain their powers and knowledge from the Devil as classical European witches were known to, but rather by dealing with fairies and sometimes by pledging themselves to the Fairy Queen.

In Scotland fairies were said to give elfshot to witches and sometimes to direct the use of it against other humans. In Ireland witches were not known to use elfshot, rather having a reputation for 'blinking' or putting the evil eye on cattle or people instead, but there were other similarities between Irish witches and fairies and it was said that witches learned from the fairies (Jenkins, 1991; Wilde, 1888)

Y

Ylfig

See: Possession by Fairies

Bibliography

Acland, A., (2017) Tam Lin Balladry Retrieved from http://tam-lin.org/

— (2015). Is Tam Lin a Rape Story? Retrieved from http://tam-lin.org/analysis/Tam_Lin_and_rape.html

— (1997) Symbols in Tam Lin: Red Roses, Green Dresses, and White Horses. Retrieved from http://tam-lin.org/analysis/symbols.html

— (1998) Alice Brand. Retrieved from http://tam-lin.org/stories/Alice_Brand.html

Al-Alim, R., (2018) Jinn Sorcery

Allen, J., (1952) North-East Lowlands of Scotland

Allingham, W., (1888) The Leprechaun; or Fairy Shoemaker. Retrieved from http://www.sacred-texts.com/neu/yeats/fip/fip24.htm

Ashliman, D., (2005) Night-Mares Retrieved from http://www.pitt.edu/~dash/nightmare.html

— (2016) Will-o'-the-Wisps

Askew, R., (1884) Bye-Gones, Relating to Wales and the Border Countries

Atsma, A., (2017) Satyroi

Ballard, L., (1991) 'Fairies and the Supernatural on Reachrai'; The Good People; new fairylore essays

Barry, G., (1867) A History of the Orkney Islands

Bauer, M., and MacDhonnchaidh, U., (2017) Am Faclair Beag

Beachcombing's Bizarre History Blog (2016) In Search of the Earliest Fairy Wings. Retrieved from http://www.strangehistory.net/2016/12/17/search-earliest-fairy-wings/

Bedell, J., (2007) Hildur Queen of the Elves, and Other Icelandic Legends

Bennett, M., (1991) Balquhidder Revisited: Fairylore in the Scottish Highlands, 1690-1990

Bergman, J., (2011) The Significant Other: a Literary History of Elves

Berk, A., and Spytma, W., (2002) Penance, Power, and Pursuit, On the Trail of the Wild Hunt

Beveridge, J., (2014) Children into Swans: Fairy Tales and the Pagan Imagination

Bitel, L., (1991) In Visu Noctis: Dreams in European Hagiography and Histories, 450-900, Histories of Religions vol. 31

Black, G., (1894) Scottish Charms and Amulets

— (1903). County Folk-Lore, vol. 3: Examples of Printed Folk-Lore Concerning the Orkney & Shetland Islands

Blain, J., (2000) Wights and Ancestors: Heathenism in a Living Landscape

Bottrell, W., (1873) Traditions and Hearthside Stories of West Cornwall, vol. 2

Bovey, A., (2006) Monsters and Grotesques in Medieval Manuscripts

Briggs, K., (1976) A Dictionary of Fairies

— (1978). An Encyclopaedia of Fairies: Hobgoblins, Brownies, Boogies, and Other Supernatural Creatures

— (1978) The Vanishing People: Fairy Lore and Legends

— (1967) The Fairies in Tradition and Literature

Briggs, K., and Tongue, R., (1968) Folktales of England

British Museum (2018) Robin Goodfellow. Retrieved from https://www.bl.uk/collection-items/robin-goodfellow-his-mad-pranks-and-merry-jests-1639

Brock, M., and Raiswell, R., (2018) Knowing Demons, Knowing Spirits in the Early Modern Period

Brosius, M., (2007). The Court and Court Society in Ancient Monarchies

Bruford, A., (1991). Trolls, Hillfolk, Finns, and Picts: the Identity of the Good Neighbors in Orkney in Shetland; The Good People

Buccola, R., (2006) Fairies, Fractious Women, and the Old Faith:

Fairylore in Early Modern British Drama and Culture

Buchan, D., (1991) 'Ballads of Otherworldly Beings'; The Good People

Buchan, P., (1828) Ancient Ballads and Songs of the North of Scotland

Bunce, J., (1878) Fairy Tales and Their Meanings

Burns, R., (1786) Poems, chiefly in the Scottish Dialect. Retrieved from https://www.scottishcorpus.ac.uk/cmsw/burns/

Byrne, A., (2016) Otherworlds: Fantasy and History in Medieval Literature

Caffrey, N., (2002) The Elfin Knight Child #2: Impossible Tasks and Impossible Love

Campbell, G., (1900) Superstitions of the Highlands and Islands of Scotland

Campbell J., (1902) The Gaelic Otherworld

Carmichael, A., (1900) The Carmina Gadelica

Carson, C. (1956) The Midnight Court

Chambers, R., (1842) Popular Rhymes, Fireside Stories, and Amusements of Scotland

Child, F., (1882) The English and Scottish Popular Ballads

— (1802) Tam Lin

C&MH (2014) Castle Life: Officers and Servants in a Medieval Castle retrieved from http://www.castlesandmanorhouses.com/life_02_officers.htm

Connor, P., (1994) Lararium

Cox, M., (1904) Introduction to Folklore

Crocker, T., (1825) Fairy Legends and Traditions of Southern Ireland

Cromek (1810) Remains of Nithsdale and Galloway Song

Cromond, W., (1903) The Records of Elgin, 1234–1800

Curtin, J., (1895) Tales of the Fairies and of the Ghost World

Cutchin, J., (2015) Trojan Feast

--- (2018) Thieves in the Night

Daimler, M., (2015) Excerpts from the Coir Anmann. Retrieved from http://lairbhan.blogspot.com/2015/08/excerpts-from-coir-anmann.html

— (2017) Echtra Condla Chaim meic Cond Chetchathaig. Retrieved from http://lairbhan.blogspot.com/2017/03/ectra-condla-chaim-meic-cuind.html

Dalyell, J., (1801) Scottish Poems of the Sixteenth Century

Davies, O., (2003) Popular Magic: Cunning-folk in English History

D'Este, S., and Rankin, D., (2012) The Faerie Queens

Deegan, G., (1999) 'Fairy Bush Survives the Motorway Planners'; The Irish Times; Retrieved from https://www.irishtimes.com/news/fairy-bush-survives-the-motorway-planners-1.190053

Dobs, M (1929) Zeitschrift fur Celtische Philologie vol. 18

Douglas, G., (1901) Scottish Fairy and Folk Tales

Drudge, C., (2016) A New Explanation for One of the Strangest Occurrences in Nature: Ball Lightning

Dúchas.ie (2018) Fairies, National Folklore Collection UCD. Retrieved from https://www.duchas.ie/en/src?q=fairies

Dumézil, G., (1974) Gods of the Ancient Northmen

Dunkerson, C., (2017) Do the Elves in Tolkien's Stories Have Pointed Ears? Retrieved from http://tolkien.slimy.com/essays/Ears.html

Dwelly, E., (1902) Faclair Gàidhlìg air son nan sgoiltean

eDIL (n.d.) Electronic Dictionary of the Irish Language http://edil.qub.ac.uk/browse

Eliot, C., (1937) English Poetry I: From Chaucer to Gray. The Harvard Classics. 1909–14

Erickson, W., (1996) Mapping the Faerie Queene: Quest Structures and the World of the Poem

Evans, E., (1957) Irish Folk Ways

Evans-Wentz, W., (1911) The Fairy Faith in Celtic Countries

Faulkes, A., (1995) Prose Edda

Firth-Green, R., (2016) Elf Queens and Holy Friars: Fairy Beliefs and the Medieval Church

Forsyth, W., (1900) In the Shadow of Cairngorm

Fortune, M., (2016) The Bow/ Banshee video at https://www.youtube.com/watch?v=ZpZBok7_f4I

Froud, B., and Lee, A., (1978) Faeries

Geoghan, S., (2005) Gobnait: Woman of the Bees Retrieved from http://www.matrifocus.com/IMB05/ireland-gobnait.htm

Gibson, J., (1837) Memoirs of the Life of Sir Walter Scott

Gill, W., (1929) A Manx Scrapbook

Gillion, A., and Smith, J., (1953) Justiciary Cases

Graves, R., (1948) The White Goddess

Gregory, A., (1920) Visions and Beliefs in the West of Ireland

Gregory, A., (2013) Rye Spirits: Faith, faction and fairies in a seventeenth century English town

Grimm, J., (1888) Teutonic Mythology volume 2

--- (1883) Teutonic Mythology volume 3

Gruber, B., (2007) Iceland: Searching for Elves and Hidden People

Guest, C., (1877) The Mabinogion

Gundrasson, K., (2007) Elves, Wights, and Trolls

Gwyndaf, R., (1991) Fairylore: Memorates and Legends from Welsh Oral Tradition; The Good People

Hafstein, V., (2000) '*The Elves' Point of View: Cultural Identity in Contemporary Icelandic Elf-tradition*; Fabula

Hall, A., (2007) Elves in Anglo-Saxon England

– (2007) '*The Evidence for Maran, the Anglo-Saxon "Nightmares"*'; Neophilogus, vol. 91

– (2007) '*The Etymology and Meanings of Eldritch*'. Scottish Language, vol. 26. pp.

16-22.

– (2005) '*Getting Shot of Elves: Healing witchcraft and Fairies in the Scottish Witchcraft Trials*'. Folklore, vol. 116, pages 19 – 36

– (2008) '*How Celtic are the Fairies?*' Kelten 37 pages 2 – 5

– (2004) The Meaning of Elf and Elves in Medieval England

– (2011) The Contemporary Evidence for Early Medieval

Witchcraft Beliefs. Retrieved from https://www.academia.edu/1528964/The_Contemporary_Evidence_for_Early_Medieval_Witchcraft-Beliefs

Halliwell-Phillips, J., (1860) Notes of Family Excursions in North Wales

Harms, D., Clark, J., and Peterson, J., (2015) The Book of Oberon

Harper, D., (2018) Hobgoblin; Online Etymology Dictionary Retrieved from https://www.etymonline.com/word/hobgoblin?ref=etymonline_crossreference

--- (2018) 'Fairy'; Online Etymology Dictionary https://www.etymonline.com/word/fairy

--- (2018) Fetch; Online Etymology Dictionary Retrieved from https://www.etymonline.com/word/fetch

--- (2018) Goblin; Online Etymology Dictionary Retrieved from https://www.etymonline.com/word/goblin

Hartland, E., (1890) English Fairy and Other Folk Tales

--- (1891) The Science of Fairy Tales: An Inquiry into Fairy Mythology

Heddle, D., (2016) 'Selkies, Sex, and the Supernatural', The Bottle Imp, Issue 20

Hierarchy Structure (2018) The Royal Court. Retrieved from https://www.hierarchystructure.com/royal-court-hierarchy/

Henderson, L., (1997) The Guid Neighbours: Fairy Belief in Early Modern Scotland, 1500-1800

--- (2016) 'The (Super)natural world of Robert Kirk: Fairies, Beasts, Landscapes and Lychnobious Liminalities', The Bottle Imp, Issue 20

Henderson, L., and Cowan, E., (2007) Scottish Fairy Belief

Hibbert, S., (1891) A Description of the Shetland Islands

Hob (2018) Merriam Webster Dictionary

Housman, A., (1922) Last Poems

Hrafnagaldr Óðins (n.d.) Retrieved from https://notendur.hi.is/eybjorn/ugm/hrg/hrg.html

Hyde, D., (1890) Beside the Fire: A collection of Irish Gaelic Folk

Stories

Jackson, G., (1883) Shropshire Folk-lore

Jackson, W., (2017) What Are the Unicorns and Satyrs Mentioned in the Bible?

Jacobs, J., (1894) More Celtic Fairy Tales

Jamieson, J., (1808) An Etymological Dictionary of the Scottish Language

Jamieson, R., (1806). Popular Ballads and Songs

JCHAS (2010) Journal of the Cork Historical and Archaeological Society

Jenkins, R., (1991) Witches and Fairies: Supernatural Aggression and Deviance Among the Irish Peasantry; The Good People

Jolly, K., (1996) Popular Religion in Late Saxon England: elf charms in context

Jones, H., (1997) Concerning the Names Morgan, Morgana, Morgaine, Muirghein, Morrigan and the Like. Retrieved from https://medievalscotland.org/problem/names/morgan.shtml

Jones, M (2003) The Wild Hunt. Retrieved from http://www.maryjones.us/jce/wildhunt.html

Keightley, T., (1850) Fairy Mythology

Kerr, J., (2012) Etymology of the Word "Glamour", Persephone Magazine, Retrieved from http://persephonemagazine.com/2012/08/glamour/

Kirk, R., and Lang, A., (1893) The Secret Commonwealth of Elves, Fauns, and Fairies

KJV (2017) Official King James Bible

Kruse, J., (2017) British Fairies

Lecouteux, C., (1992) Witches, Werewolves, and Fairies: Shapeshifters and Astral Doubles in the Middle Ages

— (1995) Demons and Spirits of the Land: Ancestral Lore and Practices

— (1996) The Return of the Dead: Ghosts, Ancestors, and the Transparent Veil of the Pagan Mind

— (1999) Phantom Armies of the Night: The Wild Hunt and the

Ghostly Processions of the Undead
— (2000) The Tradition of Household Spirits: Ancestral Lore and Practices
— (2018) The Hidden History of Elves & Dwarves
Lenihan and Green (2004) Meeting the Other Crowd
Locke, T., (2013). The Fairy Doctor. Retrieved from http://www.irishabroad.com/blogs/PostView.aspx?pid=4404
Logan, P., (1981) The Old Gods: The Facts about Irish Fairies
Lyle, E., (1970). 'The Teind to Hell in Tam Lin', Folklore, vol. 70
Lysaght, P., (1986) The Banshee: The Irish Death Messenger
— (1991) Fairylore from the Midlands of Ireland; The Good People
MacCoitir, N., (2003) Irish Trees
— (2006) Irish Wild Plants
MacCulloch, J., (1911) Religion of the Ancient Celts
MacDonald, L., (1993) People of the Mounds. Dalriada Magazine
MacGillivray, Deborah. (2000). The Cait Sidhe
McKay, J., (1940) More Highland Tales
MacKenzie, A., (1899) The Prophecies of the Brahan Seer
MacKenzie, D., (1935) Scottish Folk-lore and Folk Life
MacKenzie, O., (1921) A Hundred Years in the Highlands
MacKillop, J., (1998) Dictionary of Celtic Mythology
MacLiammoir, M., (1984) Faery Nights Oicheanta Si: Stories on Ancient Irish Festivals
MacManus, D., (1959) The Middle Kingdom: The Faerie World of Ireland
MacNeill, M., (1962) Festival of Lughnasa
MacQuarrie, C., (1997) The Waves of Manannán
Marshall, R., (2013). Clare Folk tales
Matthews, J and C (2005). The Element Encyclopedia of Magical Creatures
McCarthy, M., (1901) Five Years in Ireland
McNamara-Wilson, K., (2012) The Dearg Due Retrieved from http://gotireland.com/2012/10/11/irish-faerie-folk-of-yore-

and-yesterday-the-dearg-due/
McNeil, H., (2001) The Celtic Breeze
McNeill, M (1956). The Silver Bough, volume 1
Memmot, M., (2013) Highway in Iceland May be Side-tracked by Elves'; NPR; Retrieved from https://www.npr.org/sections/thetwo-way/2013/12/24/256863444/highway-in-iceland-may-be-sidetracked-by-elves
Merriman, B., (1780) Cuirt an Mhean Oiche
Mikl, A., (2004) Fairy Paintings in 19th Century Art and Late 20th Century Art: A Comparative Study Retrieved from http://www2.uwstout.edu/content/lib/thesis/2004/2004mikla.pdf
Miller, J., (1877) A History of the Witches of Renfrewshire
Miller, J., (2004). Magic and Witchcraft in Scotland.
Milton, J., (1877) The Poetical Works of John Milton: Paradise Lost
Monaghan, P., (2009). The Encyclopedia of Celtic Mythology and Folklore
Morgan la Fay (2018) The Camelot Project; University of Rochester. Retrieved from http://www.kingarthursknights.com/others/morganlefay.asp
Murray, J., (1885) The Romance and Prophecies of Thomas of Erceldoune: printed from five manuscripts
https://archive.org/stream/romanceprophecie00thomuoft/romanceprophecie00thomuoft_djvu.txt
— (1918) The Romance and Prophecies of Thomas of Erceldoune
— (1922) The Complaynt of Scotland
Mushroom Appreciation (2016). Fanciful Fairy Rings
https://www.mushroom-appreciation.com/fairy-rings.html
Narvaez, P., (1991) The Good People: New Fairylore Essays
NPR., (2006) The Wee Fairy Doors of Ann Arbor, Mich Retrieved from http://www.npr.org/templates/story/story php?storyId=5393277
O Crualaoich, G., (2003) The Book of the Cailleach: Stories of the Wise-woman Healer

— (2006) 'Reading the Bean Feasa', Folklore, vol. 116

O Donaill, (1977) Foclóir Gaeilge-Béarla

O Giolláin, D., (1991) The Fairy Belief and Official Religion in Ireland

O hOgain, D., (1995) Irish Superstitions

— (2006) The Lore of Ireland

O Súilleabháin, S., (1967). Nósanna agus Piseoga na nGael

O'Sullivan, S., (1966) Folktales of Ireland

Old Farmers Almanac (2012) Cat Sidhe. Retrieved from http://www.almanac.com/calendar/date/2012-08-17

Olsen, K., and Veenstra, J., (2014) Airy Nothings: Imagining the Otherworld of Faerie from the Middle Ages to the Age of Reason

Ostling, M., (2018) Fairies, Demons, and Nature Spirits: 'Small Gods' at the Margins of Christendom

Parkinson, D., (2013). Phantom Black Dogs Retrieved from http://www.mysteriousbritain.co.uk/folklore/phantom-black-dogs.html

Pattie, T., (2011) Medieval People, Titles, Trades, and Classes retrieved from http://go.vsb.bc.ca/schools/templeton/departments/socialstudies/MsRamsey/Documents/Medieval%20People.pdf

Pennick, N., (2015) Pagan Magic of the Northern Tradition

Pitcairn, R., (1833) Ancient Criminal Trials in Scotland

Pocs, E., (1999) Between the Living and the Dead

Purkiss, D., (2000) At the Bottom of the Garden: a dark history of fairies, hobgoblins, and other troublesome things

Quinn, E., (2009) Irish American Folklore in New England

Reppion, J., (2016) Spirits of Place

Rieti, B., (1991) ''The Blast' in Newfoundland Fairy Tradition'; The Good People

— (1991) Strange Terrain: The Fairy World in Newfoundland

Rhys, J., (1907) Celtic Folklore Welsh and Manx

Robertson, C., (1905) Folk-lore from the West of Ross-shire

Rodriguez, A., (1998) Old Testament Demonology https://www.ministrymagazine.org/archive/1998/06/old-testament-demonology

Rogers, C., (1869) Scotland Social and Domestic: Memorial of Life and Manners in Northern Britain

Ross, A., (1976) The Folklore of the Scottish Highlands

Rossetti, C., (1862) The Goblin Market

Sanford, F., (1919) Ignis Fatuus; Scientific Monthly vol. 9 no 4 Retrieved from https://www.jstor.org/stable/6287?seq=2#page_scan_tab_contents

Sands, Brymer, Murray, and Cochran (1819). The Edinburgh Magazine and Literary Miscellany, vol. 83

Scott, W., (1802). Minstrelsy of the Scottish Borders

--- (1820). The Abbott

--- (1827) Chronicles of Canongate

--- (1828) The Fair Maid of Perth

--- (1830) Letters on Demonology and Witchcraft

--- (1857) The Poetical Works of Sir Walter Scott in One Volume

Seo Helrune (2016) Essays from the Crossroads

--- (2017) 'Maran, Night-Walkers and Elves, Oh My!', Retrieved from http://www.seohelrune.com/2017/09/maran-night-walkers-and-elves-oh-my.html

Shakespeare, W., (2004) A Midsummer Night's Dream

--- (1974) The Complete Works of William Shakespeare

Sikes, W., (1880) British Goblins: Welsh Folklore, Fairy Mythology, Legends, and Traditions

Silver, C., (1999) Strange & Secret Peoples: fairies and Victorian Consciousness

Simpson, J., and Roud, S., (2000) Oxford Dictionary of English Folklore

Skjelbred, A., (1991) Rites of Passage as Meeting Place: Christianity and Fairylore in Connection with the Unclean Woman and the Unchristened Child; The Good People

Smith, D., (1921) *'Mr Robert Kirk's Note-Book'*; The Scottish

Historical Review

Smyth, D., (1988) A Guide to Irish Mythology

Sneddon, A., (2015) Witchcraft and Magic in Ireland

Spenser, E., (1590) The Faerie Queene

Stokes, W., & Windisch, E., (1897) Irische Texte

Suggs, R., (2018) Fairies A Dangerous History

Syv, P., (1695) Et Hundrede Udvalde Danske Viser

Talairach-Vielmas, L., (2014) Fairy Tales, Natural History, and Victorian Culture

Thomas, J., (1908) The Welsh Fairy Book

Thoms, W., (1884) The Book of the Court: Exhibiting the History, Duties, and Privileges of the English Nobility and Gentry.

Tobar an Dualchais (2018) University of Edinburgh Retrieved from http://www.tobarandualchais.co.uk/en/;jsessionid=6F20F7929222504F5BC5373DE3F6AB16

Towrie, S., (2018) Orkneyjar: the heritage of the Orkney Islands. Retrieved from http://www.orkneyjar.com/

--- (2018) The Selkie Folk. Retrieved from http://www.orkneyjar.com/folklore/selkiefolk/index.html

--- (2019) Finfolk. Retrieved from http://www.orkneyjar.com/folklore/finfolk/index.html

--- (2019) The Nuckelavee: Devil of the Sea. Retrieved from http://www.orkneyjar.com/folklore/nuckle.htm

Towrie, S., (2013) The Wild Hunt

Vallee, J., (1969) Passport to Magonia

Walsh, B., (2002). The Secret Commonwealth and the Fairy Belief Complex

Wedin, E., (2010) The Si, the Tuatha De Danann, and the Fairies in Yeats' Early Work

Westropp, T., (2003) Folklore of Clare

Wilby, E., (2005) Cunning Folk and Familiar Spirits: Shamanistic Visionary Traditions in Early Modern British Witchcraft and Magic

-- (2010) The Visions of Isobel Gowdie: Magic, Witchcraft, and

Dark Shamanism in Seventeenth Century Scotland

Wilde, E., (1888) Ancient Legends, Mystic Charms, and Superstitions of Ireland

— (1920) Visions and Beliefs in the West of Ireland

Williams, M., (2016) Ireland's Immortals: A History of the Gods of Irish Myth

Williams, N., (1991) 'Semantics of the Word Fairy: Making meaning out of thin air'; The Good People

Wilson, G., (2018) The Dearg Due: The Legend of the Irish Vampire Retrieved from https://hubpages.com/religion-philosophy/Dearg-due-the-legend-of-the-Irish-vampire

Wimberly, L., (1965) Folklore in the English and Scottish Ballads

Wooding, J., (2000) The Otherworld Journey in Early Irish Literature

Wright, A., (2009) Puck Through the Ages Retrieved from https://www.boldoutlaw.com/puckrobin/puckages.html

Yeats, W., (1962) The Celtic Twilight

— (1888) Fairy and Folk Tales of the Irish Peasantry

— (1892) Irish Fairy Tales

— (1959) Mythologies

Young, S., (2018) The Fairy Census 2014 - 2017, Retrieved from http://www.fairyist.com/wp-content/uploads/2014/10/The-Fairy-Census-2014-2017-1.pdf

Young, S., and Houlbrook, C., (2018) Magical Folk: British and Irish Fairies 500 AD to the Present

MOON
BOOKS

Other Titles by Morgan Daimler

Brigid
Meeting the Celtic Goddess of Poetry, Forge, and Healing Well
978-1-78535-320-8 (paperback)
978-1-78535-321-5 (e-book)

Gods and Goddesses of Ireland
A Guide to Irish Deities
978-1-78279-315-1 (paperback)
978-1-78535-450-2 (e-book)

Irish Paganism
Meeting the Celtic God of Wave and Wonder
978-1-78535-145-7 (paperback)
978-1-78535-146-4 (e-book)

Manannán mac Lir
Meeting the Celtic God of Wave and Wonder
978-1-78535-810-4 (paperback)
978-1-78535-811-1 (e-book)

Odin
Meeting the Norse Allfather
978-1-78535-480-9 (paperback)
978-1-78535-481-6 (e-book)

The Dagda
Meeting the Good God of Ireland
978-1-78535-640-7 (paperback)
978-1-78535-641-4 (e-book)

The Morrigan
Meeting the Great Queens
978-1-78279-833-0 (paperback)
978-1-78279-834-7 (e-book)